American Society for Training

IN ACTION

Managing the Small Training Staff

TWELVE

CASE STUDIES

FROM THE

REAL WORLD

OF TRAINING

ASTD

JACK J. PHILLIPS

SERIES EDITOR

CAROL PRESCOTT MCCOY

EDITOR

Ordering information: Books published by the American Society for Train-ing & Development can be ordered by calling 703.683.8100.

Library of Congress Catalog Card Number: 98-070301
ISBN: 1-56286-082-8

Table of Contents

Introduction to the
In Action Series

A s are most professionals, the people involved in human resource development (HRD) are eager to see practical applications of the models, techniques, theories, strategies, and issues the field comprises. In recent years, practitioners have developed an intense desire to learn about the success of other organizations when they implement HRD programs. The Publishing Review Committee of the American Society for Training & Development has established this series of casebooks to fill this need. Covering a variety of topics in HRD, the series should add significantly to the current literature in the field.

This series has the following objectives:

- *To provide real-world examples of HRD program application and implementation.* Each case will describe significant issues, events, actions, and activities. When possible, the actual names of the organizations and individuals involved will be used. In other cases, the names will be disguised, but the events are factual.

- *To focus on challenging and difficult issues confronting the HRD field.* These cases will explore areas where it is difficult to find information or where the processes or techniques are not standardized or fully developed. Also, emerging issues critical to success in the field will be covered in the series.

- *To recognize the work of professionals in the HRD field by presenting best practices.* Each book in the series will attempt to represent the most effective examples in the field. The most respected organizations, practitioners, authors, researchers, and consultants will be asked to provide cases.

- *To serve as a self-teaching tool for people learning about the HRD field.* As a stand-alone reference, each volume should be a very useful learning tool. Each case will contain many issues and fully explore several topics.

- *To present a medium for teaching groups about the practical aspects of HRD.* Each book should serve as a discussion guide to enhance learning in formal and informal settings. Each case will have questions for discussion. And each book will be useful as a supplement to general and specialized textbooks in HRD.

The topics for the volumes will be carefully selected to ensure that they represent important and timely issues in the HRD field. The editors for the individual volumes are experienced professionals in the field. The series will provide a high-quality product to fill a critical void in the literature. An ambitious schedule is planned.

If you have suggestions of ways to improve this series or an individual volume in the series, please respond directly to me. Your input is welcome.

Jack J. Phillips, Ph.D.
Series Editor
Performance Resources Organization
Box 380637
Birmingham, AL 35238-0637

Preface

In this era of so-called rightsizing and cost consciousness, organizations are expecting people to do more with less. Many companies that are looking to trim payrolls staff their training departments with only one or two people. In some cases, the trainer may have broader human resources responsibilities and therefore be able to focus on training only part of the time. However, even small training departments are expected to make significant and noticeable contributions to their organizations. Trainers in these small organizations often feel like Lone Rangers and in many instances are lone trainers. Business executives often expect these lone trainers to come up with the famous silver bullet to solve critical business problems.

Many lone trainers are new to training or have been used to functioning as part of larger staffs. As with several of the authors in this casebook, lone trainers are often former businesspeople who express an interest in training and who learn to be trainers by trial and error. No matter what their background, trainers in small departments need guidance on how to make the most of their resources and how to keep from being overwhelmed by unrealistic expectations and demands from senior management and customers. Small training departments can succeed in improving an organization's performance if they understand the key business challenges, focus on priorities, form partnerships with internal and external resources, and maintain a positive attitude. By following the strategies outlined in the chapters in this book, lone trainers can survive and even thrive in today's challenging business environment.

The Origins of This Book

My interest in this topic grew out of my experience as a lone trainer managing a small Human Resource Development (HRD) Department in Chase Manhattan's International Consumer Banking Division for three years in the mid-1980s. When I started that job, I transferred from a department of over 20 people. I had excellent instructional, delivery, and consulting skills, but little awareness or appreciation of the challenging task that lay ahead of me in creating and managing a training department of one person responsible for training in 15 counties. In the course of the assignment, I worked my way from discouragement to confidence that I could make a difference despite my department's size. I knew there were other people like me facing similar challenges who could benefit from my experience, so I gave a presentation—Creating an Effective Small Training Department: You Can Do More Than You Think—at the American Society for Training & Development (ASTD) National Financial Services Conference in Boston in 1989.

As a result of that talk, I received an invitation from the publisher Jossey-Bass to write a book, *Managing a Small HRD Department: You Can Do More Than You Think,* which was published in 1993 and provides guidelines, tools, and brief real-life examples of trainers who have made positive contributions with very limited staff. In researching the book, I sent a survey to people who had attended my initial ASTD presentation, and I interviewed over 30 trainers who faced similar challenges. The interviews revealed a variety of approaches that trainers use to meet the challenge of resource limitations. Writing the book proved to be one of the most rewarding and profound learning opportunities I have ever had. It has been heartening for me to hear how helpful the book has been in providing useful ideas as well as inspiration.

In the middle of writing my previous book, I decided to head north to Maine to work for UNUM Life Insurance Company of America. At UNUM America I have had the pleasure of managing a small staff, which has ranged in size from 1.2 full-time equivalents (FTEs) to 4.2 FTEs. After being a one-person department, it was an exciting opportunity for me to work with resources who actually reported to me, rather than relying on myself and my internal and external training network. While working at UNUM, I have learned more about working in a small training department in a very different culture. By using a balance of consultants and our two trainers and a train-the-trainer strategy, our small staff provided training for 3,000 employees on cross-company training needs, such as customer service, leadership, people management, change management, developing others, and communicating effectively. In addition to my work at UNUM, I have learned from teaching a course, Managing Training and Development, which I offer through the University of Southern Maine's Continuing Education Department, and numerous workshops that I have offered through ASTD.

When Jack Phillips asked me if I would like to edit a casebook on being a lone trainer, I jumped at the offer. This would provide a great opportunity to build on my previous experience, to learn how training had evolved since my previous research, and to offer other trainers a chance to share their learning and to experience once again the "joys" of writing for publication.

Purpose of This Casebook

The goal of *Managing the Small Training Staff* is to provide practical ideas for action and in-depth examples of what training departments that range in size from one part-time employee to five full-time people can accomplish. Representing a wide range of industries, the cases explain the challenges and opportunities small training departments face and describe specific success strategies and tactics that have proved useful. Because a major challenge of being in a small department is overcoming discouragement, this book also offers trainers a sense of optimism about contributions they can make, even with limited staff. Finally, because the book provides insights into the real world of working in a small training department, it can help with decisions about career paths—whether to pursue working in a small training department or whether to be a lone trainer on the inside or outside of an organization.

Target Audience

This book should interest anyone who works in a small training department, whether as the manager, trainer, or part of an administrative support team. It would be helpful to anyone struggling with the issue of meeting pressing organizational training needs with few resources. Readers will gain an understanding of a variety of ways to approach the tasks of determining needs, developing programs, and implementing and evaluating training with minimal resources. Readers will gain an appreciation for the joys and struggles of such a position—what it feels like to work in small training departments.

A second audience is all the people (managers as well as individual contributors) in organizations who work with small training departments and stand to benefit from their services. The book helps to clarify the vital role that nontrainers have to play in contributing to training efforts as subject matter experts who help to identify and prioritize needs and help to design and deliver training. It also explains the importance of the business partnership with training and how managers must sponsor and support training efforts so that training takes hold and makes a difference in an organization's success.

A third audience is external consultants who work in a one- or two-person training organization or who provide training support to organizations with small human resources and training departments. Many chapters address the issue of working with external resources to meet training needs. The book provides helpful clues about the realities of being a lone trainer as an external consultant. Readers also can get a feel for what it's like to work as a part-time trainer inside an organization and maintain an external consulting practice or spend more time on other pursuits.

Another audience is HRD instructors who teach programs or seminars on training and training management. The book should prove to be a helpful reference and supplementary text for programs in managing HRD at the undergraduate or graduate level. Students can use the cases as a basis for discussion about the approaches used in the case and explore alternative ways of meeting training needs for similar organizations.

Types of Cases

The 12 cases come from a variety of settings and industries, including financial and investment services, insurance, automobile manufacturing, motorcycle service, chemicals, paper recycling, metals manufacturing, telecommunications, and beauty products. The cases include organizations with sophisticated computer equipment and telecommunications networks, such as Nortel, and less technologically sophisticated organizations. You will find examples from small centralized departments in small organizations (such as Collagen, Logitech, Norway Savings Bank, and Rock-Tenn) and small decentralized training departments in business units or functions that are part of larger organizations (such as Nortel's Broadband Business Unit's training; Monsanto's Muscatine Plant; Navistar's Springfield Plant, and UNUM America's Human Resources Training Department). In one instance, Anne Monnin, a principal with STRATEGIES FOR THE 90's, is acting as an independent consultant—an "Outsourced Director of Training and Development"—for several companies. In another instance, Carolyn Balling works part-time as Collagen's training manager and part-time as an external consultant. In some cases, the departments were start-ups (Collagen, Rock-Tenn, Logitech, Louisiana Workers' Compensation Corporation, and Norway Savings Bank), whereas other departments had existed for some time and were being revitalized (Navistar) or had been significantly affected by downsizing (American Honda). The cases also represent different types of training, including soft-skills training and management training (Collagen, Rock-Tenn, UNUM America, and Kidder, Peabody) as well as technological training and job-skills training (Monsanto and American Honda).

Case Authors

Finding authors to contribute to this casebook and convincing them to submit a chapter has been an amazing challenge. One thing I knew for sure: Being a lone trainer or a trainer in a small department affords little extra time to write articles. What I had not fully appreciated was the difference between asking people to speak with me on the phone for one or two hours of research and asking them to write a chapter for publication. I am deeply indebted to all 12 authors who devoted their time, thought, and care to write and rewrite chapters for this book. I know that finding this time meant burning the midnight and the predawn oil.

Acknowledgments

This book would not be possible were it not for the creativity, insight, and diligence of the authors who contributed chapters: Raquel Fornoles Arnold, Carolyn Sorensen Balling, Barbara "Bobbi" J. Buisman, Millar Farewell, Michael J. Gettle, Karen L. Jost, Randy Maxwell, Anne Monnin, Nancy G. Nunziati, Kathryn S. O'Neill, Joanne Rogovin, and Debra T. Taylor. All of them took precious time from fighting the daily training battles to share with others what they've learned from working in small departments. I appreciate their hard work, their willingness to reveal themselves, and their responsiveness to my numerous requests for more information and for changes to their manuscripts.

I would like to thank Jack Phillips for inviting me to edit this book, and to acknowledge Jack's staff for helping to shepherd me through the editorial process. I appreciate Jack's support and encouragement as well as his leadership. Jack has set the standard for producing casebooks for trainers and other HRD professionals.

Thanks go to my colleagues and friends who have listened to endless stories about my writing trials and tribulations and who have offered me words of encouragement as well as constructive criticism. In particular, I would like to thank Mike Norton, Kathleen Jacques, Carol Ryan Ertz, Susan Fenton, and Michelle Boucher for taking the time to read my sections of the book and for providing me with thoughtful comments.

I would especially like to acknowledge Marlene Silva for her support and encouragement. As always, Marlene has provided me with many creative suggestions, and in my moments of doubt, she has given me the inspiration to work through my struggles as a writer. I appreciate her perspective, her patience, and especially her friendship. I know that the book is richer because of her ideas.

A special thanks goes to my sister, Kathryn Joy, who is learning more about HRD than she ever imagined. I appreciate her constant support and encouragement as well as her editorial suggestions, even though I don't always seem to welcome them. Kate helps me to find ways to do more than I ever thought I could.

Finally, I would like to acknowledge the support and inspiration of Marilee Marrinan and Nancy Mackay, both of whom helped me to maintain my perspective and sense of humor, and to remember what is truly important in life. They helped to bring enthusiasm, fun, and joy to this project.

Carol Prescott McCoy
Falmouth, Maine
March 1998

How to Use This Casebook

Case Organization

One of the unique features of being a small training department is that the departments are as varied as the individuals themselves. These cases represent the possible approaches in managing a training department ranging in size from a part-time person to a staff of four people. Each department's mission includes training and development, but several of them also include organizational development, performance management, and other human resources functions. Target groups for training programs vary from all employees to managers to technical specialists.

The cases do not presume to represent the ideal approach. Readers can identify areas for improvement and refinement within each one. Authors also share what they learned and in each instance how they would do things differently in the future. As part of the learning process, you can explore how you might apply their work in your organizations.

Each case begins with a broad overview of the author's organization and industry, including the training department, its purpose, programs and services, and general strategies. Authors also describe the challenges and opportunities they perceived. The cases then explore in more detail one successful intervention and analyze what contributed to the success. In the conclusions, the authors describe the lessons they learned. The cases end with review questions to stimulate the reader's thinking. Table 1 presents basic descriptions of the cases in the order in which they appear in the book.

Using the Cases

This book will be helpful to anyone who wants to see real-life examples of training in a small department. Following are some possible uses:

- The book provides HRD professionals with a basic reference on needs assessment, program development, and delivery and evaluation,

Table 1. Overview of the case studies.

Case	Industry	HRD Programs and Case Focus	Situation	Target Audience
Collagen Corporation	Beauty and health products	Quality training	Start-up HRD; part-time	All levels of employees
Rock-Tenn Company	Packaging	Leadership development	Start-up HRD	Officers
Kidder, Peabody	Brokerage	Ethics and leadership	Crisis situation	Managers
UNUM Life Insurance Company of America	Insurance	Leadership development	Changed direction and narrowed focus	Officers and managers
Louisiana Workers' Compensation Corporation (LWCC)	Insurance	Needs assessment, job-skills training, and staff growth	Start-up HRD and staff growth	Employees and supervisors
Logitech	Technology	Time management	Start-up	Employees and supervisors
STRATEGIES FOR THE 90's	Independent consulting	Quality training and directing training from inside or outside a company	Revitalization, downsizing, out-sourced training	All levels of employees

Table 1. Overview of the case studies (continued).

Monsanto, Muscatine Plant	Metals manufacturing and chemicals	Performance-based technical training	Changed direction to performance-based training	Plant technicians
Navistar—The Springfield Assembly Plant	Truck and auto manufacturing	Technical training; creating a training advisory board and a learning center	Revitalization of the training function	All levels of plant employees
American Honda	Motorcycle service	Technical training (electrical repairs)	Downsized staff	Dealer service technicians
Nortel Corporation, Atlanta Broadband Unit	Telecommunications	Technical training in emerging technologies	Ongoing HRD and technical training in a high-tech environment	Engineers
Norway Savings Bank	Financial services	Product and sales support	Start-up HRD	All branch employees

given a small staff. The book explores strategies for determining priorities, for using internal and external resources, and for creating effective partnerships inside and outside the organization.

- The book is useful in stimulating discussion about training in today's organizations. The questions at the end of each case are a starting point on how to approach various training challenges and factors to consider in making important decisions about training and HRD.

- The book supplements other training and HRD textbooks. It provides the additional dimension of real-life cases, which show the dedication, excitement, frustration, and results of small training departments.

- The book also is a valuable tool for an additional audience—managers and others who do not have primary training accountability, but who support training as sponsors, subject matter experts, trainers, and designers or some other way. The book describes the requirements for effective training and the results of effective training.

Organizations have training requirements that are unique and specific to their situation. What is effective for one may not be effective for another, even in similar settings. The authors do not recommend that specific approaches or technique be duplicated precisely. Instead, the book provides well-crafted tools and ideas with which small HRD and training departments can build.

Note

Because of space limitations, some cases are shorter than the author and editor would have liked. Some information regarding background, assumptions, and results had to be omitted. For additional information on a case, readers may get in touch with the lead author, whose address appears at the end of each case.

Managing a Small Training Department

Making the Most of Your Resources

Carol Prescott McCoy

Today's organizations are expecting people to do more with less. Training departments are no exception. In fact, one-fourth of all training departments in the United States consist of only one trainer. With small businesses on the rise, there are likely to be even more small training departments in the future. How can a training staff of only one to three people—with a broad range of responsibilities—ensure that it makes a significant contribution to its organization? This chapter explores strategies that trainers in small departments have used successfully. Readers will learn keys to working with internal subject matter experts through a train-the-trainer process as well as keys to working with external consultants and other external resources.

Successful strategies of small training departments are as varied as the individuals involved. Much more so than in large departments, trainers in small departments have a chance to place their unique stamp on an organization. The cases in this book illustrate the variety of approaches small departments use to ensure a big impact. The following key strategies are essential to the small training organization's success:

- determining priority training needs
- establishing your credibility and building a strong base of support for your efforts
- determining the best resource strategy for using internal and external resources
- maintaining your resilience and a positive attitude.

This chapter briefly explores these strategies, which the case authors and other trainers in small departments have used successfully. In addition, it will provide detailed guidance about establishing an effective train-the-trainer process for internal resources and selecting and working with external resources to expand your staff's capacity and capability.

Determining Priority Training Needs

The foundation for a successful small training department is a thorough training needs assessment that identifies the specific training needs that if met or unmet have the most impact on the organization. In doing a needs assessment, it is essential to use a variety of methods, both formal and informal, to gain a clear, complete picture. The cases in this book illustrate the range of methods for conducting a needs assessment. Strategies may include using paper-and-pencil written surveys, interviewing employees and managers, analyzing problems encountered, or doing research related to the problem or issue. A critical strategy in assessing needs and implementing performance-based training is conducting a thorough job and task analysis of performance requirements. See Michael J. Gettle's Monsanto case for an excellent introduction to developing performance-based training. Companies that are pursuing ISO quality certification can identify training needs by creating job profiles and training plans relating to ISO certification. For more information on ISO certification and how it relates to training needs, see Gettle's chapter on Monsanto, Carolyn Sorensen Balling's chapter on Collagen, Randy Maxwell and Karen L. Jost's chapter on Nortel, and Anne Monnin's chapter on STRATEGIES FOR THE 90's. Another helpful approach to assessing needs and clarifying priorities is to create a training advisory board. The chapters by Raquel Fornoles Arnold on Navistar, Debra T. Taylor on the Louisiana Workers' Compensation Corporation (LWCC), and Carol Prescott McCoy on UNUM provide insights into how advisory boards can be help set your direction.

Other approaches to needs assessment are more informal. For example, personal intuition on the basis of your experience in the business is valuable in helping you identify needs or training strategies. The cases on American Honda, Nortel, and Logitech all illustrate how the authors used their experience in the company to help them understand training needs. Listening to your internal customers also can help identify problems that might have training implications. Teaching or facilitating training allows the lone trainer to get a pulse of the organization and learn firsthand about the issues facing employees. Tuning into the recommendations of employees who attend outside training programs provides clues about potential high-impact training interventions. Nancy Nunziati discovered a training program that ultimately helped to move Logitech's culture to one of increased accountability because she listened to employees who had attended a time management program and given it rave reviews.

In many instances, a small organization may not have the internal resources needed for a detailed needs assessment that can identify the best way for training to support the business objectives. Taylor's chapter on LWCC is an excellent example of using a consultant, who already had the ear of the company president, to conduct a training needs assessment. Taylor shows that as a result of documenting needs, she was able to gain four additional training staff members. Kathryn O'Neill at Rock-Tenn and Millar Farewell of American Honda also relied on outside consultants to help them clarify a business need and determine the best approach to solving a training problem.

A key part of conducting a needs assessment is determining priorities because of the importance of focusing training resources where they can do the most good. First, it is essential to examine business data that indicate the severity of problems or highlight potential opportunities and their potential impact on the business. Farewell's case on Honda is a good example of how to collect data to determine the impact of electrical troubleshooting skills on service to motorcycle owners.

A second aspect of clarifying priorities is to determine problems where training can actually have an impact and to identify all the solutions needed to change performance. Sometimes the best solution is not a training program, but training along with other interventions—such as increasing the staff or providing appropriate incentives to perform in the desired way. Other follow-up actions often must accompany training to change employee behavior. See McCoy's case on UNUM to learn how call monitoring by supervisors following telephone skills training can lead to improved customer relations.

A third part of identifying priorities is clarifying the priorities and expectations of senior sponsors who pay for training and champion its value. Assessing the receptivity of the organization's senior management to training is essential in determining whether or not training can have an impact. Monnin's chapter illustrates why it is so important to understand the real expectations of an organization's senior management. Management's lack of commitment to training ultimately led to the elimination of the position of training director. Monnin was able to provide useful services to her previous employer as an outsourced director of training once she understood the real expectations. Furthermore, she learned to identify better customers for her services—companies where training could have a more significant impact because they had senior managers who recognized the requirements for meaningful training and were willing to support training more actively.

Training advisory boards, which include key senior sponsors, or interviews with senior managers can be very helpful in determining senior management's priorities. For example, after reviewing company data, UNUM's training department was not sure whether the initial leadership development efforts should be on current managers or aspiring managers as the primary target audience. After meeting with the senior sponsorship group, however, it became clear that current executives and people managers were the most critical audience. O'Neill's chapter on Rock-Tenn provides helpful insights in how she worked with senior management to clarify its priorities. For additional information on conducting a needs assessment, readers may refer to Allen (1990); Kaufman, Rojas, and Mayer (1993); McCoy (1993); Phillips and Holton (1995); and Zemke and Kramlinger (1989).

Establishing Your Credibility and Building Support for Training

Building buy-in or ownership for your strategy is essential. The first step in building support is having a business perspective— being able to think like a businessperson, understanding the dynamics and performance indicators of your organization's business, speaking the language of your company's business, and showing how training and other performance interventions are critical to your business's success. A well-planned and well-executed needs assessment is essential in developing this business perspective. At first, unless you have had line experience in the industry or your company, you may have a steep learning curve and may need to immerse yourself in company documents, reports, and industry publications to help gain a clear understanding of your organization's business. A key component of business understanding is talking to people throughout the organization and asking the right kinds of questions. All the cases illustrate the importance of knowing the business. Bobbi Buisman's case on Norway Savings Bank, for example, shows how the human resource development (HRD) manager learned about the business by being an active member of several critical bank committees.

An equally important step is a well-planned evaluation strategy so you can demonstrate the value of training and how training contributes to the business. There are some excellent resources to help you understand training evaluation. (See, for example, Phillips and Holton, 1995.) In some cases, the business will want to see a training activity report showing the numbers of people who have been trained (as in LWCC), whereas in other cases, it will want to see more bottom-line data (as in Nortel).

Nourishing partnerships with critical players who need to support training or who are the target audience for training will create support for your training approach. For example, sponsors may or may not provide the budget needed to develop and deliver training; and managers may or may not allow their employees time to participate in training or take care to reinforce and reward the use of newly learned skills and behavior on the job. For people to champion and support training, they need to believe in its value. Gettle's Monsanto case describes in detail his approach to building relationships at all levels throughout the Monsanto plant in Muscatine, Iowa. Because the technicians were essential to both program development and implementation, Gettle took a bottoms-up approach to building support. Another good example of building ownership for training is Arnold's creation of a broad-based training advisory group, the Progressive Education Council, at Navistar's Springfield Plant. This advisory group, which consisted of representatives of union and management, validated needs and even solved training-related problems, such as improving the effectiveness of the Interactive Learning Center. At Rock-Tenn, O'Neill did such a good job of creating officer involvement that the group wanted to create its own vision of management development, rather than one proposed by an external consultant.

Becoming an expert at managing expectations and being clear about requirements for success are essential parts of maintaining credibility in a small training department. Peter Block's classic book, *Flawless Consulting* (1981) provides excellent guidance on the critical skill of contracting. It helps you to distinguish between what is good business that can succeed and make a contribution and what is bad business that is doomed to failure. In setting expectations or contracting with your training customers, it is essential that you be clear with people who request training about what you can and cannot do for them, about whether or not training is the right solution to their problem, and about what they need to do to supplement any training intervention with needed business actions to ensure that training has an impact.

Training alone will rarely improve performance. Frequently, it will be necessary to ensure that clear standards, appropriate tools and job aids, measures of performance and rewards, and incentives are in place to encourage people to use the skills, knowledge, and behaviors learned in training. Gettle's case on Monsanto illustrates well how to ensure that training is integrated with on-the-job performance by using job aids and job procedures as the training tools. Joanne Rogovin's case on Kidder Peabody provides a wonderful example about the limits of ethics training in changing behavior when there are far too many incentives for people to behave unethically. Refer to Robinson and Robinson's (1996) *Performance Consulting: Moving Beyond Training* for help in analyzing the business situation to ensure all the needed solutions in addition to training are applied to address any business problem.

Determining the Best Resource Strategy

One thing is sure: To be successful in a small training department, you cannot do everything yourself. Finding and making the best use of resources that are not directly under your control is a critical competency. You will need to take advantage of both internal resources and external resources. Internal resources include subject matter experts (the real workers), other human resource professionals, and other internal suppliers who can help you with everything from assessing needs, determining priorities, selecting vendors, designing and developing materials, borrowing training materials, delivering training, marketing training, providing follow-up coaching and reinforcement to arranging for training logistics, such as facilities or required technology to use alternative delivery. Maxwell and Jost's case on Nortel is an excellent illustration of using internal partners to expand the technological capabilities of a training unit. Whether or not you are charged for using the services of employees in your organization, there is definitely a cost to using internal resources—lost production time while people are working on activities that are not part of their primary work accountabilities. You can use external resources for many or all of the same activities, but normally you have to pay an explicit fee for outside resources.

How do you decide whether to use inside or outside resources? Several factors are important to consider in making the decision: time, budget, need for involvement, required expertise, need for outside perspective, resource availability, track record of success, and skepticism about work done by outsiders (the not-invented-here-syndrome). Often it is best to use a combination of internal and external resources in developing and instructing training programs. (See table 1 to help you make your resource decisions.) All the case studies in this book provide examples of how to make the most effective use of your resources. The following sections describe in more detail how to work with internal resources (and train nontrainers to train) and how to work with external consultants.

Internal Resources: A Train-the-Trainer Strategy

With a small training department and a large customer base, you can train a critical mass of people in time to meet business needs by training people who are not in the training department to deliver your programs. These "trainers" may be other human resource professionals, line managers, regular employees, or trainers who are dedicated to specific lines of business or functions. The cases by Gettle on Monsanto, Balling on Collagen, O'Neill on Rock-Tenn, Rogovin on Kidder, Peabody, and McCoy on UNUM are all good examples of using nontrainers to train.

Table 1. Making resource choices.

Use Internal Resources When	Use External Resources When
• You have severe budget constraints.	• Budget is available.
• You have time to guide subject matter experts, develop text materials	• You have little time to develop a program or materials.
• You need specific expertise found only inside your organization.	• The expertise required is found only outside of your organization.
• Qualified and credible resources are available and committed to the program.	• Outside resources will have more credibility as authorities on the subject.
• You want to build sponsorship and ownership through involvement.	• You need a fresh, detached, and objective outside perspective.
• Your organization can produce high-quality materials quickly and inexpensively.	• You lack the capacity to produce the high-quality or technologically sophisticated materials required.
• The organization tends to mistrust programs not invented here.	• A relevant, proven, tested, and credible program is readily available.

Benefits in Training Nontrainers to Train

There are many advantages to developing the training skills of others outside your department. First, by increasing resources who can deliver training, you can reach more people faster. Second, resources who are close to the business have the credibility that comes with business expertise, and they can tailor the training material to real-life situations and deliver the training so that it meets the specific needs of that business. If the target audience works on different shifts from the training department, using people who work on the shift to deliver the training meets a critical logistical need. In addition, people have an increased sense of ownership of training that is taught by one of their people versus someone from an ivory tower. Furthermore, training employees with subject matter expertise to deliver programs means that you don't have to be an expert in everything. Gettle's case of the Monsanto Muscatine Plant is an excellent example of increasing effectiveness and ownership of training and overcoming logistical challenges of various work shifts by using technicians in the plant to deliver on-the-job training (OJT). Another excellent example of using a train-the-trainer strategy with an executive population is Balling's case, in which she used vice presidents (VPs) to introduce ISO certification to all Collagen employees. Using the VPs as trainers ensured ownership, enhanced credibility, and helped achieve an aggressive implementation schedule.

An additional benefit of training others to train is that the newly developed trainers get to learn new skills. Developing training and facilitation skills can be a tremendous opportunity for nontrainers. One of the best ways to learn about a subject is to teach someone else—people usually deepen their expertise in topics that they teach. As the UNUM case shows, the manager of UNUM's 1-800 Call Center learned to be a master trainer of Communico's MAGIC® of Customer Relations telephone skills program, and as a result she significantly sharpened her ability to satisfy customers as well as her ability to coach others on their phone skills. Also, improved facilitation and presentation skills can help improve people's ability to lead and influence others outside of training situations.

Challenges in Training Nontrainers to Train

Some major challenges exist in training people outside of the training department to become effective trainers. First, gaining organizational support for others to do training can be a challenge in itself. Nontrainers have other priorities besides training: Their priority is to make products or provide support services for these products. It takes time for nontrainers to learn new skills and then apply those skills in training situations. It may be difficult to persuade nontrainers to take on additional job responsibilities, especially in downsizing situations when people are already overloaded with the work of others whose jobs have been cut.

Second, it is difficult to ensure the quality and effectiveness of programs that nonprofessional trainers teach. How do you go about identifying people who are willing to teach others and are likely to be effective trainers? In general, line managers have not learned to teach. To those who have never done it, training often looks deceptively easy. People may underestimate the required preparation and consequently may not become sufficiently familiar with the training material or take enough time to practice to ensure an effective delivery. Also, subject matter experts may know so much that they fall into the trap of lecturing and answering all the questions themselves, rather than acting as facilitators who draw on the expertise of the group.

Finally, getting administrative support for decentralized programs can be a big challenge. When another area offers training, the business unit may need to provide administrative support as well as instructors for the programs. Administrative assistants who are not in a training department are usually unfamiliar with the trials, demands, nuances, and detailed follow-up required to ensure that training programs run smoothly. It takes time as well as specific knowledge to provide smooth logistical support to programs. You need to train the administrative support people as well as the trainers.

Finding the Right People to Be Your Trainers

So, how do you go about finding people who would be successful trainers? First, you need to be clear about the criteria for an effective trainer for a specific program. Although your specific requirements will vary somewhat, there are some standard criteria for selecting trainers. A critical requirement is knowing enough about a subject to have credibility with your target audience. For example, you want to make sure that the people you choose to teach leadership skills are perceived to be effective leaders and that those who teach customer service are known for their skill with customers and their customer orientation. Often you can ask the business sponsor or the human resource representative from a particular business to name the credible experts. Sometimes you can identify these people on your own observations in and out of the classroom. In the classroom, look for people who demonstrate solid program understanding in training exercises and who show excellent presentation skills when they volunteer to share information or act as spokespersons for a group after a break-out session activity. Stay attuned to the quality of information that people share with you when you conduct a needs assessment interview or speak with them in a casual phone conversation.

Another important requirement is the trainers' enthusiasm about the subject and their desire to teach others about it. Are they willing to put the time and effort into learning how to teach a program about a particular subject? Often people will let you know that they would be interested in teaching a subject.

Keys to a Successful Train-the-Trainer Process

Making trainers out of nontrainers (subject matter experts, or SMEs) is not easy. There are, however, a number of steps that can ensure that employees and managers who learn to teach your programs succeed in delivering effective training. First, it is essential that you have a selection process and criteria to help you choose the right people who have the credibility, talent, and interest in teaching a particular subject. Businesses are often reluctant to part with their real SMEs and may want you to be content with any warm body as a trainer, not the person who would do the best job. You'll need to convince managers that in the long run having the best qualified SME teach would have the most positive impact on the business because that person would teach an effective program, whereas someone less qualified is likely to provide poorly delivered training, which ultimately leads to errors, ineffective business processes, and costly rework.

Next, it is important to provide everyone who teaches training with the right tools and learning to ensure they succeed. An effective train-the-trainer process for SMEs might include the following steps:

1. Clarify the expectations of the training certification process with the SME and the SMEs' managers. Let SMEs know that it takes time, effort, skill, and practice to become an effective trainer. Let them know that not everyone participating in the certification process may succeed in being certified as a trainer.

2. Ensure that the SME is exposed to the program prior to teaching it. It is helpful to require that the SME attend the program as a participant in order to understand the content, flow, learning dynamics, and pitfalls of the program. This may not always be possible if the

SME needs to teach the pilot program. In that case, the SME may learn about the program by playing a significant role in program design.
3. Provide a clear, user-friendly instructor's manual or leader's guide that explains the learning objectives, key learning points, training materials, and training activities for all content. In some cases you can use job aids and job procedures if trainers are providing OJT.
4. Provide a train-the-trainer workshop that teaches the appropriate content and facilitation skills. Keys to a successful workshop include creating a safe and supportive learning environment; helping people to assess their own skill levels as trainers; providing many opportunities to practice and improve by videotaping practice segments and providing constructive feedback and improvement ideas.
5. Observe new trainers and provide coaching. One way to do this is to require new trainers to teach programs with an experienced co-trainer or cofacilitator who can provide on-the-spot coaching and assistance. Tracking the program evaluations to identify areas where new trainers need to improve is another method.
6. Create a certified trainer network that allows line trainers and SMEs to share ideas about what works and what doesn't work in delivering training. Be sure to follow up with trainers to help them solve any problems they encounter.
7. Reward and recognize the contributions of SMEs who contribute to training either as designers or instructors.

Working Effectively With Outside Resources

There are many resources outside of your organization that might help you with training. Outside resources could include consultants and vendors, graduate students seeking an internship in HRD, high school or undergraduate students who participate in work-study programs, and temporary help. You can obtain excellent services from students wishing to learn HRD in action as part of various study programs. At UNUM, we recently used a University of Southern Maine graduate student in HRD who wanted some company experience to develop a self-study writing skills module as part of an employee certification program—we could have never made the deadline or kept the budget without additional free help. Arnold of Navistar has used graduate students on several occasions to help with needs assessment and program development.

How can you find outside resources who can help? One helpful strategy is to keep a network with other trainers and human resources professionals within your company and other organizations. You can also ask your colleagues for referrals for competent external resources. Joining the national American Society for Training & Development (ASTD), in Alexandria, Virginia, and the local ASTD chapter can provide you with useful contacts. You may find consultants by attending national or local conferences. Frequently, training conferences will include expositions of vendors that could be future resources for you. ASTD publishes a consultant directory and also maintains an online service, ASTD Online, which can serve as another source for consultants. Once you've joined any professional training organization or attended a training conference, you will be added to a myriad of mailing lists. Take time to review the catalogs, fliers, and "junk mail" that you receive because they may include precisely the resource you will need at a later time. Finally, the Internet may be a possible source of consultants.

Consultants can be a good way to deliver training if you have the budget and know external consultants that have the credibility and skills to get the job done. Perhaps you can score a quick win with an off-the-shelf program. These programs can be helpful in meeting generic skills, such as communicating effectively, managing time, preventing sexual harassment, managing others, and the like. Nunziati's case on Logitech is a good example of using a generic time management program. Sometimes vendors offer special deals on their programs and allow some employees to attend their programs for free or a nominal fee in order to build interest.

A key to successful use of consultants and vendors is having a well-thought-out selection process to ensure that you hire the right one. See O'Neill's case on Rock-Tenn for an excellent discussion of how to work with consultants. Important steps in selecting a consultant to develop a program include the following actions:
1. Locate potential resources and create a candidate list. Having more than one consultant provides options, a better chance to get the most cost-effective solution, the potential to gain ideas from more than one source, and a back-up strategy in case your first choice falls through for any reason.
2. Create a vendor selection committee. Sharing the responsibility for selecting the right vendor with the business not only improves your selection, but also creates a sense of business ownership for the training.
3. Create selection criteria to help you choose the most appropriate consultant. Criteria might include expertise, familiarity with your

industry, proven track record, capacity of the company to produce high-quality training materials using a variety of delivery mechanisms, capacity to produce training quickly, solvency of the vendor (to ensure that it lasts throughout a long program development time), the quality of their instructors, and your gut feeling about how it would be to work with them.

4. Create a request for proposal (often referred to as an RFP), which includes design specifications that detail your requirements. (See McCoy, 1993; and Abella, 1986 for more information on design "specs.")

5. Review proposals and work samples. Make sure that you review written proposals and sample training materials to get a feel for the consultant's style, approach, and competence.

6. Check references. It is amazing what you can learn by speaking with other people who have worked with the vendor. It can help you avoid a disastrous decision or learn how to work most effectively with the consultant that you hire.

7. Meet with the finalists and make sure that you speak with the people who will actually do the work, not just with the salesperson. If you are selecting a consultant to deliver training, make sure that you observe the instructor to ensure that he or she is competent and that there is a fit with your organization. If you cannot observe the person teaching a live program, you can usually do so on videotape.

8. Negotiate with the consultant to ensure that you get the best deal before making your decision. In one instance, I had a consultant reduce his fee by $40,000 to beat out a competitor's bid.

Hiring the right consultant is only half the battle. When you are short of resources, it is tempting to think that a consultant will do all the work for you. With customized programs, consider the time and effort required to manage consultants. Although consultants have expertise, they require guidance and monitoring. Unless they understand your business, the consultant's programs won't truly meet your business's needs. Farewell in the American Honda case mentions that he selected a consultant who rode a motorcycle and that ongoing communication with this consultant helped contribute to his project's success. Consultants' contributions vary tremendously depending on how you manage them. Even though consultants are outside your organization, they should not appear to be external or out of touch with your organization's issues and culture. This connection may require considerable coaching from you. You should not let consultants run loose throughout your organization. If you have hired them, they represent you.

Some keys to working well with consultants include the following steps. First, make sure that you create a well-thought-out contract that clearly specifies the roles and responsibilities of the consultant and your organization. Next, it is important to build a project plan with regular milestones and clarify expectations of how you and the consultant will work together. It is essential that you provide an orientation and introduction to your organization. For a program to be effective, it is important that the consultant understand and fit within your organization's culture. See Nunziati's case on Logitech and O'Neill on Rock-Tenn. Be sure that you follow up at significant milestones to ensure that the consultant is progressing on schedule. Finally, it is helpful to have a safety valve and a back-up plan in case the consultant fails to meet deadlines or does not work out as planned.

Maintaining Resilience and a Positive Attitude

Having a positive attitude is essential to your success. Your attitude affects your ability to think of possibilities, to influence others, and to build key partnerships inside and outside your organization. It also is a source of sustained momentum and energy that you will need to overcome obstacles and the foundation for your mental and physical well-being. A key challenge in a small training department is facing all the demands and keeping up with the constant work pressures without being overwhelmed. Sometimes it is easier to notice all that you cannot do rather than what you can do. Given the size of the responsibilities you face, you can feel like "a tiny speck of dust in the universe" to quote the words of Ed Asner on the *Mary Tyler Moore Show*. This pitfall of feeling small, inconsequential, and powerless can be particularly compelling if you have previously worked in a very large HRD department or if your department has been downsized significantly.

A key part of resilience is taking care of yourself so that you have the energy to work long hours. Balling has written a book, *Fit to Train* (1997), and offers seminars at various conferences that offer advice on eating and exercise habits that help maintain your physical and emotional health. Balling's case on Collagen shares some of her tips for maintaining her positive outlook. Keeping a sense of humor is key. In addition, finding time to do activities that restore you can go a long way in regenerating your spirit. Monnin, for example, makes sure that she allows time to play tennis or ski, depending on the season. I find that working in my garden and watching or participating in sports is very restorative. If you travel as part of your job, take advantage of opportunities on those trips to learn about different cultures and take in local sights. For those of you who are open to it, polarity therapy can be a wonderful way to relax yourself, tap into your creativity, and focus your energy. This therapy involves a mixture of light massage, work with crystals, and a variety of relaxation techniques. For more information on polarity therapy, get in touch with the American Polarity Therapy Association, in Boulder, Colorado.

When you're in a small department, it is easy to get into a reactive mode in which you respond to urgent demands for your services and stay in a constant state of crisis. Being in constant crisis can be very exhausting and discouraging and can lead you to feel that you aren't making a meaningful contribution because you stay focused on short-term requests, rather than on important longer term priorities that are not so urgent. Having a longer term focus helps the organization you serve and helps you stay true to your values and priorities. By staying focused on what you want to accomplish and how you can make a difference, rather than dwelling on what you cannot do, you can make a big difference in your own attitude. On a personal note, my entire outlook on my job at Chase changed when an executive in our business in Brazil told me that he valued my advice and that I would be much more effective if I focused on what I could do rather than what I could not do. This attitude shift not only helped increase my effectiveness as a consultant but also buoyed my spirits and confidence.

Books and workshops can be wonderful ways for you to refocus yourself on important goals and to restore needed balance in your life. I've found that reading *The Path of Least Resistance: Learning to Become the Creative Force in Your Own Life* by Robert Fritz (1989) and attending his workshops are helpful in realizing my aspirations. You can learn to take actions and put supports in place that make it much easier for you to succeed. Fritz teaches the importance of visualizing your important goals on a daily basis and taking actions that make it easier for you to focus on your goals. For example, I was having a hard time working on my previous book partly because I felt tired and my environment distracted me from writing (my computer was set up at an uncomfortable desk and chair next to my very comfortable bed). Not unlike many writers who experience writer's block, I wasted time berating myself for procrastinating. After taking one of Fritz's workshops, I took mental and physical steps to help redirect myself back to my goal. First, I visualized the book being completed and how pleased I would be: Visualizing success made me feel happy and energized. Next, I bought an ergonomic chair and desk, and learned to take breaks to restore my energy. After those changes and learning to respect my own natural working cycle, I was able to work for much longer periods. This same principle helped me in my business work as well.

Stephen Covey's books, audiotapes, and workshops also encourage people to make choices to respond to what's really important in their lives, rather than what is merely most urgent (see, for example, Covey, 1990). Learning by listening to audiotapes is a great way to change your perspective or learn new skills while traveling. I was very inspired by listening to Covey's audiotape "First Things First" as I drove to work in the morning. It was a much better way to start the day than listening to the news disasters of the day or the latest country hits.

Participating in learning activities of all types helps to build your skills and give you a new perspective. Stephanie Burns, author of *Artistry in Training* (Burns, 1996), advocates the value of learning a completely different skill unrelated to your job, such as learning how to play a musical instrument or how to sky dive, to keep your mind sharp, to build your own flexibility, and to enhance your awareness of what's involved in the learning process itself.

One excellent way to build your skills, increase your personal network with others who have common interests, and refresh your enthusiasm is to speak at various training conferences, present courses or workshops at a local university, and write books and articles. Since writing *Managing a Small HRD Department* (McCoy, 1993), I have spoken about that topic and other topics at local and national ASTD conferences, at an International Quality and Productivity Conference, and at a local conference, "Women in Management," sponsored by the University of Southern Maine in Portland. In addition, I teach Managing Training and Development at the University of Southern Maine's School of Continuing Education. It's very rewarding for me to share what I know and to learn from others in the HRD profession. Connecting with people outside of my current organization keeps me plugged into organizational and business trends, and also gives me a broader context for my work. Publishing can be a wonderful way to share knowledge and learn at the same time. I've enjoyed interviewing and working with other trainers as part of writing and editing books. Finally, I've found it enlightening to work with publishing companies as an HRD expert who reviews potential manuscripts.

Summary

In conclusion, there are several strategies to keep in mind so you can thrive in a small training department. First, you need to ensure that you have identified the priority training needs and that you focus on these priorities. Second, you need to take steps to establish your credibility and build a strong base of support for your efforts by getting to know the business and creating partnerships with key players inside your organization. Third, have a resource strategy that takes advantage of all potential resources inside and outside of your organization. This strategy will greatly expand your capacity and effectiveness in providing training support. Finally, you will get much more done in your work life and feel much more satisfied and healthy if you find ways to keep your outlook balanced and positive and your activities focused on your important goals.

References

Abella, K.T. (1986). *Building Successful Training Programs*. Reading, MA: Addison-Wesley.

Allen, E.L., editor (1990). *ASTD Trainer's Toolkit: Needs Assessment Instruments*. Alexandria, VA: American Society for Training & Development.

Balling, C.S. (1997). *Fit to Train: How to Succeed at Training Delivery Without Really Tiring*. Minneapolis: Lakewood Publishing.

Block, P. (1981). *Flawless Consulting: A Guide to Getting Your Expertise Used*. San Diego: Learning Concepts.

Burns, S. (1996). *Artistry in Training: Thinking Differently About the Way You Help People to Learn*. Warriewood, New South Wales: Woodslane Press.

Covey, S.R. (1990). *The Seven Habits of Highly Effective People: Powerful Lessons in Personal Change*. New York: Fireside Books, Simon & Schuster.

Fritz, R. (1989). *The Path of Least Resistance: Learning to Become the Creative Force in Your Own Life*. New York: Fawcett Columbine.

Kaufman, R., Rojas, A.M., and Mayer, M. (1993). *Needs Assessment: A User's Guide*. Englewood Cliffs, NJ: Educational Technology Publications.

McCoy, C.P. (1993). *Managing a Small HRD Department: You Can Do More Than You Think*. San Francisco: Jossey-Bass.

Phillips, J.J., and Holton, E.F., III, editors (1995). *In Action: Conducting Needs Assessment*. Alexandria, VA: American Society for Training & Development.

Robinson, D.G., and Robinson, J.C. (1996). *Performance Consulting: Moving Beyond Training*. San Francisco: Berrett-Koehler.

Zemke, R., and Kramlinger, T. (1989). *Figuring Things Out: A Trainer's Guide to Needs and Task Analysis*. Reading, MA: Addison-Wesley.

Involving Vice Presidents as Trainers in a Worldwide Training Effort

Collagen Corporation

Carolyn Sorensen Balling

This chapter illustrates that even a part-time trainer can make a significant contribution to an organization, and it explores the advantages and challenges of working as a part-time one-person training department. Carolyn Sorensen Balling shows how she meets priority training needs for Collagen and still has time for a rewarding external consulting practice. Using the introduction of the ISO-certification process at Collagen as an example, Balling describes how to build executives' ownership and involvement in a large-scale training intervention. Balling also offers some excellent advice on how to maintain one's perspective and positive outlook.

Company Background

Collagen Corporation develops, manufactures, and markets biomedical devices for the repair of damaged or aging human tissue. Established in 1975, Collagen is based in Palo Alto, California, the cradle of Silicon Valley. The company is best known for its injectable face products, which are used, as the sales literature says, to correct soft-contour facial deformities, or as most people say, to fill in, or "plump up," wrinkles. Our primary customers for these products are plastic surgeons, facial plastic surgeons, and dermatologists, whom we train and approve to use our products before they begin injecting patients.

The injectable collagen products are derived from bovine collagen, extracted from the hides of a "closed herd" of steers located

This case was prepared to serve as a basis for discussion rather than to illustrate either effective or ineffective administrative and management practices.

in the northern reaches of California. Having a closed herd means that we know the lineage, diets, and habits of every member of the herd and that other animals do not commingle with ours on the range or in our harvesting facility. Collagen established both the herd and the slaughterhouse in the early 1990s to ensure a high-quality, safe product. The injectable collagen products are all manufactured in our plant in Fremont, across San Francisco Bay from the Palo Alto headquarters.

Following approval of the Food and Drug Administration (FDA) in the mid-1990s, Collagen began producing collagen-based products for nonfacial applications, such as urinary incontinence and bone grafts, that other firms market. The company also acquired a Swiss-based company that makes breast implants, currently available only in Europe, and beginning in 1996, added noncollagen-based facial products to its line of goods. As of 1997, Collagen had approximately 400 employees in 13 countries (with more than half of those working in two Bay Area locations). Distributors sell our products in another 26 countries.

The Beginnings of the Training Function

Collagen's Training and Development Department was established as part of the Human Resources (HR) Department in August 1989, when I was hired from the outside as a part-time employee working 20 to 25 hours per week. I originally reported to the vice president of HR, but I started reporting to the director of HR when the vice president's responsibilities expanded to include Administrative Services. While at times the Training and Development Department has included a part-time training administrator, mostly I've been on my own, borrowing necessary administrative support from HR. At Collagen, HR is a lean group, with three full-time employees, two other part-time employees besides myself, and one part-time contract employee.

The training department was established mainly in response to a desire for systematic supervisory and management development. Most employees in management positions at Collagen hadn't had previous management jobs or worked for companies large enough to provide management training. Training and development were seen as a means of helping to increase managers' effectiveness. For about two years leading up to the creation of the training department, Collagen had provided occasional management training through external consultants and an off-the-shelf, modular, management skills program. HR and other internal staff who had completed the vendor's training-for-trainers course have delivered several of those modules.

By 1989, Collagen wanted someone focused specifically on training and development. Training provided up to that point had gone well, but training needs were met more sporadically than the company wanted because coordinating and organizing training was not any person's primary priority. Staffing a training function on a part-time basis was an appropriate solution, given the company's size and age.

I liked the idea of being a part-time internal department. At that time, I had just left a position as director of human resource development and was working as an associate with a consultant. Working part-time at Collagen offered me a chance to be both internal and external. I was ready for such an alternative work arrangement that would allow me to have a more flexible schedule to continue my associate relationship and take on independent consulting jobs and would also give me fewer days with long commutes and, I hoped, less job stress. As much as I liked the flexibility and independence of consulting, I was also attracted to working internally. Besides offering steadier income than consulting, being internal would bring with it camaraderie, group synergies, and even staff birthday parties—it would meet my affiliation needs. An internal position would provide me with the opportunity to watch an organization change and individuals develop over time, too, partially as a result of the work I would do. Finally, working inside a company would make it easier to stay plugged into changes in corporate America. Being both internal and external would offer me the best of both worlds.

My background was relevant to the challenge. When I joined Collagen, I had had about 14 years of training experience, all in small to medium-small companies (or small pieces of larger organizations), all with minuscule to small staffs (of one to six employees). My training career began in my first job out of college, when I worked in Montana for a Girl Scout council, and training adult members was one of my job responsibilities. Successive jobs included stints as training manager for a Girl Scout council with 2,000 members (including 400 adults) north of San Francisco; a stock brokerage firm with 800 employees in 20 California offices; a property-casualty insurance company with 2,400 employees in seven western states; and a life insurance company with 725 employees.

In all my previous positions, being a trainer meant handling all parts of the process, from needs assessment through evaluation. Collagen was looking for the same one-stop-shop approach to training that I was used to. The departments I'd worked in before were either newly created or being returned to days of former glory. I'd been involved with and enjoyed starting up or revitalizing training functions. The Collagen job reflected pieces of every job I'd had before so I had no concerns about my ability to do it. Rather, I was intrigued with tackling the task part-time and being an external consultant part-time. I didn't consider becoming a department of one-half as a step backward. I was ready to take a side step off the corporate ladder. Even so, I had some concerns. I was worried about not being as involved in the organization as full-time employees usually are. Having less time on site would give me fewer opportunities to work the "white spaces" of the organization and keep up with the ebb and flow of corporate life. The job would also be a step removed from the decision-making access I had been used to in my previous jobs. All in all, the pluses of the job still outweighed the minuses.

Training Mission and Services Provided

During my first few months on the job, in between developing and delivering a course on interviewing skills, completely revising the new-hire orientation, and laying the groundwork for relaunching the management skills program, I developed a mission statement for the department. It was based on expectations that senior management (especially the vice president of HR) had for a training function, on input informally gathered from participants in former HR-provided training programs, and on my perspective on the role of a training function. It served to set a direction for training at Collagen and helped to educate the company about the products and services the Training and Development Department would provide. In its abbreviated form that mission is

> **Training and Development** seeks to maximize the continued performance of employees and the organization, so that Collagen Corporation achieves its goals and objectives.
> Towards that end, **Training and Development** creates, supports, manages and integrates purposeful learning experiences designed to strengthen needs and anticipated skills of employees.
> **Training and Development** operates within the context of the company, analyzing and addressing voiced and identified needs that relate to performance issues.

Embedded in the mission is a summary statement, inspired by the American Dental Association's standard statement about toothpaste: "Our basic belief is that training is an effective means of improving performance and developing employees that can be of significant value when used in a conscientiously applied program of communicated expectations, adequate resources, and regular management feedback and support."

Since 1989, the training department has provided services that tend toward the generic—knowledge and skills needed by employees regardless of their level or function, such as:

- overview of our business for new hires
- supervisory and management skills training
- HR-related workshops on topics that include interviewing skills, sexual harassment, performance appraisals, compensation plans, and policy manuals updates.

Staff in other departments handle training on specialized or technically oriented topics. For instance, the Facilities Department schedules and tracks safety training; Information Services offers system and software applications workshops; Operations provides sessions on good manufacturing practices for staff involved with manufacturing; and the Sales and Marketing Department handles its own product training for the salesforce.

With each of these groups I'm an occasional consultant, providing advice or direction in the development, administration, or delivery of training it provides. Such consulting might involve helping to find an external vendor to conduct a specific course, such as a writing skills, or advising a group on plans for its own training. Other internal consulting projects have involved facilitating department interaction and team building or rebuilding efforts. Much of the internal consulting work I do is for HR. In that role, I take on tasks that others don't have the interest or experience to complete, such as managing the redesign of the performance appraisal process; reviewing and improving internal processes in HR; and analyzing the results of hiring decisions and related turnover.

How the Training and Development Department Operates

My general needs assessment strategy involves meeting with officers, directors, and key managers to discuss business issues for an upcoming period. I do this formally every other year. Some years we've had so many must dos related to HR and general company issues that there has been no reason to determine other specific needs—we wouldn't have been able to address them all anyway. I stay current with needs and issues informally by keeping up on company developments and communications, tracking existing company measures, and interacting with employees at all levels. Because Collagen is relatively small, training priorities and training courses are generally set on the basis of the number of people they affect (needs that cross most lines), the calendar, looming deadlines, or special circumstances. For instance, training programs for new hires are scheduled once enough new hires are on board. In any given year, the number of these workshops varies. The budget and approximate timing of these sessions is based on projected openings given the current turnover rate.

The courses may be developed in-house, purchased off-the-shelf, or created by consultants. Training delivery is typically via classroom. We have a few underused audiotaped and videotaped tutorials, primarily dealing with computer applications programs, in the company's Information Center. Internal course delivery usually involves managers or speakers from other areas working with me. That gives us a chance to share the load and credibility and to provide exposure for managers in the role of trainer.

The extent to which course evaluation occurs depends on the course. At a minimum, I use reaction evaluations for all courses. Frequently, evaluations of learning take place, especially with skill- or knowledge-building programs. Besides product training, which uses paper and pencil tests, evaluations occur through skill practice sessions, role-plays, discussion, and problem-solving exercises. Several times when a workshop has dealt with perceptions, I have taken before and after measures of opinions to gauge the impact of training. In a few instances, I've measured behavior changes with postcourse evaluations, in written, electronic, or oral formats. Although I have been able to see clear improvements, the small numbers involved may mean the results are not statistically significant.

In general, Collagen values learning. Employees take advantage of internal offerings and of external opportunities as well. Collagen employees attend external seminars, conferences, and other professional development opportunities with the approval of their managers. I'm not involved in these decisions unless I'm suggesting sources for the employee or manager to contact. As with many companies, higher level employees can travel farther, stay longer, and pay more in registration fees for their learning opportunities. Tracking of training at Collagen has shown us that on average nonexempt employees receive just over 50 hours of training per year (most of it delivered internally, on the job); exempt employees (excluding executives) receive about 59 hours; and executives receive between 70 and 100 hours per year. Departments often bring in consultants or trainers to help with particular, technically oriented issues.

Despite all those hours of training, Collagen would be characterized more as training light than training heavy. The company is not intent on creating an internal corporate university, being on the cutting edge of training technology, or transforming itself into a learning organization. The training function at Collagen doesn't jump on many human resource development (HRD) bandwagons or grab on to many training fads. Training and development at Collagen can help fill appropriate, generic gaps—and they do. Although my work arrangement at Collagen is innovative, I often think that the company's training could be more plentiful and cutting edge. However, doing more and being different would require pushing more and getting more resources than are available within the current bounds and expectations of the job. The training that we do offer is high quality, well received, and well regarded. I wish we could do more.

The Fun and Challenge of Being a Part-Time Trainer at Collagen

In the years I've been in the job, the positives and negatives have remained the same. A continuing positive is autonomy. In addition to support and respect, I have tremendous independence in everything I do, from picking the hours and days I work to providing training services. The hardest part of being a part-timer is not feeling as plugged into the company as I'd like. The people I've reported to have had the seat at the decision-making table that I have had in previous jobs. Although they've kept me clued in on company news (as does the company overall, through its regular communication channels), it's not quite the same. Because I'm not always around, I have to fight to avoid being invisible. Although it takes more effort and time to be visible, the obvious payoff is keeping training in existence and me in employment at Collagen.

The scariest aspect of being a part-time employee is having truncated timelines. A project with a deadline that's a month away translates into two and a half weeks maximum for me. Because I've mostly had no staff, there is usually no one to move projects along when I'm out. A big challenge is establishing a flow at the start of a project—determining what needs to be done when, what can be done without me, or at least what isn't affected by my absence. In between my days at Collagen, I'm usually doing work for other companies, and that can be mentally taxing. The simplest way I've found to cope is to keep many to-do lists—per project, per quarter, per day, for the present and the future. It's not very exotic, but it works.

My employment with Collagen is the longest I've ever worked for one company. Several reasons account for my longevity. The key reasons are the work environment and autonomy as well as the respect for my skills that I experience throughout Collagen. Working part-time is a contributing factor, too. The change of pace and variety I get through consulting make variety in internal assignments less important. I don't mind giving the same course over and over at Collagen, as I did when I worked full-time in other places.

Collagen's culture is another reason I've remained with the company. At Collagen, my colleagues and I talk a lot about the importance of "fit." For us, fit has to do with compatible work styles; preference for action, interaction, and getting things done; and comfort with a lean, open organization with little pretense. It's often hard for employees who come from larger companies to make a successful transition to Collagen. They often feel it doesn't offer enough in terms of support, organizational policies, or practices. In contrast, I've always felt that I fit Collagen well and have been able to adapt to its myriad changes over the years. I like what I do at Collagen, the business we're in, how we go about that business, and the people who carry it out.

Success Story—Introducing ISO Certification

During the fall of 1994, training and development took on a training effort that would within a few months involve training all of Collagen's 300 employees worldwide. Because of the relative vastness of the undertaking and the smallness of the department—two part-time employees at that time—that assignment provides a good case study in tackling a big task with limited resources.

The Business Need and Challenge

In September 1994, Collagen Corporation decided to pursue ISO 9001 certification, a designation, established in 1987, that recognizes manufacturing companies who meet expectations of quality in their internal processes. Being ISO certified is a step toward achieving a CE mark. Having both ISO certification and a CE mark signifies that a company meets required standards for quality manufacturing and management, and helps to reduce regulatory hurdles for products in Europe. These designations are now considered necessary for any company selling manufactured goods in the European Community.

Collagen wanted and needed both. Nevertheless, the challenge of seeking ISO certification was daunting. To receive certification, Collagen had to demonstrate that it had numerous, defined processes clearly described, followed, and thoroughly documented. The company wanted to be certified by June 1995. True to its corporate style, Collagen was attempting to prepare for an audit and certification in nine months, compared to the recommended 12 to 24 months.

An ISO Certification Team in the regulatory affairs/quality assurance (RA/QA) area was handling preparation for the three-day audit leading to certification. That group had to document existing company processes, conduct internal audits to uncover areas needing process improvement, and schedule training (outside vendors give) for employees in manufacturing and research and development on critical aspects of ISO that were related to their job duties and functions. As part of the preparation process, senior management decided that all 300 worldwide employees needed to receive baseline training about ISO. The management group wanted every employee in the company to understand the purpose of ISO and its basic tenets, the reasons for certification, steps involved in becoming certified, Collagen's quality policy, and how each job related to the company's quality focus. Given its other responsibilities, the ISO Certification Team did not have time to provide such an ISO overview course. Even if it did, its members didn't have the background to design or conduct the training. Although there was money for consultants, those dollars seemed better directed toward the technical aspects of the certification process.

Senior management asked the Training and Development Department—composed of myself and a part-time administrative assistant—to design, develop, and administer an ISO-overview training course. The course represented Collagen's first-ever, worldwide training effort since the company had gone global in 1991. Senior management wanted the department to create a solution to this training need much as it had handled other all-employee interventions, such as sexual harassment workshops during the summer of 1992. It left every decision about ISO-overview training to the department—timing, format, approach, content, presenters, and evaluation.

Developing the Training Intervention

As soon as we were given the assignment, we developed the basic approach. Central to our plan was to involve vice presidents (VPs) of the company as the presenters of the information, especially to the staff in their own functions. We had several reasons for making this decision. Primarily, we wanted the VPs attached to the message about ISO—we didn't want the ISO-overview sessions viewed as HR programs. We felt the VPs' involvement was critical to the credibility of the officers as well as of the ISO certification effort. At that time, many employees were skeptical about whether the officers were united in the drive for certification or were even knowledgeable about details of ISO. Placing VPs in the role of trainer would help allay that skepticism. It would also ensure that the officers all had a similar base of knowledge about the certification process. Finally, we felt that the VPs were in the best position to answer questions from their own staffs about how individual jobs related to ISO certification.

After developing the general approach, I sketched out a design for a short overview course. In drafting the design, I considered several factors: what employees (myself included) wanted and needed to know about ISO as it pertained to Collagen; the internal communication about ISO up to that point; and the connection most employees had to ISO certification (which wasn't much), and what it needed to be. I also included the key points the ISO Certification Team wanted all employees to know—information that the auditors were likely to ask randomly selected individuals. The design was for a one-hour session— about the maximum for a fairly directive, knowledge-based (not skill-building) session. We wanted every employee to have a similar, general knowledge base about ISO, however simplified. This would be better than the current situation in which a few employees knew a great deal at a very detailed level, whereas others knew close to nothing. There were four simple objectives. Specifically, by the end of the session we wanted participants to be able to

1. repeat Collagen's Quality Policy
2. name at least two places where a written copy of the Quality Policy can be found
3. list the three primary criteria of ISO standards and explain what each means
4. explain the relationship of Collagen's quality management system and the ISO guidelines to their own jobs.

Armed with an overall strategy, a general outline, and session objectives, I presented my proposal to the VP of HR and Administrative Services. She gave it a green light. Next, I tested the plan with the VP of RA/QA, who headed the ISO Certification Team. Then I met one-on-one with the other officers to enlist their support for the course overall and, mostly, for being the course trainers. Everyone supported the concept and said that they were willing to deliver the sessions.

The task was then to develop a short course that met the objectives and that the officers could present comfortably. Because we had done something similar with the sexual harassment workshops two summers before, I knew the officers would want a scripted presentation (even if they didn't follow the script) as well as a general outline and plenty of visuals to support their remarks. The core of the program, the refrain to repeat, came from an explanation given at a company meeting about the essence of ISO: "Say what you do. Do what you say. Keep good records." Basically, the overview course had to communicate that message and explain it. Every employee needed to know that phrase and what it meant. To flesh out the design details, I bought the simplest book I could find on the subject (Patterson, 1995). I also borrowed materials from the ISO Certification Team and met with the members to fill in my gaps in my knowledge about ISO.

Gaining Management Approval

Once I developed the script, I had key VPs and internal experts review it for accuracy and tone. The finalized script went to all VPs prior to a mid-January 1995 senior management meeting. At that meeting, they would approve the script and reach decisions about session schedules and whether VPs would conduct presentations alone or in teams of two. We recommended scheduling about 20 Bay Area workshops from the end of January through March, including two regional sales meetings for field sales representatives. We also recommended shipping scripts and visuals overseas by March, giving our Collagen International employees two months to conduct the overview session before the audit date. (Because no auditors would be meeting with Collagen employees outside the United States, we weren't as concerned with international implementation. Our primary concern was ensuring that employees who were likely to run into auditors would be well informed.)

The critical manager meeting occurred on January 17. At that meeting, the CEO stated that he wanted one session conducted each day from March 15 to April 15, during the final push before the May audit so the information would be fresh in employees' minds. The group that day decided that it would train in teams of two, and that none of them would be able to deliver the session at either regional sales meeting. I came out of the meeting with script approval, agreement on the general approach, and a clear time frame. The only unknown was a strategy for training the salesforce. We needed a new solution for that group because the VPs wouldn't be presenting at the regional sales meetings. We ended up gaining several weeks to complete the project because the first workshop would begin in two months, rather than by month's end as originally planned.

Dealing With Logistics

In those remaining two months (more like one month for us, as part-timers, though), we dealt with logistics issues and polished the program materials. Logistically, scheduling speakers and attendees involved several steps. We scheduled rooms and equipment for 14 one-hour sessions, for each Tuesday, Wednesday, and Thursday between March 14 and April 12. We assigned each VP to present three or four sessions as either a primary or secondary presenter. Employees would be invited to attend a session at which their VP was the primary presenter. We sent initial communication about upcoming sessions to all employees and sample announcements to the executive coordinators of each VP for them to customize and send to their employees. (Executive coordinators, not the Training and Development Department, were responsible for ensuring that employees responded and for making sure that all the employees in their function attended one of the 14 sessions.)

Polishing the course materials involved finishing the session script and creating colored-ink overheads using PowerPoint, the computer software program, for visuals. Finally we assembled binders for each VP trainer, containing the following:

- narrative script, with points indicated for discussion with the audience
- overheads (including a few ISO-related Scott Adams's Dilbert series cartoons)
- reduced-size hard copy of overheads with room for presenters to note key points they wanted to make
- schedule of all sessions and presenters
- sign-in sheets for attendees
- reminder of their responsibilities as trainers (including finding their own substitute, if they need one)
- tips on presenting the session and on using equipment effectively.

As we put the finishing touches on the program, we also decided that, although not ideal, the best way to inform our 30 field sales representatives in the United States and Canada would be to videotape one of the VP-led sessions. We contracted an external video service to record the session by our new company president and the VP of regulatory, the VP most knowledgeable about ISO, which was to be given to the inside sales reps, marketing group, and customer relations employees. (The videotape would serve to introduce the salesforce to the new president as well as to ISO.) The national sales manager flew in to attend that session, too. She worked with the cameraman to tape a message to edit into the beginning of the video as an introduction for the salesforce, and asked questions as an audience member would during question-and-answer periods. We alerted the salesforce and the regional sales managers that the tape would be coming and needed to be watched by May 1. Tapes went out to each sales rep, along with a letter from the national sales manager, within two weeks of the recording.

We also assembled and shipped binders to each of our country managers. Their assignment was to schedule and conduct sessions, or at least discuss the materials with all their employees by May 1. Some country managers had to have the script and overheads translated in order to complete that assignment.

The Results and Lessons Learned

Our plan worked! Every scheduled session occurred as planned. VPs delivered the programs with no apparent problems. They found their own substitutes; customized communication to their staffs about the program; altered times of sessions to best meet the needs of their groups; took responsibility for the courses, and kept us informed. The VPs let us know what modifications or customizations they wanted in the overheads (and we made the changes and sent the updates to all VPs). We noticed that the sessions seemed to get shorter the more often the VPs presented them, no doubt because they learned the points to emphasize and the places to skip. We also noticed that the message was getting through—employees knew that ISO could be summarized as "Say what you do. Do what you say. Keep good records." They knew Collagen's Quality Policy and where to find it in writing. The objectives were met!

We did not include evaluation forms as part of the session package because we didn't want the presenting VPs to compete for high evaluation scores on reaction evaluation forms; we just wanted employees to find out about ISO. In hindsight, I wish we had included reaction evaluations, however simple. Evaluation data would have helped us measure the success of the project from the employees' perspective.

We also regretted doing little to follow up with the field sales reps or the overseas groups. Our task had been to develop the course and turn it over to the officers to implement. The VPs were supposed to follow up with staff in their areas of responsibility, including field sales and overseas offices, but their schedules and priorities interfered. In hindsight, I wish we'd had a process for tracking out-of-area implementation.

The most positive lesson we learned was that we could carry out a global training effort for 300 employees. With a plan that made sense and that had buy-in from our senior management and other key players, we could accomplish a great deal, even as two part-timers. We were pleased that we were able to keep our involvement in that intervention nearly hidden from employees. We designed and implemented a plan that let the VPs take center stage and reap the rewards, precisely our desired outcome.

Every employee attended a workshop or received a tape. Everyone heard what the purpose of ISO was and why Collagen was pursuing certification. Our employees were informed in time for the ISO audit. By helping bring all employees up to speed on ISO and the certification process, we contributed to Collagen's receiving its ISO certification and a CE mark, following our successful May audit. We completed the task and lived up to our department's mission in doing so. What training department, of any size or configuration, could ask for more?

Some Final Advice

Shortly before starting my job at Collagen Corporation, I came across a quote attributed to Pope John XXIII. It offered me the perfect advice as I headed into being a training department of one-half. Thinking back over the six other training jobs I've had in the past 20-plus years, I realize it applies to each of them as well. The perfect guidance for an HRD professional, unwittingly offered by Pope John XXIII, is "See everything. Overlook a great deal. Correct a little."

Like the process of training itself, I find that advice powerful in its simplicity, yet often difficult in its execution. Here's my elaboration on the advice based on how I've tried to put the words into action throughout my training career.

See Everything

Observe your organization and the people in it. Keep an eye on your company's customers and their needs as well as your own department's customers and their needs. Watch processes and how they work as well as where they crack and what drops through when they do. Note what and who gets reported, rewarded, ignored, and erased. Keep fingers on several pulses. Listen as well as see.

See things outside your company as well. Plug into training organizations. Keep up on reading or at least scan titles and look at captions. Stay tuned to issues faced in the training field by your colleagues in other firms and your company's industry. This learning through observation will not only help you be a more effective manager and employee but also help you design and implement HRD interventions that stand a chance of success.

Overlook a Great Deal

Know that everything isn't important. In fact, lots of things don't even matter. Learn the difference between what's important and what's not in your company. Pick your spots and your battles. Use your limited time, energy, and resources wisely—spend them on interventions and actions that will make the biggest difference for the company and will bring the greatest return. Think optimal, not ideal. Choose your crusades wisely, too—avoid being the perpetual champion of lost causes.

Correct a Little

Everything that isn't working quite right isn't broken, bad, or in need of major corrective surgery. In fact, everything that's broken doesn't deserve fixing. Again, pick your spots. Correct the correctable. Correct only what others are committed to correcting (that could include correcting their lack of commitment). Your job isn't to create a perfect organization. Your job is to help the organization do best what it does.

Shortly after starting at Collagen, I began a new lunch hour routine that's made all the difference in maintaining a positive perspective and avoiding burnout. I walk a couple of miles with Collagen employees from other departments as often as possible. What a difference 40 minutes and fresh air can make! Problems that loom large before lunch shrink away after a walk. Everything becomes more tolerable after a break, time outside, and a little exercise. Few HRD issues can't wait until after lunch to be addressed. In two decades in the business, I have yet to be called away from my desk for an emergency needs assessment. Solutions and needed insights often appear during walks, either from discussion with other walkers or on their own. If you want balance in your life, if you want others to have balance, you need to model it by creating it. Getting out, giving yourself time for your physical side, does that. Walking makes lunch taste that much better, too.

Questions for Discussion

1. What does the mission statement of Collagen's Training and Development Department position the function to do in the company?
2. The training department at Collagen Corporation chose to enlist vice presidents as trainers for the ISO-overview course. What other approaches would have been appropriate?
3. What are the advantages and disadvantages of a training department choosing a behind-the-scenes role for an intervention, as Collagen's department did with the ISO-overview training project?
4. When would it make more sense for a small company to outsource training rather than hire part-time employees, and when would the opposite make sense?
5. In what ways could Collagen's Training and Development Department have evaluated the presenters and the ISO-awareness training course to determine the effectiveness of each?

The Author

Following several years as a training manager in a variety of industries, Carolyn Sorensen Balling now splits her time between being a one-person internal training department at Collagen Corporation, a biomedical firm in Silicon Valley, and an external consultant, working with companies on issues relating to performance and training. Previously Balling started and headed the Training and Development Department for AMEX Life Assurance Company; managed the Corporate Training and Development departments at Industrial Indemnity, a property-casualty insurance services firm, and Sutro & Co. stock brokerage; and served as training director for Napa-Solano Girl Scout Council. A frequent presenter at national training conferences and a member of the advisory board for Lakewood Conference's Training Director's Forum, Balling is also an instructor in University of California, Berkeley, Extension's Training and HRD Certification Program and the author of *Fit to Train—How to Succeed at Training Delivery (Without Really Tiring)*, 1997, Lakewood Publications. Balling holds a B.A. in psychology from University of California, Berkeley, and an M.S. in education from California State University. Carolyn Balling may be contacted at Collagen Corporation, 2500 Faber Place, Palo Alto, CA 94303; phone: 650.354.4658; fax: 650.354.4932; or at her own business, Training That Fits, 6743 Banning Drive, Oakland, CA 94611; phone or fax: 510.339.9039.

References

Balling, C.S. (1997). *Fit to Train—How to Succeed at Training (Without Really Tiring)*. Minneapolis: Lakewood Publications.

Patterson, J.G. (1995). *ISO 9000—Worldwide Quality Standard*. Los Altos, CA: Crisp Publications.

Developing People at Rock-Tenn

Rock-Tenn Company

Kathryn S. O'Neill

This case illustrates how a one-person training department can support the development of managers. Kathryn O'Neill shows how she selects and works with outside vendors to ensure she has the best resource for any human resource development (HRD) intervention. She describes how she created an effective partnership with senior management in planning to implement enhanced management development training at Rock-Tenn. Having worked previously in a small training department, O'Neill shares her thoughts on how to build your own skills to succeed in this role.

Company Background

Based in Norcross, Georgia, Rock-Tenn Company is one of North America's leading manufacturers of packaging, 100 percent recycled paperboard, and laminated paperboard products. Product lines include folding cartons, corrugated packaging and displays, and thermoformed plastic packaging. Over 70 manufacturing facilities in the United States and Canada employ approximately 8,000 people who are supported by the small Home Office Group of 200, as the company lives by a lean-and-mean philosophy. About one-third of the plants are unionized.

Since its founding in 1973, the company has grown by acquisition, with the merger of Rock City Box Company of Tennessee and Tennessee Paper Mills, creating a vertically integrated company. The papermill produced the paperboard, and the folding carton plant converted it to products of higher value for external customers. In 1976, Bradley Currey Jr., the current chairman and CEO, joined

This case was prepared to serve as a basis for discussion rather than to illustrate either effective or ineffective administrative and management practices.

A. Worley Brown, the retired chairman, to assist in running the company. Since their first acquisition of a Texas papermill in 1979, the company's sales have grown from $88.5 million to $1.2 billion. In 1994, Rock-Tenn became a public company, traded on the New York Stock Exchange.

The company operates with a decentralized structure, with considerable decision-making responsibility located in the divisions and plant network. Seven divisions produce different products. The Recycled Fiber and Mill divisions produce raw materials that they sell internally to converting divisions and externally to other converters. Paperboard converting divisions include folding carton, paperboard product, corrugated, and partition. The Plastic Packaging Division gathers its own raw materials to recycle, and it produces roll stock as a raw material for itself and external customers and thermoformed plastic packaging. The company's governing body is the Management Committee, consisting of the CEO and other senior executives. Plant general managers (GMs) in most divisions have profit-and-loss responsibility and considerable decision-making authority for their sites. Capital expenditures gain approval through a multilayer decision-making process, but most other decisions are made locally. Few programs and approaches are mandated from the top. For example, top management sets corporate-wide safety targets, but GMs create their own plans to reach the goals.

The company's mission is "To provide cost effective solutions to customers' needs. Our success is based on adherence to realistic and challenging objectives which guide the way we do business." In 1976, Brown and Currey created a statement of the company's core values, which were published as objectives in the 1994 Annual Report. The top five of Rock-Tenn's 12 objectives appear in table 1.

Among other achievements, these objectives have guided management to the position of industry leader in safety with a record of injury prevention that is 70 percent better than the industry average. Value for people is expressed through the yearly ritual of service awards, during which Currey and Jay Shuster, president and chief operating officer (COO), make the rounds of the plants with divisional executives and shake the hand of every employee. Most sites have standing teams with rotating membership from all levels in the plant that oversee quality and safety and make recommendations for improvement.

The Training Function

The position of director, training resources, was created in 1993 as part of the Risk Management Department at the Home Office Group.

Table 1. The top five of Rock-Tenn's 12 objectives.

Objectives	
Customer	Customers are the lifeblood of our business. With them we can be anything; without them we are nothing. We will do things for our customers that our competitors cannot or will not do.
People	The most valuable resource of the company is the people who make up the Rock-Tenn Team. We must maintain an environment that will attract and retain quality people and encourage their personal development.
Safety	Injuries bring suffering and devastation to people and their families. Safety is a primary concern of Rock-Tenn, and our goal is no less than zero personal injuries.
Quality	Quality is the key to satisfying customers. Our objective is to be recognized by our customers as the quality leader in the products and services we provide. All facets of our business are employing continuous improvements to achieve this objective.
Environment	Rock-Tenn people recycle recovered paper and other materials. Recycling, source reduction, and proper disposal of waste materials help Rock-Tenn contribute to the preservation of natural resources.

At that time, the manager, risk management, and his manager, the chief financial officer (CFO), were engaged in assisting the company to build awareness of and compliance with environmental laws. In this process, they were conducting environmental familiarization training that wasn't as effective as they required. In addition, the need to improve supervisory skills at the plant level was growing, and these managers could anticipate increasing future needs as a result of growth. The original mission of the training position was to improve existing training and to assist management in making effective choices for future training. The incumbent would be expected to position the function effectively, given the structure and culture of the company, and to find ways to work with management so as to create processes and knowledge for making training decisions.

Rock-Tenn delivers traditional human resources services as an educational function, not a compliance function. Consistent with the corporate lean-and-mean staffing philosophy, a small staff in each human resources functional area acts to educate field managers and to consult with them in solving problems. Benefits administration, including medical and pension, is centralized as part of risk management. Along with benefits, risk management also includes safety and environmental compliance, administration for workers' compensation and other insurance policies, and two positions that provide consultation on labor and employee relations problems. Because human resources functions are located in the Risk Management Department, training was added to that department. (See figure 1.) The director, training resources, is a one-person shop that reports to the vice president, risk management and administration. In this position, I share the services of an administrative support person with the director, labor and employee relations. At the time the position was created, there were no other employees at Rock-Tenn with a training title.

Because the divisions operate autonomously and vary in size, they are free to make training choices at individual plant sites. Several divisions have added divisional training coordinators, but these positions are designed as developmental and focus primarily on facilitation and training delivery. Typically, incumbents move on from the training role to plant line management. The Marketing Services Group has also added a training group that creates and delivers product knowledge techni-

Figure 1. Organization chart, risk management and administration at Rock-Tenn.

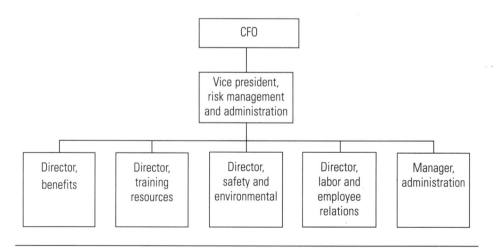

cal training for sales representatives and team building training for interdivisional project teams. Inside the Home Office Group, a training group now operates in the Information Services Department. This department creates job aids and other written guides for software installation and operation, and recently it designed and delivered training to support sales force automation and the installation of Windows 95 at the Home Office Group. None of the other training groups report to the director, training resources, who is the only person with training as a career focus. I maintain consulting and support relationships with the other groups and often help them to locate and select resources.

Several training efforts have a corporate-wide focus through a consensus of Management Committee members. In making the decisions regarding what programs to use, I have found training options that fit the company culture and the objectives of the project, and I have facilitated the decision-making process with the Management Committee. Rock-Tenn uses Zenger Miller *FrontLine Leadership* for training frontline supervisors and *Dimensions of Professional Selling (DPS)* from Carew Positional Selling for sales training. As a master trainer for Zenger Miller, I train and certify facilitators at the plant level. As one of six certified trainers for Carew DPS, I coordinate the delivery of DPS workshops as needed by divisional hiring; the training is delivered by certified working salespeople from the divisions. Once a plant trainer is certified for Zenger Miller, delivery of the training becomes a turnkey operation at the site level, and plants organize their own sessions, including purchase of materials.

If a project originates with management, I source training options and assist in making and implementing a choice. Currently, I consult with a subcommittee of the Management Committee to locate providers who will custom design management development training directed at plant GMs and others in positions of equivalent responsibility. I also act as an entrepreneur and originate projects where I see an opportunity. For example, after identifying a need for training in coaching skills for sales managers, I raised the issue with divisional sales managers and found interest in five of seven divisions. I then assisted in sourcing vendors and coordinating implementation for their chosen option. Budget for the position has grown to approximately $300,000. This figure includes funds for materials and facilities costs for two yearly consolidated Zenger Miller workshops for frontline supervisors, for facilitator certification workshops, for sales training workshops as necessary, and for a resource library for facilitators and managers. Salary costs for me and for my administrative help are additional.

Challenges and Opportunities

As in any start-up, a primary challenge is establishing awareness and utility of the function in the minds of the line management clientele. At Rock-Tenn, my first work projects were within Home Office Group and within risk management in particular. Early projects involved redesigning environmental training and working with staff members in information services who were involved in training plant employees on new software installations. Outside of the Home Office Group, the pace was slower. Several months passed before a corporate-wide project emerged. This project involved training frontline supervisors in participative management skills. Sponsored by the president and COO, the project had its origins in the company objectives for people and quality. Management expressed a need for supervisors to work with employees in such a way as to foster their participation in improving operations, including safety and quality.

Because Rock-Tenn produces a commodity, it always has to keep costs low in relation to those of its competitors. As the company has grown, it has developed an increased need to professionalize its salesforce and to draw upon the knowledge of all employees in its quest for quality improvement. Like management in most organizations, Rock-Tenn's management has a need for people to learn more quickly and to use what they have learned immediately. Training that had been designed and delivered according to an academic model was ineffective in turning training into action, and that experience led to the decision to add a professional trainer. As the company learns to expect and identify quality learning experiences and sees real returns on training, managers will be more open to additional people-development strategies and to forecasting development needs through strategic planning.

Because the training function was new, I had to establish myself as a credible resource for optimal training design and delivery. Beyond immediate needs for training, I also wanted to establish the utility of general HRD practice, including facilitation, front-end analysis as a precursor to performance improvement, and the maintenance of the company's culture. There were few women in management, so I felt exceptionally visible and was particularly concerned about avoiding early missteps.

Although I had previous experience in other industries, I entered Rock-Tenn with eight years in banking and was wary of differences in culture and thinking that might affect how I identified opportunities and positioned the culture. For example, the banks in which

I had worked were very centralized with decisions made at the top and implemented universally in the organization. At Rock-Tenn, few initiatives were mandated throughout the company; even when they were, choices about implementation were typically left to the divisions and sites. I was very excited about moving from banking to manufacturing, and from managing a staff to being an internal consultant as a single practitioner. Although I had worked as a one-person training department before, Rock-Tenn's decentralized structure offered me the opportunity to develop my consulting skills. I think of my practice as my own small business within Rock-Tenn, and count my successes as business won and lost within my customer base of line managers. I value the variety of my work, and I am constantly challenged to improve my listening, thinking, and communication skills.

Providing Value to the Organization

Often in a start-up situation many high-priority needs exist, and it is possible simply to survey the target populations for perceived needs and preferences. If senior management has no preferred starting point, it can motivate the targets of the training to participate in making the decision about where to start. I have used this methodology in the past. At Rock-Tenn, however, the picture was not so simple because of the decentralized structure. Needs assessment methodologies differed by project and population.

For example, to assess the needs of managers and supervisors in the Home Office Group, I used a multirater 360 feedback survey from a vendor to assist in establishing training priorities within the group. For this project, I consulted with my boss, his peers, and the CFO, their manager. I searched for an instrument that we could use both with managers who supervised one or more subordinates and with single professionals that had no direct reports but many internal clients. I found one satisfactory option, and the managers accepted my recommendation. We administered the survey, kept the groups separate, and listed needs in order of priority for both groups. The results indicated a skill gap for managers in delivering performance appraisals and a need in the professional group for problem-solving skills. I recommended a performance appraisal skills workshop, which I teach, and chose two problem-solving modules of the *Front-Line Leadership* for the professional group.

For the current management development project, I recommended to the Management Committee that we conduct a front-end analysis before beginning the design. This analysis would provide us with specifics about the target jobs and incumbents to enable consensus among the divisions and to focus the design effort. I located three possible providers for the analysis, who were interviewed by an appointed subcommittee of the Management Committee. From the vendor they chose, we commissioned a front-end study of the GMs' job, which produced a competency profile based on interviews with the Management Committee and identified exemplars.

I have also used my own observations of performance and practice to suggest projects such as sales management training to managers. At this point, management is not calling on me to improve performance for a given population, but I expect to develop its awareness of HRD practice to that point.

Services of the Training Resources Department

Prior to the closure of Waldorf Corporation, Rock-Tenn's largest acquisition to date in December 1996, my manager asked me to write a capability statement for training resources for use by both companies' managers in the effort to complete the acquisition. The request was an opportunity to update the original mission with specifics. This list constitutes the services I provide to the organization in fulfillment of my mission to improve existing training and to assist management in making effective choices for future training in ways that fit the structure and culture of the company. The list is as follows:

- facilitator certification for Zenger Miller *FrontLine Leadership* supervisory training
- coordination for participation in Carew sales training
- coordination for participation of newly promoted and hired supervisors in Fundamentals of Supervisory Leadership for those plants that have finished work on the initial seven *FrontLine Leadership* modules
- consultation, information, and assistance in addressing training needs and projects, including the following: needs and front-end analysis; design of training; delivery and instructional skills; coordinating use of outside vendors for training, including identifying and evaluating possible choices; identification and work with appropriate facilities for training; providing a library of predesigned training activities, including ice breakers and other participative exercises
- consultation in specific skill areas, including the following: sales; sales management; conducting appraisal meetings; documenting discipline; termination procedures; preventing sexual harassment; negotiation skills; supervisory skills; train the trainer; problem-solving process, tools, and techniques for teams and team leadership.

Program Development and Consulting Process

As I have worked with Rock-Tenn managers and employees, I have found that projects originate in one of two ways: with the client or with me. The consultation process varies depending on whether the client or I initiates a project.

Projects Originating With the Client

When a project originates with a client, my consulting process consists of the following six-step process:
1. consideration of corporate identity
2. definition of training needs
3. defining options
4. making a choice
5. implementation of the choice
6. evaluation

These steps are graphically depicted in figure 2. All training choices begin with a consideration of fit with the corporate culture and goals. The needs that the project will address depend upon consultation with the "champion," or executive sponsor, including the existing climate in the group to be trained. I find and offer at least three options, which to date have always been outside vendors and I assure managers that they can be successful with any of the three. They make a choice and individual divisions may opt to include themselves in the project or not. I then assist with implementation and evaluation.

To date, projects have addressed universal training needs that are common to all organizations, such as supervisory training, for which programs from outside vendors are satisfactory. In a very few cases, such as assessing skills in use and review of neglected skills, I have provided design and delivery services myself. In my experience, it is common in start-ups to find basic needs throughout the organization for which there are both pent-up needs and existing solutions. These projects, such as supervisory skills or basic sales training, are a matter of implementation, with minimal data collection and analysis. For the current management development project that will involve custom training design, I helped management select consultants to perform data collection and analysis because of limitations on my time. We are using this front-end analysis data to interview and select a design partner, which will probably be a local university.

As the organization becomes more sophisticated about training activities, management is likely to charter more projects that would require the use of the six-step consultation process. As expenditures increase and management sees more opportunity for an organized

Figure 2. Corporate training decisions model.

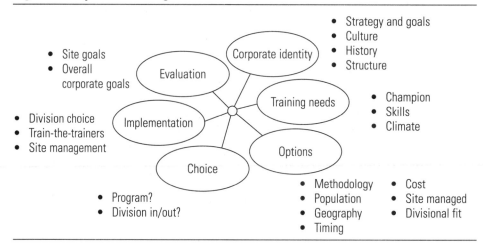

approach to job skills and performance improvement, the demand for evaluation should increase. This increase would emphasize the importance of the contracting step, and custom-designed projects would lead to data collection and analysis. The current status of HRD as the installer of programs to meet basic needs is attributable to its youth as a function in the organization. Management is learning through experience what HRD can do, what to expect, and what management itself must do to make it successful.

Projects Originating With Me

If I originate a project, the process works somewhat differently. First, I must attract the attention of managers and raise their interest in the project. To do this, I may circulate materials or prepare a proposal for presentation to Management Committee members. For example, after attending a sales management workshop that the provider of our basic sales training offered, I heard several attendees express their disappointment. The workshop assumed we had far more structured human resource processes—one with formal job descriptions, for example—than we had. In addition, it assumed that attendees had the willingness and time to create additional structure. Several attendees told me that they had merely wanted to know how to use the information in the fundamental sales course to coach salespeople.

To answer their expressed needs, I circulated materials from several vendors to divisional sales managers and probed for their interest.

Sales managers from five divisions were interested. Based on their expressed interest, I confirmed my perceptions and conclusions about the scope of the workshop with a few brief questions assuring that all had similar interests and needs. I coordinated a meeting with them and representatives of three vendors. From my clients' questions and statements, I learned more about their preferences and specific needs so that I could help to clarify their choices. When a choice of vendor was made, I coordinated the training dates and arrangements with the vendor. Vendor costs were stated up front and were split among the participating divisions according to their numbers of participants.

To continue the improvement of training quality at the plant level, I would like to form a trainer network of the certified Zenger Miller facilitators throughout the company. We would convene a trainer conference once a year to build skills in training design and facilitation, and distribute new training materials to members of the network throughout the year. For this plant trainer network and the associated train-the-trainer conference, I found managers in two divisions with whom to consult in the determination of need and opportunity. From them I determined that they believed the projects were needed and that they would support the effort. After conversations with them, I prepared a proposal that recommended forming a project development group composed of the two other managers and myself. This proposal is currently waiting for presentation to the Management Committee for endorsement.

Program Evaluation and Tracking

Most program evaluation combines end-of-workshop evaluations with 60 to 90 day postworkshop surveys of managers and participants. End-of-workshop evaluations ask for "liked best," "liked least," "suggestions for improvement," and a request for the three to five items that participants intend to do back on the job. I am seeking opportunities to improve what we do, and to gauge participants' intent to transfer skills and learning. In one workshop, I use a "Letter to My Boss" activity that participants complete and I mail. Thirty to 60 days after the workshop, I sample participants and managers for application stories. I circulate summaries of these activities to plant GMs and the Management Committee. At this point, we have not conducted any sort of quantitative study of effectiveness or application. I will be establishing a detailed cost-tracking system for training activities in anticipation of our need for more quantitative evaluation.

Success Story
Background

One strategically important project began with a comment from the president and COO to the senior vice president (SVP), marketing and planning. The president remarked that he would like to see training for plant GMs that would give them more strategic vision and planning skills and enhance their leadership skills so that they could accomplish their plans. The SVP, marketing and planning, headed a project steering committee, composed of volunteer Management Committee members, which included my manager and myself.

This project was crucial for two reasons. First, it centered on a critical layer of management, the plant GM, who in most divisions wields great authority and operates with autonomy and wide decision-making power. Most GMs are senior managers who have worked their way up to the position. If something is to happen at Rock-Tenn, the plant GMs must support it. Second, this project represented the first-ever corporate-wide training directed at senior levels. If this project went well, future training would be positively anticipated and received. If it didn't, there would be negative consequences far into the future. The company's unique culture, the expectations for the target group, and the importance of achieving results called for a custom-designed experience centered on Rock-Tenn culture and operating issues. Outside vendors and partners would have to be sought to design the training.

Selling the Front-End Analysis

The initial consulting meeting took place between the SVP marketing and planning, my manager, and myself. My goal for the meeting was to convince them that we should begin with a thorough front-end analysis. If we simply had decided as a small group what to teach, we would have been shooting in the dark because there were no job descriptions or written expectations for the plant GM position (or for any position in the company). Additionally, plant GMs operated differently in various divisions. In several divisions, the candidates for the training would be at a divisional level rather than a plant level. Finally, although I felt certain that every Management Committee member knew what a GM did, I wasn't sure that all the members had the same picture. We needed a front-end analysis to describe the GM position so that we could gain consensus on job content and target specific areas for training. After a brief explanation of my rationale, a few questions, and a brief discussion, I was successful in persuading the SVP and my boss. We decided that I would make a case for the front-end analysis at an upcoming Management Committee meeting. The SVP would describe the project in its early stages using some preliminary ideas of his own and the subcommittee's, and then I would propose the front-end analysis. This strategy worked, and we were off and running.

Finding the Right Vendor

The next challenge was to locate a vendor to do the front-end analysis because I had neither time nor staff to perform the project myself. I selected three possible vendors based on colleagues' recommendations and my knowledge of local providers, and scheduled meetings with them and the SVP, my manager, and myself. I selected widely varying options so that my clients could see that there was more than one way to approach the project. Before meeting with my internal clients, I spent time with the selected vendors answering their questions and telling them about Rock-Tenn and the project.

The next step was to hold meetings with the potential vendors and my clients. At these meetings, the questions that clients ask the vendors always give me a better idea of what to offer in the future. The vendors I had selected included a local practitioner who is a one-person shop, the executive development consulting office of a nationally known local university, and a well-established local firm with some national accounts that specializes in competency-based analysis and training. The SVP and my manager judged the one-person shop as too limited and unsophisticated for the project. We ruled out the university representatives because they talked only about designs they had already produced and seemed not to understand our need for a thorough front-end analysis. Because the competency-based firm understood our need well, we invited representatives of that firm to visit with the subcommittee.

At the meeting, the representatives presented a plan that included two rounds of interviews, one with all members of the Management Committee and one with exemplars of high-performing plant GMs they would identify in their divisions. At the end of the project, we would have a detailed description of the GM's job and a suggested curriculum for addressing all parts of the job. The subcommittee approved the plan and championed it to the Management Committee as a whole. We got approvals up the line, and the project got started.

Conducting the Needs Assessment

Interviews with the 13 Management Committee members went well, even considering their heavy travel schedules. The information we gathered enabled us to structure the second round for maximum effectiveness. Each of the seven divisional GMs on the Management Committee identified at least two plant GMs or people with equivalent responsibility for the second round, for a total of 16 people. Because we paid $40,000 and travel expenses for the vendor, I held my breath waiting for my clients to see the value of the interview process and the resulting analysis.

When the vendor presented its timely report, which included a suggested curriculum map, members of the subcommittee were surprised and energized by the picture of the GM's job that emerged. The scope for the project enlarged as a result of the vendor's information. Instead of accepting the vendor's proposed curriculum, the subcommittee created its own vision (see table 2) and decided that all plant GMs would need a grounding in fundamentals before proceeding to more advanced topics. In addition, the report they presented assisted us in gaining consensus among all Management Committee members on the content of the GM's job and the training. I felt relieved when my boss told me that "we had more than gotten our money's worth."

Finding a Partner for Program Design and Delivery

The next step was to find a partner who could design the program and help coordinate program delivery. The subcommittee visited with three vendors whom I chose: the same local university executive development office, a large national training provider, and a local practitioner with a national practice. I invited the university back because it had experience dealing with executive audiences and had an excellent reputation for doing good work for other large companies, and its forte seemed to be design. Also, our CEO is chair of its board of trustees. The other two vendors were a large national training company with consulting capabilities and experience in working with senior audiences and a local consultant with extensive experience in training simulations for senior audiences. The latter two came from interviews with the vendors, consultation with local colleagues, and my own knowledge of providers in the local market.

All the vendors represented themselves well, and the single practitioner turned out to be a frequent subcontractor with the university. All vendors featured action learning projects and simulations as

Table 2. Management development training vision.

Why?

Rock-Tenn is a company of winners. It has always been better than the pack. As the markets Rock-Tenn serves become more competitive and change at a faster pace, the company's superior performance depends on its investment in people—taking better advantage of skills, experience, and potential of its key leaders. Current and future leaders need to be prepared in new ways to lead their teams with a clear vision of the future of their plant, area, or division.

What?

The management development process will enable leaders to:
* work with their teams to determine where to compete and how to compete
* communicate those decisions up and down the line
* turn those decisions into actions that secure a successful future for that leader's business

How?

To accomplish the above goal, Rock-Tenn will use its role models, real Rock-Tenn cases, and outside resources to design and deliver training modules for several important skill areas.

Who?

Each division will decide which leaders are responsible for choosing where and how the business competes. Those leaders will be invited to participate in management development training.

When?

Rock-Tenn hoped to begin training its leaders before the end of 1997.

---

core learning experiences. To ensure that we had the best university provider possible, we interviewed executive education providers at three other local universities. At present, we are pursuing partnership with the original university group with the goal of presenting the first workshop by the end of the first quarter of 1998. There is a possibility that pieces of the final project will also include the other two vendors.

Keys to Ongoing Success

This story, which is ongoing, is a success because it is following a solid design path that should get my clients the results they want. I am pleased with my effectiveness as a consultant so far because my clients seem satisfied and confident with the choices they have made. I am looking forward to the learning I am sure to receive in the course of designing and delivering the training. Finally, I am pleased with the opportunity to demonstrate to the Management Committee how a solid training development process takes place, and I hope to work with it to establish evaluation opportunities as a part of the process. Committee members are learning about such developmental tools as multirater 360 feedback and simulations that expand their awareness of effective possible approaches to skill development. Finally, this project can go far in establishing my credibility and skill with the Management Committee so that I may expand my practice areas inside the company.

Advice to Lone Trainers

- *Be selective and fast.* When you're first in the position, cherry-pick projects that are important to management but won't require a long development process. You can speed up the process by using vendors. Even if your budget doesn't allow doing business with a major vendor, you can buy already designed seminars and books of activities that give you rights to reproduce materials. With these, you can quickly design and deliver an effective, participative, skills-based experience for several major groups, such as sales and supervision, or in several major topic areas, such as service delivery and team skills.

- *Be a business partner.* Be sure to learn the business of your company and how it operates. Think of part of your job as helping management to learn how good training and development operates in a company, including the value of front-end analysis and posttraining evaluation. Don't be shy about making direct references to key business drivers or parts of the strategic plan that may depend on growth in skill and knowledge for their full accomplishment. Don't let management—or participants—forget that training is an important business activity by building in management involvement before and after the training.

- *Be customer-service oriented.* Think of yourself as a service provider with customer expectations to meet. This perspective doesn't mean that you slavishly do whatever management wishes. With its need for results in mind, you can suggest alternatives and give assurances with supporting data of the effectiveness of your chosen alternatives.

- *Attend to your own growth and development.* Read, read, read. Improve your skill at local chapters of the American Society for Training & Development and the International Society for Performance Improvement and at conferences and seminars. There is science to training, and your skill and knowledge base must be genuine to be credible. You must earn your seat at the table as a business specialist with a record of success and with demonstrated understanding of what is important to your clients and to the organization.

Recommended Reading

Broad, M., & Newstrom, J. (1995). *Transfer of Training*. Reading, MA: Addison-Wesley. This book is an excellent model for planning manager and trainee involvement before, during, and after training. It includes a "Letter to My Boss" template to build manager involvement and facilitate evaluation 60 to 90 days after training, plus many other practical ideas. The authors also include a simple nine-box model you can use to consult with clients on activities for themselves, the trainees, and the trainer to ensure transfer of skills and knowledge to the job.

Block, P. (1992). *Flawless Consulting*. San Diego: University Associates. This book is excellent for all consultants, including lone trainers functioning as internal consultants. Block explains a step-by-step process very thoroughly, and his chapter on dealing with resistance is excellent.

Gilbert, T. (1996). *Human Competence: Engineering Worthy Performance*. Amherst, MA: HRD Press. Gilbert provides a great front-end analysis approach for skills-based training, a good tool if you have the opportunity to establish yourself as a performance consultant.

Phillips, J. (1995). *The ROI of Training*. Houston: Gulf Publishing. Not every program can or should be evaluated quantitatively, but it's good to have a grounding in how to do it at least one common way with return-on-investment. This book also provides excellent guidance in setting up your files and tracking systems for true training costs, which is easier to do earlier than later. Knowledge of the numbers associated with your training will also assist your credibility with your management clients.

Robinson, D.G., and Robinson, J. (1992). *Training for Impact*. San Francisco: Jossey-Bass. The Robinsons provide another excellent model for front-end analysis so that your training relates to genuine business needs. This model also has the advantage of identifying other variables in the work situation that affect performance so that the success rate for training needed is increased.

There are lots of good resources out there for quick and simple design. Richard Chang's training series is one example, but there are others. Get on several good catalog lists (yes, there is actually good junk mail!). Call Pfeiffer/Jossey-Bass at 1.800.274.4434; HRD Press at 1.800.822.2801; and HRDQ at 1.800.633.4533.

Questions for Discussion

1. How do you work with your client managers to accomplish a project? In Peter Block's terms, are you a "pair of hands," "an expert," or a "collaborator"? In what way do your clients see you as a resource?
2. What do you like to do as a practitioner—design? delivery? consulting? As a single practitioner, you are likely to do a little bit of everything. Too much time spent in design and delivery, however, limits your ability to do other things. Where should you spend your time?
3. What sort of budget will you have for training? Having budget money available means that you'll be able to use outside resources more often.
4. What basic needs exist that you can fill quickly? What are the next steps you intend to take as the appetite for more sophisticated training increases?
5. How much do your clients know and appreciate about training? Teaching management what you do and how to use your skills is part of your job. What strategies will you use to teach them?
6. What is your plan for your own professional development?
7. How well do you understand your company's business? How will you learn what you don't know so you'll understand the problems line management faces?
8. How do training projects originate in your company? How do you initiate a project?

The Author

Kathryn S. O'Neill is currently director, training resources, for Rock-Tenn Company. She has been in the business of training and development since 1978, when she started as the first and only person with a training title at a large daily newspaper. Since that time, she has started up the training function at organizations in several other industries, including home building, banking, and manufacturing. She is currently at work on a Ph.D. in human resource development at Georgia State University, and looks forward to a retirement career in academia. For fun, she sails, goes to the movies, spends time with her two adult children, and volunteers. She can be contacted at: Rock-Tenn Company, 504 Thrasher Street, Norcross, GA 30091; phone: 770.368.7654.

Managing the Small Training Function: Ethics and Wall Street— Not an Oxymoron

Kidder, Peabody

Joanne Rogovin

This chapter provides a fascinating look at what can be done in a small training department as well as at the limits of ethics training. The case illustrates how Rogovin built her credibility and made the best use of external consultants and internal subject matter experts to develop and deliver training solutions. Rogovin explains how she approached the daunting task of providing ethics training to a challenging audience. Whereas Rogovin developed a program that built awareness of ethical dilemmas and provided a framework for making ethical decisions, ultimately no ethics program could change the behavior of some employees who were overwhelmed by their desire for financial gain at any cost.

Introduction

This is something of a morality tale. Morality tales classically teach us about good and evil. This story, set in the tumultuous financial services environment of the 1980s, can teach us about what may happen when there is a lack of vigilance against the forces of greed, deceit, and corruption. It speaks to the impact that strong corrective actions can have, but only if there is unwavering attention to and support for them. It also raises questions about how much impact training can have and whether the training function could have done more to prevent the relapse that proved fatal to the firm.

This case was prepared to serve as a basis for discussion rather than to illustrate either effective or ineffective administrative and management practices.

Many of us in human resource development (HRD) and training think about our work in terms of the value added to our organizations' pursuit of success. Rarely, however, is our work tied intimately to the very existence of the company. In this case, a training program became part of the collective response to a scandal that threatened the firm's survival. The program was directly linked to a series of initiatives that the Securities and Exchange Commission (SEC) required as the result of an insider-trading disaster, and it served as a vehicle for communicating a new set of imperatives about ethics and adherence to regulatory requirements. The case will describe how Kidder, Peabody lost its way, recovered, and, in a postscript, how it lost its way again.

Organizational Background

Founded in Boston in 1824, Kidder, Peabody & Co. Incorporated was a leading international investment banking, brokerage, and financial services firm. It barely survived the crash of 1929, but under the astute management of new partners, it began a new era of expansion, building a successful capital markets practice underwriting initial public offerings of emerging companies. Growth continued through strategic acquisition and international expansion.

The firm remained a partnership until 1986 when General Electric bought it for $600 million and it became a subsidiary of GE Capital. At that time, the firm employed over 7,000 people. With the reduction in investment banking opportunities and the impact on the brokerage business of the October 1987 "market correction," the firm, by 1988, reduced the staff to approximately 5,000 through attrition, selective office closings, and limited hiring. Most of these reductions were in the National Sales division with 1,200 brokers, 700 sales assistants, and numerous support staff, followed in size by Investment Banking. Other lines of business included Equity Sales and Trading, Fixed Income Sales and Trading, Financial Futures, Research, and Asset Management. In addition, several hundred people worked in the so-called back office of Operations, Finance, and Management Information Systems (MIS). There were 50 branch offices across the United States and offices in London, Paris, Geneva, Zurich, Hong Kong, Cairo, Osaka, and Tokyo.

Kidder, Peabody's underwriting revenues ranked it as a second-tier investment bank, behind "bulge bracket" powerhouses such as Merrill Lynch, Goldman Sachs, Lehman Brothers, Salomon, and First Boston. Its peers in the second tier were Smith Barney, Bear Stearns, and Prudential Securities.

Because the firm was part of GE Capital, no separate financial figures are available except as indicated in GE's Annual Report of 1994, the last full year of Kidder's operation. In that last year, Kidder, Peabody enjoyed the strongest balance sheet in its history and a well-balanced portfolio of financial service businesses. Its strength was in part the result of its strong response to the insider-trading scandal involving Martin Siegel, at one time Kidder's stellar investment banker, which is the subject of this case. It was another breach in propriety that toppled the firm in 1994. The end for Kidder, Peabody came quickly. GE management liquidated the firm as the result of yet another huge ethics lapse—the alleged booking of false profits in government bond trading by Joseph Jett, a managing director in Fixed Income. A large proportion of Kidder assets were sold to Paine Webber, and many employees joined that firm; other bank employees have found employment in financial institutions and outside the industry.

Kidder, Peabody was structured traditionally with lines of business and support areas reporting functionally to managing directors. (See figure 1.) The Management Committee, headed by Chairman and CEO Michael Carpenter (now CEO of Travelers Life Insurance) consisted of the heads of the business lines noted in the preceding paragraphs as well as the chief financial officer (CFO), chief counsel, and managing director, Human Resources. The National Sales organization's 50 branches were geographically grouped and headed by three regional managers. During the course of this case, Charles Sheehan, chief financial and administrative officer, to whom Audit reported, was given the additional role of executive managing director of the National Sales. One of the managers that General Electric installed, he embodied the commitment and strength of character needed to help redirect the firm's attention to compliance and exemplary business practices.

The First Ethics Problem

What was it in the firm's culture that allowed Martin Siegel to operate with such impunity? There was, first of all, a great deal of autonomy and entrepreneurship within the environment. It rewarded individual actions and results. With bonuses running into seven figures for contributions to the bottom line, the environment was ripe for excess. Kidder, however, had always prided itself as a collegial, above-board place. It was a "conservative investment house; we didn't hire fast buck artists," Andrew Barfuss, the vice president of auditing at Kidder in the late

Figure 1. Kidder, Peabody & Co. Incorporated organization chart.

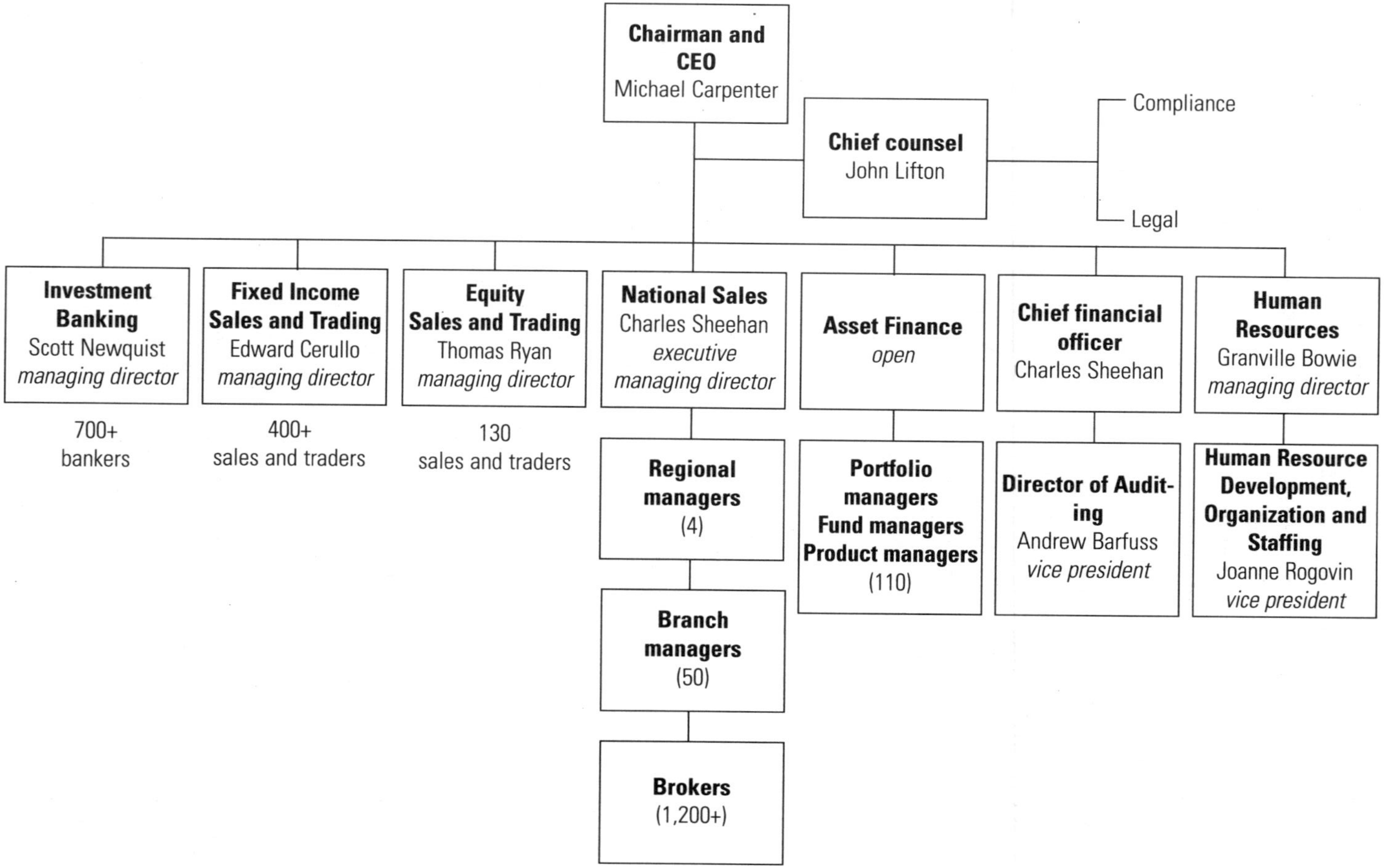

1980s, told me. This belief in the ultimate trustworthiness of its people had created a complaisant, laissez-faire attitude about scrutiny. Prior to his arrest, Marty Siegel, the managing director of Mergers and Acquisitions in the 1980s was something of a hero at the firm. He had developed a unique product for the firm, an original form of defense against unwanted takeover attempts. Known as the tender defense, Martin Marietta Corporation first used it in fending off Bill Agee's Bendix attack. This product put Kidder, Peabody on the map in the heated merger and acquisition climate of the 1980s. It was this willingness to trust that allowed the firm to ignore the uncanny hit rate of Siegel's recommendations.

In June 1987, rather than engage in a long and costly legal fight, a very angry General Electric settled with the SEC for a record $25 million, terminated the CEO, president, and general counsel and replaced them with proven GE managers. It also named a new Audit director. Kidder got a new CEO, Michael Carpenter, a former head of GE strategic planning who was executive vice president of GE Capital Corporation.

General Electric also created two new powerful functions within the firm: a Compliance Review Board to which all business units reported on matters of business conduct, policy, and compliance; and an external ombudsman to collect anonymous information from employees concerned about the ethics of certain practices. The Compliance Review Board was empowered to investigate irregularities and overrule business unit management when it saw fit. It often did so.

The situation was extremely demoralizing to the firm. The GE acquisition had provided for generous payouts to the Kidder shareholders over two years. Once that time was up, they could leave with no consequences, and they did, taking much of the corporate culture and memory with them. It would take until mid-1989 for the firm to restabilize and put new programs in place that would set it back on course. In this atmosphere of turmoil, anger, and demoralization, the company developed and implemented the Compliance and Ethics Program described in this case study. It was at this time, in the fall of 1988, that I joined the firm from the New York Stock Exchange.

Training Function

In June 1988, General Electric appointed Granville Bowie, a GE veteran, as managing director for Human Resources. He quickly determined a need to upgrade the training function and replace the existing director. Our mandate was to deliver the highest quality, most relevant development for over 5,000 employees. Only broker training was outside the scope of our effort.

The corporate function, prior to 1988, focused on traditional course offerings—supervisory skills, business writing, interpersonal communications—that were predominantly off-the-shelf purchases that internal staff or external consultants presented. The key audience for these offerings were supervisors and managers in the firm's support areas—Operations, Finance, MIS—with little interest from or involvement of those on the revenue-producing side.

As my initial discussions with managers began to reveal the extent of the firm's training and development needs, we agreed that the incumbent junior trainer would be replaced by a more senior professional. In January 1989, Chuck Kovach, now with Smith Barney, joined the staff as senior training specialist. (He was promoted to assistant vice president in 1990.) There was, at this point, no plan to expand the department, and this remained the case throughout the firm's remaining years.

Based on a relationship model, Chuck and I assumed primary responsibility for different clients. His target population was Operations, Finance, and MIS; mine focused on Investment Banking, Legal and Compliance, Equity and Fixed Income Sales and Trading. I want to stress that we collaborated extensively on all projects, and this division of labor was strictly to provide our internal clients with a single point of contact. Our initial priority was building relationships with key players.

The budget for training was approximately $450,000. This included staff salaries (with the exception of that of the vice president), use of consultants and purchased materials, expenses for off-site meetings, and the overhead for the training room. The department title, Human Resource Development, Organization, and Staffing, was meant to convey the scope of the effort: training and organizational development, performance management, and succession planning. There was no evidence that the firm cared about or saw much value in development, and building a constituency was the first, and hardest challenge.

Challenges and Opportunities

In the Wall Street tradition, there had been little, if any, linkage between training and the firm's core businesses. Strategically, my approach to building the human resource development function can be summarized as follows:

- Build relationships with the revenue-producing side through consulting and partnering on business issues.
- Provide relevant, timely, customized programs and interventions at all levels that improved organizational capability to meet business objectives.
- Identify visible, high-impact, *achievable* opportunities to create credibility for the effort.

Our greatest challenge lay in the fact that investment banks are just not interested in anything that takes them away from doing deals. The truth is that any time away from the business is seen as money lost to them and the firm. There had never been any leadership development, management training, or team building, and no one was clamoring for it. Then along came GE, with its world-renowned reputation for training, its commitment to using development as cultural glue, and its expectation that all of its businesses would be professionally managed. As one Kidder managing director told me, "We just learned how to spell management!" So the idea of management development was as remote for them as taking a walk on the moon.

Now, there were compelling business reasons for upgrading the abilities of senior officers. Kidder's investment banking effort was adrift. Business opportunities were shrinking, and the investment banking teams were not hitting home runs. The equities market was still recovering from the 1987 crash. Brokers were struggling to reinstill confidence in investors. Only the Fixed Income area, with the emergence of new products like mortgage-backed securities, was showing promise and profit. Additionally, there were unrealized synergies with GE Capital and other GE businesses. I saw in this an opportunity to provide training solutions to serious organizational problem

I had determined that we could meet a number of key objectives by using GE's Crotonville Management Development Center for our leadership programs. First, it is an exceptional facility, creating a perfect environment for learning, dialogue, relationship building, and recreation. Even more important, I felt it was a way to break down some of the antipathy toward the parent company. I had learned from my work integrating corporate culture and values into leadership development at The New York Stock Exchange the power of executive development in leveraging the human capital of the company. As with many acquisitions, the hoped-for synergies between General Electric and Kidder, Peabody had gone unrealized because of vast, unresolved cultural and operational differences.

I also hoped to engage GE Capital in a collaborative effort. My idea was that our populations were similar enough that a customized program for our combined groups could have exceptional payoff. However, the head of GE Capital training elected to send his people to the generic GE programs, and so this potential was never realized. It was, I believe, a lost opportunity to bridging some of the gaps between the two entities.

Undaunted, we forged ahead. In collaboration with both Crotonville development professionals and Robert Eccles, professor of management at the Harvard Business School and author, with Dwight Crane, of *Doing Deals,* we developed a customized, case-driven three-day leadership event that included multirater 360 feedback, an outdoor challenge, extensive teamwork, and emphasis on the leader as catalyst for change and growth. There was limited enthusiasm on the part of many attendees. Two things helped, I think. The 360 feedback was about them, and what could be more interesting! And my deal was that if it was not worth their while by noon on the first day, they were free to leave. No one ever did. This program, attended by officers at the senior vice president level and above, fulfilled its objectives: It helped inform participants about their leadership role and helped forge relationships across organizational lines, and it also broke down the barriers between HRD and the firm. It became the springboard for many other, highly successful initiatives.

Providing Value to the Organization

To fulfill our strategic objectives, the following approach was applied for all major programs and projects:

- data gathering and analysis through interviews, focus groups, review, where appropriate, of performance appraisals, succession plans, turnover rates, error rates, and so forth
- presentation to division senior management of findings and recommendations
- formation of a Design Team of internal and, where needed, external subject matter experts (SMEs)
- implementation of pilot program, then evaluation, and changes as needed
- rollout and follow-up evaluation.

Our commitment was to serve the total organization. There was heavy use of in-house experts as trainers, and train-the-trainer sessions were required for participation. This maximized the effectiveness of a small training function with a very large mandate and added credibility to the work. For many of the presenters, their involvement allowed them to showcase their abilities to senior management. One of the most complex and forceful programs we developed using this process was Finance for the Financial Industry. Kidder's controller had identified a need to build business expertise in the accounting and tax functions. Working with Harbridge House, an international consulting and training organization based in Boston, and a team of internal SMEs, we developed a three-hour per week, 13-week case-driven course taught exclusively by internal managers. Presenters gained visibility before the Management Committee members who attended the course's final case presentations. Enrollment was expanded to include professionals in Operations, Compliance, and Audit, and the program ran twice a year.

Another example of the successful use of the process was Best of the Best, a classroom and self-study multimedia program for the 700 sales assistants who supported brokers. This Design Team consisted of senior sales assistants, branch managers, branch administrators, brokers, external instructional designers, and training and development (T&D) staff. As with the finance course, National Sales professionals attended train-the-trainers sessions and assumed full responsibility for the course. We provided administrative and materials support.

Evaluation of the impact of training is at best an art, not a science. During long programs, we implemented interim feedback reports and made adjustments as indicated. We conducted pilots, reviewed feedback, and revised as needed. I don't believe "happiness sheets" at the end of a program tell us much. With all programs, we conducted a three-month follow-up with participants' managers to identify more long-term effects. For the finance course, managers reported tangible increases in competencies, as did branch managers for the sales assistants' program. These are hard to summarize. My sense is that because efforts were so targeted and customized, and because we kept being asked to do more, the firm felt that the impact was positive.

Case Study: Becoming Aware: An Ethics and Compliance Workshop

Kidder, Peabody & Co. Incorporated is a leading international investment banking, brokerage and financial services firm. By applying the highest level of innovation, service professionalism and integrity, Kidder, Peabody aims to help clients realize their financial goals.

This is how Kidder described itself in a 1992 recruitment brochure. The company had traveled a long and hard road since the dark days of 1987 and 1988 when it was rocked by what was then the largest insider-trading debacle in Wall Street history. How it had reached this low point in its history, and how a dynamic training program helped restore and support a climate of integrity and trust is the subject of this case.

Background

"We've been waiting for you to get here." With these words, Andrew Barfuss, vice president, Audit, and James McVey, the head of Compliance, entered my office at Kidder, Peabody, just after my arrival, in September 1988, as vice president, Human Resource Development, Organization, and Staffing. Their sense of urgency was well founded. In May 1988, the SEC had settled an insider-trading case involving Martin Siegel, managing director of Mergers and Acquisitions, levying a $25 million fine on the firm and requiring that a full-scale compliance and ethics training program be implemented for all KP professionals. This meant that 3,000 Equity and Fixed Income Sales and Trading staff, brokers, investment bankers, portfolio managers—everyone who had direct client contact—would be required to attend. The order by the SEC stated: "The Firm should develop a prioritized plan for the conduct of employee training covering broader expectations inherent in the Firm's formal policies and procedures." The wording made it clear that attention to the spirit as well as the letter of the law was to be addressed. The firm's SEC-approved review team of Coopers & Lybrand and the law firm of Weil Gotshal and Manges would carefully scrutinize the training effort. Its potential impact on the organization's ability to put the past behind it and move forward in restoring client and regulatory confidence was very significant. The meeting with Andy Barfuss and Jim McVey was the start of an extensive collaboration reaching across all organizational lines and resulting in a process that far exceeded the organization's expectations.

The insider-trading scandal created tremendous reverberations throughout the firm. Compliance with regulatory requirements was assumed, and not a great deal of attention was given to either training or communicating about this issue. There had been lack of attention to upgrading computer technology to track compliance concerns and little investment made in upgrading tracking systems for trading, sales, and portfolio management. There was a dedicated staff of compliance officers and auditors, but the numbers and systems were insufficient for a firm of this size and complexity.

It was in an atmosphere of increased scrutiny by regulators and the media that the situation occurred. The excesses of the 1980s were beginning to show unwelcome dividends—the unmasking of insider trading and stock manipulations by the likes of Marty Siegel, Ivan Boesky, Michael Milken, Dennis Levine, and the like. Confidence in the marketplace was eroding. As a result of the machinations of these and others, venerable firms like Drexel, Burnham, Lambert, were forced to shut down. Individual investors left the marketplace for the safety of mutual funds and money market funds. The mergers and acquisitions business dried up and with it the hefty fees that had bankrolled investment banking firms to never-before-realized profits. Junk bonds became suspect. The companies that had used them for raising capital were riddled with debt, and investors had not had the long-term, high-yield payoffs these instruments had promised. There was, therefore, not only a legal and regulatory reason for addressing the issue but also was a business imperative that everything possible be done to restore customer confidence in the market and the firm.

Meeting the Challenge of Developing an Ethics Program

So, there we were—miserable situation, hateful subject, fear and loathing among the troops, and me new to the firm. I couldn't even throw myself on the mercy of friends because no relationships had yet been built. I made an early decision. This was not going to be some bad-tasting medicine that everyone had to swallow. If we had to do this, I was going to make sure that it was worth everybody's time and effort, and that it had a positive impact on the firm. The only way to do this was to enlist key players as partners in the project, and to approach the undertaking with energy and creativity. The challenge was to gain more than just compliance from them, but to get them to provide the resources in time and staff to create a meaningful product. I was naïve about the resistance we would encounter and how much people wanted to avoid this painful subject. My objective, however, was clear from the beginning: Make this program relevant, challenging, and dynamic for the over 3,000 professionals who had to attend. This would require the identification of external resources and the quick assimilation of these experts into Kidder's culture and business.

The question I asked was, "What would make it worthwhile for your people to spend a day attending an ethics and compliance workshop?" The answer, although not enthusiastic, was consistent across the firm: Make it relevant, use Kidder cases, make it real, help them understand the consequences of their actions. There was also agreement that awareness of consequences was even more important than becoming an expert in compliance law (which was never a program objective!). It was Mike Ciasca, head of Compliance for National Sales, who told me that most problems occur because of "inadvertent negligence" rather than a deliberate intent to defraud. This became our mantra: Make people so aware of the consequences of their actions that the likelihood of inadvertent negligence would be minimized. This would lead to the development of one of the program's most innovative tools, a dynamic model for ethical decision making (see figure 2), and it gave us our workshop title, *Becoming Aware: A Workshop on Ethics and Compliance.*

Although there was a sense of urgency, Compliance and Audit were also willing to examine various ways of approaching the problem. I had strong support from Andy Barfuss and Jim McVey to investigate how other organizations approached ethics training. A survey of financial services firms yielded no results. A review of the literature about corporate ethics programs turned up either product liability or whistle-blowing. Then I hit pay dirt. Ron Berenbeim, the senior research associate for business and education research at The Conference Board offered us a number of possibilities. In the end, it was a *Harvard Business Review* article that became the anchor for the program. It will be described at length later on.

Internally, I met with each business unit's managing director and compliance officer. They then selected staff members to work with us on development of cases for the program. An attorney from the legal department, Mary Chamberlin, took the lead in reviewing technical content, and her support and input were invaluable. By this time, I had identified an instructional designer, Merle Goldstein, who took incredibly dense and complex materials and turned them into elegant learning tools. She worked fast and smart. We first met on December 7, 1988, and entered into an agreement on December 12. By January 23, 1989, she had completed initial interviews for the customized handbooks, read and analyzed the compliance manuals, and had completed a first draft of the generic handbook that was an integral part of the workbook. The program will be described in detail. A timeline tracing the activities that brought the program to fruition appears in figure 3.

Merle Goldstein and I divided up responsibilities. She delved into the technical side of the material, pouring over dense compliance

Figure 2. Ethical decision-making model.

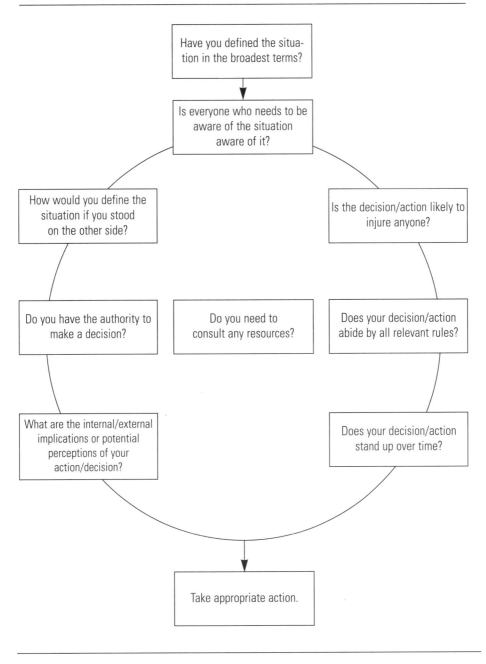

Figure 3. Timeline of activities for *Becoming Aware: A Workshop on Ethics and Compliance*.

Action	Time Frame
Initial compliance meetings and research	September–November 1988
Selections of instructional designer; initial meetings with content experts	November 1988–January 1989
Material development: customized section, CEO videotapes, case studies, decision tree model	January–March 1989
Development and review of National Sales pilot materials; creation of leaders' guides, train-the-trainer materials for National Sales	March–April 1989
National Sales pilot	April 1989
National Sales train-the-trainer	May 1989
National Sales implementation	June–September 1989
Program review by Coopers & Lybrand; final approval	July 1989
Firmwide implementation	August 1989–March 1990

manuals to ferret out salient information. She was guided in this by the business unit compliance officers who told her which areas of the regulations were pertinent to their business. Working with corporate Compliance and Auditing, she also zeroed in on those areas of the law that were generic, that applied across the board to all aspects of the firm's operations. From this research emerged two handbooks for each business unit's training program: a generic one capturing laws, regulations, and policies fundamental to running our business, and a customized set of guidelines for each of our businesses. I wish I could truly communicate the Herculean nature of this effort. The compliance manuals filled bookshelves. They contained some of the most dense and yet often vague body of law ever enacted. It was no wonder that managers avoided referencing them. They were virtually incomprehensible and of little utility. Merle bravely waded into this morass and emerged with documents of great clarity and serviceability. She also conducted initial interviews with bankers, traders, and branch managers to determine suitable case material. We worked as real partners, collaborating on cases and reviewing each other's products.

Finding a Powerful Ethics Dilemma to Stimulate Awareness

We settled on a *Harvard Business Review* (HBR) article, "The Parable of the Sadhu," written by Bowen H. McCoy, as the catalyst for the ethics portion of the program. Based on McCoy's actual experience, the article describes a situation during a Himalayan climb that posed ethical and practical conflicts. The article had received more reader response than any HBR feature to that point.

Here's the story: Bowen "Buzz" McCoy, a managing director at Morgan, Stanley, had taken a six-month sabbatical to make some decisions about his life. It would be easy to dismiss this as some midlife crisis, but what happened had some potentially life-changing implications.

Part of McCoy's time away was to be spent climbing in the Himalayas in the company of a friend and, of course, guides. After many months of preparation, considerable expense, and 30 days of climbing, McCoy and his team were positioned for their final assault on the summit. The weather, always a critical factor in that region, was changing. It was warming up, creating the likelihood that the ice pass over which they had to climb would begin to melt, preventing them from achieving their goal. Just as they were about to embark on this final phase, a climber who had been ahead of them appeared with the body of a Nepalese holy man, a Sadhu, in his arms. The Sadhu, dressed in rags and barefoot, was suffering acutely from exposure. The climber dumped the body at the McCoy team's feet and returned to his group. McCoy, as leader of the group, had to make a decision. Among the choices were

- leave the Sadhu and hope someone else would help him
- take him with them, severely taxing their resources
- take him partway down the mountain to a lean-to passed on the climb and hope that subsequent climbers would help
- take him to safety and medical help and forfeit reaching the summit.

I am sure you can think of other options. There was great time pressure in the situation. Altitude sickness compromised their ability to think clearly. In the end, McCoy went for the summit; his friend took the Sadhu to the lean-to and joined him at the top. It was only when the friend, who happened to be a Quaker, confronted McCoy about the implications of their actions that he stopped to consider the consequences and, perhaps more important, what had led to the decision.

On video, the climb and pivotal incident are re-created, followed by a Socratic discussion led by Arthur Miller of the Harvard Law School.

It proved to be what I hoped, the catalyst for lively, often heated discussion. Knowing the population—short on time and attention span—I felt the video would energize the groups more than the article, and this turned out to be true. During the presentations, the tape was stopped at several critical junctures to allow for discussion. We talked about what happens to our thinking when we are so focused on a goal that we screen out potentially challenging information. The time (if not weather) pressures of the case struck home. A critical piece of awareness concerned the implications of taking actions that affect people who are "remote" from us. It was hard for McCoy to relate to the Sadhu. One of the questions Arthur Miller posed is, "What would you have done if it was a white woman?" For us it was, " How does a banker or a trader or a broker keep those who are impacted by his or her decisions in mind when they are unknown and invisible to him or her?"

Although "The Parable of the Sadhu" would set the context for the program, it was essential to bridge the material back to the firm and its reality. I finalized business-unit-specific case material by meeting with content experts across the firm. All the cases were actual Kidder incidents with identifying details disguised. They ranged from a situation in which a new investment banker at Kidder found himself representing a client interested in acquiring a former client of the banker, raising both insider information and potential conflict-of-interest issues to a new broker being caught up in a scam perpetrated by a client. No matter how we tried to disguise the material, there was the inevitable situation where someone in the group blurted out that that was him! There was a moment of silence...and then he said, " and you got it exactly right."

The program consisted of the following elements:
1. introduction and videotape of Michael Carpenter, CEO
2. overview of the workshop
3. *The Parable of the Sadhu*: videotape case study and discussion
break
4. the current business and compliance environment for financial services—lecturette and discussion
5. Kidder, Peabody Case #1
small group discussion
large group discussion
6. Kidder, Peabody Case #2
break

7. Kidder, Peabody Case #3
8. Kidder, Peabody policies and procedures—presentation and Q&A with Legal/Compliance officer
9. closing remarks and conclusion

Demonstrating Support for the Program

The visible support of senior management was crucial to the program's success. It had to come not only from the CEO but also from all formal and informal organization leaders. Carpenter agreed to take a lead role in communicating the program's importance. His introductory video stressed the importance of questioning activities and behaviors that seemed out of the ordinary. The Ethical Decision Making Model (figure 2) was designed to raise awareness of how critical it is to question and assess consequences. Also, a letter from Carpenter welcomed each participant and spoke about the firm's commitment to integrity at every possible occasion. Most important, Carpenter told his managing directors to visibly support the training.

The response, however, varied. In all cases attendance was mandatory. Some business unit heads attended their unit's sessions. In some cases, it was clear that this was a forced march, and that the managing director in charge was antagonistic to the whole effort. Part of this is understandable. The deed had been done in the investment banking area. Why should everyone be punished? It was like being kept after school because one person had acted up! However, there also was support from many quarters, both internally and externally.

The SEC decree had mandated the naming of an ombudsman for the firm, someone to whom employees could go in confidence and discuss concerns about ethical and compliance issues. Sam Scott Miller, a partner at Orrick, Herrington and Sutcliff law firm, was appointed to the post. The firm was not Kidder's outside counsel, and so independence was maintained. Miller also appeared on the introductory videotape and was featured in the internal employee newsletter. His role was to be a confidential sounding board; with an employee's permission, he could delve further into an issue and help resolve any potential problems. He became a trusted, external source for advice and consultation, and lent considerable support to the development of the workshop. I made it a point to keep the consultants from Coopers & Lybrand apprised of our perspective and progress. The last thing we needed was a surprise from them at the end, telling us this was not what they wanted.

Refining the Program and Planning to Meet Logistical Challenges

All employees with client contact were required to attend the program. In April we conducted the first pilots of the program, introducing the workshop to a group of newly hired brokers. I led these sessions with either Mike Ciasca, the compliance director for National Sales, or David Worley, an attorney from the firm's legal department. The pilot, for which we rehearsed as though it was a Broadway opening, helped refine the program and the leaders' guide into the successful product it became. We also created a monitoring system to track participation.

That still left us with a logistics nightmare. There were over 3,000 people to train; they were located in 50 offices around the country. For the traders, daytime training was impossible—they were glued to their computers from 9:30 a.m., when markets opened, until 4:00 p.m., when they closed. There were a limited number of attorneys and compliance people to conduct the technical side of the workshop, and there were significant time constraints for them.

The answer was both obvious and scary: For National Sales, train the branch managers to deliver the program, and enlist regional and branch compliance officers to handle the critical task of applying rules and regulations to real-life situations. I would conduct training at Kidder, Peabody headquarters in New York City for Investment Banking, Equity and Fixed Income, Asset Management, Financial Futures, and Research as well as for the new brokers, with the promise of a lawyer or compliance officer to present the technical material. I also agreed to conduct sessions for those non-National Sales businesses with offices outside of New York. For example, Investment Banking and Fixed Income had people in California and Chicago.

At the end of March, Merle Goldstein began working on the leaders' guide. Although many of the potential presenters had experience in running staff meetings, few had any formal background in training. The guide was to cover all the planning, logistics, and technical sides of setting up the sessions as well as comprehensive guidelines for discussion of the Sadhu article and the cases.

Several activities continued in tandem. Second drafts of guidelines and case studies went to content experts. There were the usual delays in getting them back. The people who were reviewing the material were, of course, the best and the brightest, and their work demands were pretty overwhelming. Also, this was not their favorite thing to do. My calendar shows that I became a world-class pest during April and May.

During this time, I contracted with an external company that would print, store, and ship materials according to our predetermined schedule. Given the highly customized nature of the materials, their ability to create and distribute the binders would make a significant contribution to the eventual program success. Murphy's Law took over, and a series of minidisasters kept us in a high state of anxiety. The problems were particularly challenging when we needed different sets of materials in the same time frame (for example, binders for investment banking in New York concurrent with binders for Fixed Income Sales and Trading in Los Angeles. We learned to be on site at the printer after having averted a major debacle by shanghaiing Kidder's printing department into an all-nighter. The lesson is, always keep the originals!

Training the Trainers

In May 1989, again, with National Sales as our partners, I began a series of train-the-trainer programs for branch managers on a regional basis. In the morning, I took the managers through the program. In the afternoon, we discussed and practiced training techniques. Managers were asked to "teach" a piece of the program. There was some resistance, which they often expressed as knowing how to do this. We then talked about the implications of the program, and the need to assure that it passed muster—Coopers & Lybrand consultants were keeping an eye on everything and were planning to attend at least one session in the branches to assess its effectiveness.

The signs of resistance showed in interesting ways. Branch managers in our western region had been scheduled for a train-the-trainer session on May 22 in San Francisco. A week prior to the session, I received word from the eastern region manager that the only time he could give me to work with his managers was May 23 in New York. Nothing would influence him to change the date. I took the "Red Eye"—the overnight flight—back from San Francisco, and at 8:30 a.m. conducted the meeting.

Implementing the Training

Corporate-wide training began in July 1989. By March 1990, all firm professionals had participated. Each new class of brokers received ongoing training. The National Association of Securities Dealers (NASD) requires an annual compliance refresher for brokers; the program we developed was deemed acceptable to fulfill this necessity, and we provided annual updates.

In some cases, senior management showed its commitment by attending sessions or kicking them off. To accommodate work schedules, many programs took place in the evening, and a few took place in the early hours of the morning. As with many successful training programs, food was a key ingredient. We kept several restaurants and caterers happy, not to mention the car service that took bankers and traders home from these nocturnal events.

The demanding schedule caused other glitches. As implementation went on, participation from Legal and Compliance diminished. I'd like to think that this was based on their confidence in my ability to do that part. I had heard it so often that there was little I could not answer. But the truth is that the sense of urgency was waning as distance grew between the precipitating events and the program. It was this reversion to an earlier mentality, a more laissez-faire approach to ethics, that laid the groundwork for the fraud that brought this venerable firm to an end.

Measuring Effectiveness

The question of how to measure the success of any program is always a tricky one. In this case, here's what we know. Everyone showed up: Over 3,000 people really did attend. The discussion was often heated and challenging, so we achieved our goal of getting people to think and become engaged with the subject. I still have a folder of letters from regional and branch managers saying that the sessions they led were the best meetings they had ever conducted. A team from Coopers & Lybrand attended the program in our Chicago branch in July 1989. Its response was a resounding rave—the program surpassed the group's expectations and fully met the SEC consent decree requirements.

Did it stop people from unethical or illegal behavior? When Mike Ciasca, National Sales compliance manager, told me that most problems come from inadvertent negligence, he also said that no training program or set of policies is ever going to prevent someone who is intent on stealing. I think we raised the level of dialogue and awareness, which is what we set out to do. I believe we made a difficult subject come alive with the Kidder, Peabody case studies as well as with the use of the "Parable of the Sadhu" case and videotape. Most important to the success of this program was the partnership that developed across the firm with business heads, Compliance, Auditing, Legal and Human Resource Development. Without that collaboration and willingness to provide the intellectual resources and time needed to bring this enormous effort to a successful conclusion, there is no way that we could have achieved the level of quality and impact that occurred.

Lessons Learned

Partnering, partnering, partnering. Unless you have the secret to cloning, there is no other way to make a meaningful contribution as a small training department. You can bring in an army of outside consultants and trainers, but in the end that most often results in training by catalog. Our goal for the Becoming Aware workshop was to provide a valuable, useful, and even memorable opportunity for dialogue and discovery that would meet a critical organizational need and be recognizable within the culture and dynamics of the firm. It was the model I have always used; I have always managed small HRD functions mandated to solve a great variety of development problems. Becoming a business partner in your company takes time and relationship building. In this case, we did not have that luxury, and so we built the relationships as we created the program. It also takes perseverance, commitment, extraordinary energy, and a thick skin. I'd like to think intelligence and creativity play a significant part. To either create demand or respond to needs in a large organization with few resources at your disposal means reaching far outside the box for solutions.

There are many roles we in training and development can choose to play. At the very least, we must provide information, diagnose and help solve people problems, and recommend and help implement change. But if we are to make a real contribution, there are other, more critical functions for us to fill: to build consensus and commitment around excellence and change; to facilitate client learning and be a catalyst for a learning environment; and, most important, to make a significant contribution to organizational effectiveness. We can do this only if we are joined at the hip to the business leaders. We can do this only if we can anticipate their needs, not just respond to them. And to do this we have to be there—attending staff meetings and planning sessions, becoming a trusted ear and advisor to management, staying current about trends in our industry and our competition, and knowing what our company's competitive advantages are, so that we can support and enhance them.

Given the exigencies of the case presented above, it was difficult to meet the criteria. In retrospect, I would spend more time with senior managers. I would have engaged content experts on development teams rather than work with them only on a one-on-one basis.

I believe that the quality of cases would have been even better had this happened. I would have pushed the implementation schedule harder. As I review the material, it feels as though it took a long time to complete the training. Half a dozen large-scale projects were happening in tandem, but given the importance of Becoming Aware, I feel we should have moved even more quickly. And, as we did in future programs, I would have engaged senior managers as trainers, not only as we did with National Sales but with other business units as well.

I hope it is clear that I like these tilting-at-windmills assignments. I like the buck-stops-here aspect of running a small function. Although there are great pressures, never enough time or resources, and—if you're doing the job—increased expectations, there is also great gratification in being an asset to the business. It requires lifetime relationship building. No matter how good we are, we are not revenue producers; we have to reestablish our value on an ongoing basis. I have found that it requires resilience, curiosity, and always a sense of humor to stick with it. In the end, working in partnership with smart, dynamic, demanding people is enormously satisfying and the greatest learning experience I have ever had.

Postscript

From 1988 to 1991, the existence of the Compliance Review Board, ombudsman, ethics and compliance training, and high expectations from the chief financial officer and director of auditing created a climate conducive to the application of ethical standards and compliance requirements. In the early 1990s, however, the CFO retired, the membership in the Compliance Review Board turned over, and Andy Barfuss was promoted out of auditing into a nonfinance role. This transition seemed quite natural at the time, and there was no awareness of any erosion in effectiveness or functionality. In retrospect, however, red flags should have gone up, signaling that the turnover in personnel undermined the sense of purpose of the board and the lack of line management commitment. As the original players were replaced by people who had not been directly involved in the earlier events, intensity and effectiveness diminished. Because both the board and ombudsman functions were classic add-ons, the sense of direction and purpose were lost over time. Integrated functions have a self-evident purpose with core activities, measurements, and accountabilities. As add-ons, these Kidder functions lacked such advantages, and despite a strong start, drifted badly after a few years.

In 1994, Kidder was undermined by a major trading fraud allegedly perpetrated by Joseph Jett, a managing director in Fixed Income Sales and Trading. The Compliance Review Board and ombudsman were caught completely by surprise. The fact that no one questioned his actions in this $350 million scam is symptomatic of an organization that relapsed into a mode of ethical insensitivity and nonvigilance. Although the organization had responded valiantly to a firm-threatening ethical lapse, the lack of sustainable momentum and vigilance led to the final, fatal blow. The ultimate training challenge is to sustain the momentum over several generations of senior management.

Questions for Discussion

1. Could training have helped the organization stay focused on these issues and perhaps avoid this relapse?
2. Should the mission of the original training been expanded to include ongoing reinforcement and involvement of management?
3. How can momentum be maintained?
4. Could our measurement criteria have been stronger, and how could we have enforced the measurements?
5. How can the objectives of training truly be baked into line management's responsibilities?
6. Were there other linkages to human resources practices that training should or could have forged in this effort?

The Author

Joanne Rogovin is currently senior executive and organization development consultant for IBM. She has extensive experience in internal and external consulting to manage change. She held the position of vice president of Human Resource Development, Organization and Staffing at Kidder, Peabody from 1988 to 1992. Prior to that, she served as managing director of Management and Organizational Development at the New York Stock Exchange, where she spearheaded a values-driven culture change effort. She has been an adjunct instructor at New York University's School of Continuing Education and at Queens College. She is a frequent conference presenter. Rogovin has a B.A. in political science and an M.A. in communications from Boston University. She holds an M.S.W. from Yeshiva University and is a New York State Certified Social Worker. She is certified by the Center for Application of Psychological Type. She can be contacted at 161 West 15th Street, New York, NY 10011; phone: 212.243.1516.

Building a Leadership Development Program: Making the Best Use of Internal and External Resources

UNUM Life Insurance Company of America

Carol Prescott McCoy

This case illustrates how a small training department made wise use of external consultants and internal experts to develop and deliver a leadership development program for the home office of North America's leading disability insurer. By building strong sponsorship through a leadership advisory group, the department was able to implement a leadership assessment and development process within a short time frame. The chapter also provides insights into how to expand your capabilities by using job sharing and temporary help and how to evaluate the success of interpersonal skills and customer relations training.

Background

Based in Portland, Maine, UNUM Life Insurance Company of America (UNUM America) is a subsidiary of UNUM Corporation, a Fortune 500 company and the world leader in disability insurance with offices in North and South America, Europe, and the Pacific Rim. As the leading provider of group disability insurance in North America, UNUM America provides long-term disability, short-term disability, life insurance, long-term care, and other employee benefits to the group and individual market. A growth company, UNUM America is recognized for its disability knowledge, risk management expertise, and distribution capabilities, which include a broad network of brokers and

This case was prepared to serve as a basis for discussion rather than to illustrate either effective or ineffective administrative and management practices.

a world-class salesforce. Licensed to operate in 49 states and Canada, UNUM America has approximately 1,500 people located in over 34 sales offices throughout the United States, and approximately 3,000 employees in its home office. The company is guided by its Vision and Values and by ambitious 1998 goals relating to shareholder value, customer satisfaction, people, and operating effectiveness. UNUM America has a fast-paced, high-performing culture and a constantly changing organizational structure. In 1997, *Business Week* magazine named UNUM America one of its top 10 family-friendly companies. Known for its market leadership and its work environment, UNUM tends to attract highly educated and motivated employees.

Training at UNUM America

At the time of this case, training at UNUM was both centralized and decentralized. The centralized training department, Human Resources (HR) Training, which is the focus of this case, had 2.2 full-time equivalent employees (FTEs). The staff consisted of myself as director, two part-time management development consultants, Carol Ryan Ertz and Kathleen Jacques—each of whom worked three days a week in a job-share arrangement—and a series of temporary employees who provided administrative support to the department. Our temporary administrative assistant was Anne Marie Quesnel, who supported our department while she was preparing to embark on her own homemade ice cream business in Portland.

In addition to the HR Training Department, there were decentralized training departments that provided technical job-skills training and some soft-skills training in the operations field organization and the various benefits organizations. Some training also came from human resources consultants (HRCs) who provided dedicated HR services, such as employee relations consulting, organizational development (OD) support, team building, and some interpersonal skills training to various departments.

Mission and Services

The HR Training Department's target audience was 3,000 home-office employees, with a primary emphasis on managers and supervisors. Our mission was to provide training that addressed companywide knowledge and skills needed to accomplish the business objectives. The mission was to do the following:
• provide employees with a common foundation and framework needed to operate effectively in today's business environment

- design and implement training programs that teach critical competencies needed to meet business challenges
- support the divisions in the delivery of corporate training programs within the business units and functions where applicable.

    Our major services included

- developing training programs that teach managers generic competencies that cut across business units and functions
- providing guidance to managers and division directors regarding appropriate training and development interventions for managers and individual contributors
- providing training programs that teach competencies that the company as a whole requires
- providing train-the-trainer support to help prepare decentralized trainers and managers to deliver training programs.

Adding Value: Needs Assessment, Program Development, and Evaluation

Needs Assessment Approach

Our approach to training involved conducting a needs assessment through a variety of means, depending on the situation. Typically we reviewed critical company documents and performance indicators, such as quarterly sales results, customer satisfaction, and retention data, or the annual People Goal survey results. For important strategic initiatives, we often created advisory groups, which provided direction and guidance on priorities. Other methods included conducting interviews with managers, implementing focus groups on specific topics, and sending surveys either on paper or over e-mail. Another important source of information was the HRCs who gave input on training needs based on their review of employee documents, such as performance plans and appraisals, and their observation of any employee relations trends.

A good example of our needs assessment approach involved assessing the training need for the Managing Effective Communications program, developed under the sponsorship of the Corporate Communications Department. To investigate the need for this program, we took several steps. First, we reviewed UNUM's Vision and Values document, which highlighted the importance of open communication. Next, we conducted interviews with senior members of corporate communications to clarify their view of the need. We also reviewed data gathered from a corporate communications survey, which indicated that UNUM was good at formal communication, but not as effective at informal face-to-face communication. To gain a more refined view, we conducted focus groups with employees to identify the specific skills required for successful communication at UNUM. To validate the needs, we created a communications skills assessment instrument, which listed critical communication skills, and then reviewed this instrument with a pilot test group to ensure that it addressed the right skills.

Program Development and Delivery

In the early 1990s, after interviewing senior managers and assessing business trends, we developed an UNUM Learning Framework, which identified core competencies that cut across businesses. In the early to mid-1990s, we developed a broad curriculum of programs on topics such as change management, customer service, and communications skills to support the learning framework. At the time, all of our programs were classroom based, ranging in length from two hours to four days. Because our target audience was located within the same city and worked similar hours, classroom training was an appropriate solution. We also used videotapes on topics such as diversity, service, mentoring, and leadership as part of classroom training or to reinforce classroom training. At the time, HR training did not use computer-based training (CBT) because people preferred classroom training, and the company was not equipped with an intranet or with CD-ROM capability. Within the past two years, the operations and benefits training areas, whose clients are primarily scattered in field locations, have made extensive use of CBT for product and role training. Currently, we are exploring using CBT for some aspects of customer service training.

Our staff has developed many of our programs, including Managing at Unum, Understanding the Impact of Change, Leading in a Changing Environment, Increasing Your Resilience, and Managing Effective Communications. Occasionally, we have used consultants to develop parts of the programs, such as case studies or skill surveys, and have worked with outside vendors to adapt external programs to Unum and to certify Unum instructors to teach them. For example, Unum's curriculum included Achieving Service Excellence (ASE) and Coaching for Service Excellence, which the Forum Corporation in Boston developed and the MAGIC® of Customer Relations, which Communico, a Westport, Connecticut, company developed.

Our department offered many programs on a regular basis and also instructed other trainers and nontrainers to teach our programs through a rigorous train-the-trainer process. It required that potential trainers attend programs first as participants and then demonstrate skills in train-the-trainer workshops. (For details about UNUM's train-the-trainer process, see McCoy's chapter "Managing a Small HRD Department—Making the Most of Your Resources.") We were able to identify potential instructors by working with business sponsors who nominated appropriate people, by observing participants in various training programs, and by using our Learning Discussion Network (LDN). Established in 1992 by an HRC and me, the LDN was made up of a group of trainers, HR professionals, and other people interested in training who were linked on an electronic distribution list and met quarterly to learn about training related topics and share best practices.

The Training Department initially marketed programs through publication of the UNUM Learning Framework, which included program descriptions. New programs and ongoing programs were announced over the company e-mail system, and the program schedules were kept on an electronic bulletin board. People also learned of training through memos and word-of-mouth from enthusiastic attendees. Senior management mandated some training, such as ASE. In this case, we trained 39 ASE instructors through a train-the-trainer certification process and ultimately trained more than 2,000 employees in ASE in two and a half years.

From 1991 to 1995, the HR Training Department offered a wide range of skill-building programs, including numerous train-the-trainer programs, to the 3,000 home-office employees. Over time, as a result of pressures on operating expenses, we offered fewer programs and our focus narrowed to two critical cross-company initiatives—customer satisfaction and leadership development.

Program Evaluation

Evaluation is a critical tool in improving effectiveness as well as demonstrating the value of training. Kirkpatrick (1994) describes four levels of evaluation: Level 1, reaction or customer satisfaction; Level 2, learning; Level 3, behavior or application of skill and knowledge on the job; and Level 4, results. Evaluation at the higher levels requires evaluation at each of the preceding levels. At the end of each of our programs, trainees completed Level 1 evaluations through a consistent evaluation form. This form collected both quantitative data and qualitative data, which allowed us to improve future programs and coach instructors who had completed our train-the-trainer process. In addition, we also collected verbal feedback and suggestions for improvement from trainees who participated in pilot training programs. The Level 2 evaluation was measured during training programs through skill demonstrations, such as role plays and other skill application exercises. In our train-the-trainer process, the Level 2 evaluation was accomplished by videotaping potential instructors who presented segments of the program and critiquing them using a facilitation skills observation form.

Level 3 was not measured consistently. In some business units, departments identified on-the-job behaviors that needed to improve as a result of Achieving Service Excellence training and were able to show a positive improvement as a result of training. Current and future programs are now taking advantage of Level 3 evaluations. For example, the new Managing Performance Workshop requires that trainees work with their managers to create a performance contract that specifies areas that need improvement such as writing clear performance objectives, writing performance appraisals, and giving effective feedback. In these performance contracts, trainees indicate how their managers will effectively assess progress after training by reviewing written performance documents, by multirater 360 feedback, or by some other means. Also, as part of our LEA Skill-Building Workshops, we have implemented mandatory follow-up sessions six to eight weeks after the programs in order to measure progress on skill growth.

Recently, we have begun to evaluate customer relations training at Level 3. One of the best ways to do this is through call monitoring, in which supervisors listen to employees' calls for their use of specific skills following telephone skills training. An excellent example of this is the implementation process for Communico's MAGIC® of Customer Relations program, which identifies 33 specific behaviors (points) that employees should use when speaking on the telephone. Communico, the Westport, Connecticut, company, has shown that these 33 points, which are listed on an observation form, correlate with customer satisfaction in a number of industries. To ensure that employees have achieved Level 2 learning, trainees are audiotaped during role plays in the MAGIC® program, and trainers rate these taped calls on the 33 points. Trainees show significant improvement from the baseline to the second role play. For Level 3 evaluation, trainees' customer calls are monitored and rated on the 33 points.

The MAGIC® training and call monitoring have been used successfully in UNUM's 1-800 Call Center. The center's manager has become certified as a MAGIC® instructor, and all of the information specialists and supervisors have participated in the program. For the past 18 months, the Call Center has been implementing a program of call monitoring in which supervisors listen to taped calls, provide coaching, and rate specialists on their use of the 33 points as part of the performance appraisal process. As a result of this customer-focus culture, the Call Center has shown improvement in Level 4 (business results) as indicated by customer surveys that measure perception of UNUM employees' courtesy, knowledge, and responsiveness. Senior management considers the Call Center a model of excellent telephone skills, and the Call Center manager, Annie O'Neil, won UNUM's prestigious President's Award for her contributions to customers' satisfaction with the Call Center's service and her support of the training. O'Neil also regularly shares her insights with other areas of the company. Because of the dramatic impact of this training process, other areas are now implementing MAGIC® followed by call observation. In the Billing Department, all managers and billing specialists attended MAGIC® training, and the managers were trained in how to observe the 33 points of MAGIC® and how to coach for improvement. After a monitoring and coaching period, managers will "certify" the billing specialists' customer relations skills by formally evaluating several tape-recorded calls. The managers are meeting this certification process with enthusiasm, whereas the billing specialists are greeting it with some trepidation. Managers have already noticed improvement in the specialists' skills in greeting customers, listening for needs, and demonstrating empathy.

Challenges We Faced

The HR Training Department has faced a number of challenges. As a result of downsizing within the Human Resources Department, training lost some precious positions. Previously we had had an additional management development consultant as well as two full-time administrative assistants. Being a good training administrator is not an automatic skill of every administrative assistant—even if someone understands the requirements of training logistics, there are specific requirements for different programs. As a consequence of losing our permanent administrative assistant, we needed to continually retrain temporary administrative help in how to provide logistical support to training.

The Human Resources organization acknowledged that as a result of the downsizing it would not be possible to offer as many standing programs as we had in the past. Instead, our department would focus on identifying the need for new broad-based programs, managing their development, conducting pilot programs, and providing train-the-trainer support so that the business units would provide their own training. Because businesses had been used to having people sign up for regularly scheduled training, some departments did not appreciate the change, which now required them to send people to outside programs or find ways to offer training themselves. As a consequence of the downsizing, we needed to focus only on the most important business priorities and manage our resources even more closely than before.

Another challenge was learning to make the alternative working arrangement of a job share work well in our small department. The two management development consultants, who worked long hours and wished to spend more time with their families, each wanted to work three days a week. Because UNUM strongly supports having a flexible work environment and because we wanted to find a way to meet the personal needs of the management development consultants, we decided to pilot the job-share arrangement. Our initial plan was for one of them to work Monday through Wednesday, and the other to work Wednesday through Friday, which would allow for a full week's coverage and one day of overlap. In reality, they sometimes needed to work the same days whenever they needed to facilitate a program together. There were challenges in making sure that all of us communicated with one another, and that nothing fell through the cracks. Phone mail updates were very helpful in bridging the communication gap, but it was challenging for me to keep in touch, given their changing work schedules. There is no doubt that UNUM has more than gotten its money's worth from this job share, as it has allowed the department to retain two experienced employees, renewed the two management consultants' spirits, helped to stimulate their creative juices, and actually increased their productivity. Overall, increases in productivity and decreases in absenteeism and sick days are well-documented benefits to effective alternative work arrangements.

Success Story—Creating a Leadership Development Program for the Home Office

The leadership development program for UNUM America's home-office employees is an excellent example of creative use of resources and building broad-based sponsorship. The goals for leadership development were to ensure the following:

- Current and future leaders had strong leadership skills to meet UNUM's business and work environment goals.
- There was a systematic process to develop leadership skills.
- There was bench strength for future leadership positions.

To understand the evolution of this leadership program, it is important to have some background.

Background

To create a career path for the salesforce and to improve sales, UNUM America had previously implemented a successful management development program (MDP), which focused specifically on the salesforce located in 34 offices throughout the United States. A senior marketing officer sponsored the field MDP, and an UNUM HRC who supported the marketing organization managed it. In creating the MDP, this HRC had worked closely with an external consultant, Tom Rand of the Rand Consulting Group, of Portland, Maine. Rand was one of the authors of a leadership assessment instrument (the Leadership Effectiveness Analysis, or LEA), which could be used for self-assessment and for 360 feedback. The LEA helped to identify the degree to which individuals used various leadership behaviors, and it focused on 22 dimensions, such as strategic thinking, innovation, communication, feedback, delegation, persuasiveness, and empathy. Rand created a customized Unum profile of success identifying dimensions that correlated with being a successful sales manager as measured by sales results, product mix, office turnover, and rankings of senior officers. The field MDP assessment process included a self-assessment of the LEA and 360 feedback on the LEA, and some additional assessment activities that measured motivation and critical thinking.

For several years, senior management in the field had offered salespeople the opportunity to apply for this elite MDP for individuals who would receive specific developmental opportunities. Those candidates who were accepted into the MDP received more in-depth leadership assessments and training, guidance on a development plan to address gaps in their assessment, and coaching from managers who were familiar with the Rand assessment tool because they had also participated in the assessment process. MDP participants also received an opportunity to get a taste of management by helping with budgeting, recruiting, and other managerial functions. MDP served as a formal "bench-strength-building" system of recruiting and training the next generation of managers. Once MDP candidates demonstrated skills necessary to be a manager, they were eligible for consideration for the next management opening. The field MDP had strong management support from the marketing organization and had considerable success in raising the management skills of new managers of the salesforce.

The Challenge and the Opportunity

UNUM America's home office had no comparable MDP for the 3,000 employees (including approximately 600 officers, directors, and managers) who worked in various jobs in customer services, underwriting, and benefits departments. Selected employees could participate in a number of training programs that could build managerial skills, but there was no common assessment process, no consistent way of selecting people with management potential, and no systematic way of preparing managers to lead others.

In 1995, senior management asked our department to create a leadership development program for the home office, based on key success principles of the field's MDP. A critical goal was to develop UNUM America's bench strength so that the company would have people with the right skills ready at the right time when management positions became available. Ultimately, we had about eight months in which to develop a leadership framework, provide assessment tools, and train a target audience of 400 managers.

Despite the challenges, there were many reasons for optimism. We had a talented, experienced, and dedicated staff. There was an opportunity to contribute to a significant initiative—to build our leadership capacity and ensure that all of UNUM's people managers honed their leadership skills to the highest level. We could learn from and draw upon the well-respected field MDP. Most important, the new operations executive, who had sponsored the field MDP and who had a reputation for getting things done, was a strong proponent of leadership. He would be a highly visible and credible sponsor who would make sure that funds and people would be made available to support our leadership development work.

Building Sponsorship and Clarifying Priorities

The first steps were to clarify the specific requirements of leadership for the home office, which differed from that of the field salesforce, and to build important relationships with potential senior sponsors. Although we needed to build on the strongly supported field MDP, we also had the opportunity to tailor and add to that program. We knew from an electronic survey of managers and employees that there was a need for a more structured curriculum and for a tool that would help managers understand the specific knowledge and skills they needed. Many managers needed to improve their skills in setting performance objectives, providing feedback and coaching, and providing documented performance appraisals. For example, only 61 percent of employees say that they received regular feedback from their managers, and only 49 percent of employees said that they knew what was required to "exceed," not simply "meet" performance expectations.

To ensure sponsorship and buy-in, we created a leadership development advisory group that helped to provide direction and validate our recommendations. The senior operations executive, who had sponsored the field MDP, led this advisory group. One of our first decisions was whether to focus on current managers with direct reports or on "aspiring managers" (MDP-type candidates) who were individual contributors who wanted to be managers. The advisory group identified the most critical audience as the 400 officers, directors, and managers who actually managed other people. The advisory group decided that starting a management development program for aspiring managers was a lower priority. The most urgent priority was approximately 38 officers who needed to receive an in-depth assessment of their own leadership skills and developmental needs. We needed to reach this group before focusing on lower-level managers so that we could create a common vision of leadership, common expectations, and a common language for people development, to ensure that all levels of managers were getting the same message. A critical message was the importance of developing leadership behaviors and skills, and the acknowledgment that everyone had some developmental needs regarding leadership.

Establishing the Core Leadership Message

The first priority involved developing the leadership skills of key executives who would sponsor the program. Succeeding at this phase was essential in establishing our department's credibility. A key group of officers, whom Rand had not already assessed, needed to be reached first. This group would work one-on-one with Rand and its own managers to receive in-depth assessments, feedback, and coaching on needed leadership characteristics. Our department played a key role in helping to negotiate the consultant contract, plan the budget, identify candidates, schedule, and track these executive assessments. Each assessment consisted of three feedback sessions with Rand, followed by a three-way session with Rand, the executive, and his or her boss, which focused on key developmental messages regarding leadership. This candidate identification and scheduling process was very time-consuming, politically sensitive, and logistically difficult. We met the goal of ensuring that these 38 key executives were assessed within a short time period by working closely with the senior sponsor and with Rand.

Developing an Action Plan

Having gained clarity on priorities from the leadership advisory group, our next step was to develop an action plan to ensure that 400 leaders received appropriate leadership assessments and messages regarding required leadership behaviors in a six-month period. Our plan consisted of several significant milestones:

- Create a UNUM home-office profile of leadership to reflect required competencies.
- Develop a leadership framework, which included all the assessment tools for the different audiences, and developmental activities to help build needed competencies.
- Communicate the leadership framework so that all executives and leaders would know what they were expected to do.
- Schedule the executives for assessment and coaching.
- Create a UNUM Understanding Your LEA Profile Workshop and then certify UNUM instructors in the LEA assessment workshop.
- Schedule LEA Profile workshops.
- Develop the leadership curriculum after completion of assessments and analysis of gaps.
- Track attendance and measure the impact and gap analysis for future interventions.

Creating the Leadership Framework

One key challenge was finding or creating assessment tools that had senior management support, that would work well together, and that would help employees. This was no small task. A "racing bike model of leadership," which Rand had used with many members of senior management, was helpful in illustrating aspects of leadership assessment. (See figure 1.) In this model, the power wheel represents functional, or business, knowledge and critical thinking skills; the steering wheel represents how leaders behave; and the pedals represent the energy and motivation to propel the bike. No leader could be successful without all three working properly.

Rand had created a specialized battery of assessment tools for the executive level, but we needed to decide on the required assessments for directors and managers. We selected three primary leadership as-

Figure 1. Leadership skills assessment model.

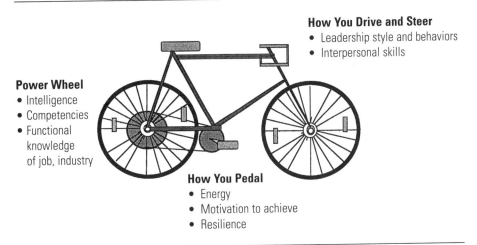

How You Drive and Steer
- Leadership style and behaviors
- Interpersonal skills

Power Wheel
- Intelligence
- Competencies
- Functional
  knowledge
  of job, industry

How You Pedal
- Energy
- Motivation to achieve
- Resilience

sessment tools for the UNUM Leadership Framework: the LEA self-assessment; a 360 feedback online leadership-behavior survey; and a knowledge and skills inventory. We included the LEA as a mandatory assessment because the senior management team strongly supported its use. However, there was one hurdle to using the LEA for the home office. There was a validated LEA profile of success for UNUM leaders in the field sales management organization, but the characteristics leaders in the home office needed were more varied and not precisely the same as those for the field. An essential tactic was making sure that the senior advisory group believed in the validity of the home-office leadership profile. To ensure their buy-in, Rand worked with the company president and his direct reports to create a specific home-office leadership profile that would apply across a variety of levels and positions.

We also incorporated two other assessment tools to give a more well-rounded picture. Another front-wheel tool was the newly developed electronic 360 feedback survey on UNUM leadership behaviors, which also had strong buy-in from the officer group. This survey was based on a Profile of Leadership developed by a group of UNUM officers who had identified required leadership behaviors in eight categories, such as inspiring a shared vision, developing others, and customer focus. As training director, I participated in a project team that created the online leadership survey and played a critical role in ensuring the survey's validity. To validate the instrument, we hired a psychology professor from the University of Southern Maine who helped us test the survey and revise it on the basis of an item analysis. The third tool, the Management Development Knowledge and Skills Inventory, measured "back wheel knowledge and skills." It compared the manager and his or her manager's ratings on specific knowledge and skills needed to manage people. One of our management development consultants developed the inventory with input from UNUM's Manager Supervisor Steering Committee, a standing group of well-regarded managers and supervisors who understood what leaders needed to do to succeed at UNUM.

In addition to these assessments, we proposed a curriculum that consisted of the following programs:

- Understanding Your LEA Profile Workshop (one day)—trainees completed the LEA as prework, reviewed their LEA profile, created a developmental plan in the workshop.
- Developing Others Workshop (one-half day)—to help people understand the three assessment tools and plan for the development of their staff.
- LEA Skill Building Workshops—six different programs, each designed to address a specific leadership behavior gap identified by people's LEA profiles.
- Managing Performance Workshop (two days)—to build performance management skills.

Once the advisory group approved the framework, we planned for a wide-scale communication of the leadership framework. To demonstrate sponsorship, four senior managers who had completed the leadership assessment process gave these communication sessions. Attendance at one of these leadership briefing sessions was mandatory because we needed officers and directors with direct reports to understand actions that they would be required to take.

Developing and Implementing the Curriculum

To develop and instruct the new leadership curriculum, we relied on a combination of ourselves, other HR employees, and external consultants. We worked with Rand to customize the Understanding Your LEA Profile Workshop and to create a train-the-trainer process to certify 13 HR professionals to instruct the workshop and interpret the profiles. An outside firm that works closely with Rand, Management Research Group (MRG), in Portland, Maine, processed the assessments. Because it was mandatory to get an LEA assessment, it was essential to track participation in this program for senior management. Our temporary assistant did a masterful job of administering and tracking participation in the LEA workshops. In a six-month period, 375 of the target audience of 400 managers completed LEA assessments either by attending an LEA workshop or by participating in an executive assessment with Rand. Given the logistical constraints and some resistance, this was an amazing feat.

From analyzing the 360 feedback survey and other data, it became clear that "developing others" was a weakness of many leaders. We wanted to offer a half-day workshop on developing others to help people understand the assessment tools and build their skills in developing their staff. I designed the workshop based on an earlier program that I had developed. I trained our two management development consultants and three other HRCs to facilitate this workshop, and we trained 120 managers in three months.

The six LEA Skill Building Workshops provided formal developmental opportunities to address gaps identified in the LEA profile, such as a need to increase persuasiveness, empathy, or strategic thinking. Tricia Nadaff of MRG designed, instructed, and administered the workshops. Although the workshops took a while to catch on, employees who took advantage of them found the sessions helpful. The two management development consultants also were certified to instruct the LEA Skill Building Workshops as well to increase our capacity to offer these programs and deepen their knowledge of the LEA. Mandatory follow-up sessions after the LEA Skill Building Workshops were a means to measure Level 3 change in leadership skills on the job.

We knew that there was a need to address performance management skills and to revise our four-day Managing at UNUM program. The initial plan was to develop a Managing Performance Workshop later in the year, but we received an urgent plea to train new managers in our benefits area by the end of August. Because our staff had no time in June and July to develop this program by the deadline, I worked closely with an outside consulting firm, The Forum Corporation, to create a new program based on our needs assessment data, using the best parts of the Managing at UNUM program and incorporating more hands-on learning as well. As with all new programs, we incorporated Level 3 evaluation into this workshop. As prework, trainees completed the Management Development Knowledge and Skills Inventory and created a results contract with their managers on specific areas they needed to improve. To help address the business need, I taught the pilot for this program with an HRC in the benefits area. Later, I conducted a train-the-trainer for three additional UNUM instructors so that the program could be offered in other areas of the company.

Results and Ongoing Evolution

In the course of less than a year, a department of 2.2 people was able to create a leadership framework and curriculum, and spread a consistent assessment process, to help build bench strength for the future. Since the rollout, the UNUM Leadership Framework has been expanded to include aspiring managers, a formal readiness phase, a rigorous application and selection process that uses an assessment center process to identify candidates for a home-office management program, and additional leadership workshops for the executive level. UNUM America has selected its second MDP class, and graduates of the first class have already assumed successful managerial positions. Early in 1997, data from all the assessments helped to shape the curriculum design and influenced the new president of UNUM America to invest more in leadership and to continue the focus on building leadership in our organization.

Meanwhile UNUM continues to change rapidly. UNUM is working toward a common definition of leadership and a common leadership curriculum, bringing together best practices across all UNUM companies. This cross-affiliate leadership development framework is leading to changes in UNUM America's leadership framework. In addition, our small training department has been merged into another department and has refocused its work on performance consulting. UNUM America is currently evaluating its training strategy and training continues to evolve.

Lessons Learned

With strong sponsorship and a mandate from senior management, a lot can be accomplished in a short period of time. Developing relationships with sponsors, focusing on their priority populations and actions, using a wide range of internal and external providers to develop and deliver programs, and having a highly organized and competent administrative assistant were keys to success in this program's development and initial implementation. Another key success factor was agreeing on a common definition of leadership, which gives leaders a clear target. The program's future success will depend on creating a partnership with a new sponsor because the previous sponsor left for a senior position with one of our affiliates. Future success also will depend on working with the other human resource levers that have an impact on leadership, such as selection, recruitment, retention, compensation, and succession planning.

A major lesson for me was just how much can be accomplished by a small training department made up of people in a nontraditional work arrangement—two part-time trainers who job share and a temporary administrative assistant. Despite the challenges to maintaining a flow of communication, there can be tremendous gains in productivity and morale by having trainers work part-time and job share. By being able to take care of other responsibilities during part of the workweek, the trainers were able to focus on the job and tackle all the training assignments with a high level of enthusiasm, creativity, and concentration. In addition, in spite of our initial frustrations, we found that it was possible to provide administrative support to training programs by using temps. Although we lost the full-time permanent head count, we were able to keep the budget to hire temporary help. Even though it was inconvenient to keep retraining temps, it was possible to find outstanding temporary employees who agreed to work on assignment for up to six months. For example, Anne Marie Quesnel needed a long-term temporary assignment while she was getting her new ice cream business up and running. When working with creative and entrepreneurial temporary employees, it helps to be flexible in allowing them to pursue their other interests as well. By planning for the needed budget and maintaining your flexibility, you may be able to take advantage of talented temporary employees who have excellent interpersonal and organizational skills.

Questions for Discussion

1. How were training needs assessed in general? What methods could you use to assess needs in your organization?
2. How does UNUM's HR Training Department evaluate training? What measures could you use to evaluate interpersonal skills and leadership skills training?
3. What challenges did this department face, and how were they overcome?
4. What are the advantages and disadvantages of having a job-share arrangement for trainers? Could you take advantage of having a job share in your organization?
5. What actions did UNUM take to ensure sponsorship and support of the leadership development program? What additional strategies could the company have used?
6. What decisions guided the resource strategy for developing the leadership curriculum?

What internal and external resources are available to your organization to assist in developing and delivering training? Are you using the most effective resource strategy?

The Author

Carol Prescott McCoy is currently manager of training quality assurance and the performance consultant for customer satisfaction with UNUM Life Insurance Company of America. Previously she was director of UNUM's Human Resource Training Department. She received her B.A. from Connecticut College in psychology and her M.S. and Ph.D. from Rutgers University, in social psychology. Before joining Unum in 1991, McCoy worked in various areas of human resource development (HRD) for Chase Manhattan Bank from 1980 until 1991. At Chase, she created and managed a small HRD department in Chase's International Consumer Banking division. In a one- or sometimes two-person department, she oversaw management training for managers in 15 countries. Before starting her career in the financial services industry, she taught psychology at Livingston College and Rutgers University and was chairperson of a one-person social science department for a nursing school in the Bronx, New York. McCoy is author of *Managing a Small HRD Department: You Can Do More Than You Think* (McCoy, 1993) and a frequent conference speaker. She can be contacted at 11 Johnson Road, Falmouth, Maine 04105; phone: 207.781.7515; e-mail: Cmccoy3333@aol.com.

References

Kirkpatrick, D.L. (1994). *Evaluating Training Programs.* San Francisco: Berrett-Koehler.

McCoy, C.P. (1993). *Managing a Small HRD Department: You Can Do More Than You Think.* San Francisco: Jossey-Bass.

Proving the Need for a Training Staff

Louisiana Workers' Compensation Corporation

Debra T. Taylor

This case is a source of hope for all lone trainers who know they need more dedicated training resources to help the business succeed. It is an excellent illustration of how one trainer in a start-up situation created a master training plan and used an external consultant to conduct a needs assessment that ultimately proved the need for more training resources. As a result of her thoughtful approach, Debra Taylor was able to increase the staff of LWCC's Training Department from one person to five people in order to meet urgent business needs of a company with over 430 employees. Readers will find that Taylor's master training plan is a helpful example of how to present training objectives and strategies.

Company Background

Workers' compensation had become a nightmare for Louisiana. Insurance companies no longer wanted to write workers' compensation coverage in the state because the cost of doing business was not profitable. In October 1991, Louisiana Workers' Compensation Corporation (LWCC), a private not-for-profit mutual insurance company, was created by constitutional amendment to save the state's failed workers' compensation system. Our company's mission was as follows:

- to guarantee the solvency of the corporation and to provide the highest level of policyholder services
- to provide workers' compensation insurance to as many Louisiana employers as possible at the lowest feasible cost
- to provide the injured worker with rapid, efficient, and complete compensation for injuries and to provide the best opportunity for a rapid return to work

This case was prepared to serve as a basis for discussion rather than to illustrate either effective or ineffective administrative and management practices.

- to manage risk and to educate agents, insureds, and employers on the value of a safe workplace
- to promote quality and efficiency with so-called Zero Waste.

As you can imagine, our mission demanded every employees' expertise and commitment. LWCC started in December 1991 with one employee, our CEO. Our work order was to open for business in October 1992. Needless to say, we had a lot of work to do in 10 months.

With insurance companies pulling out of Louisiana; we were fortunate to gain some of our workforce through downsizing of other insurance companies. Even though we hired the best and the brightest, there was still training to be done. We had to do it better and differently than those that had left the state. We had to do it according to our mission—the promise we had made to Louisiana businesses, our policyholders.

The Beginnings of the Training Function

While hiring claims and underwriting staff, the human resources (HR) director was just as busy hiring staff for the HR area. The employment manager and the benefits manager were hired in April and May, respectively, and I was hired as the training coordinator in July 1992. My job description, simplified, was to handle all the training that employees needed to hit the ground running. Although I reported to the HR director, I purposely chose my office on the floor that housed the major departments of our company—claims and underwriting. I needed to be located where it happened—where money came in and went out—where I could hear and see the needs of the employees.

My first day at LWCC was also the day the corporation installed the new phone system. Instead of doing new-hire paperwork, I was taking notes in a train-the-trainer session on our new phone system. This was major training because the telephone was the tool that the corporation would use to conduct a large percentage of its business transactions. Because there were only 60 employees at the time, I handled this training with no problem.

On every desk was a personal computer loaded with Windows 3.0. The employees came from a variety of desktop environments, which resulted in my second major project—computer training. Because I was the only trainer, I reached reality quickly and began outsourcing the training. Several companies had heard about our new company, so there was a pool of resources to choose from. I reviewed bids from external sources and made my selection. A computer train-

ing lab with eight PCs was set up, and training began shortly there-
after. With this external vendor, LWCC had increased its investment
in training. It was important to know and document that we were
meeting the needs of the participants. Every participant of the computer classes signed in and completed a multiple-choice training evaluation form that asked if the course fulfilled the student's purpose;
how useful it was in helping the participant perform his or her job;
how the instructors rated overall and on preparation, accuracy and
knowledge, ability to maintain interest, pace of instruction, and clarity. The questionnaire also asked students to estimate by what percentage they would increase their job effectiveness as a result of the
course, and it asked students to write in what they could do to make
the course better.

After the training, all participants had significantly increased their
skill on Word for Windows, and there was an immediate transfer of
skill to the job. Employees as well as supervisors commented on the
change in behavior as a result of the training.

Even though the external sources were plentiful, they could not
handle all the training challenges of the company. We had specialized in-house software, developed specifically for our business, and
the computer skills needed for it would be highly technical. It was
obvious that once this software was up and running, more extensive
training would be required. Fortunately, there was a group of individuals who played an integral role in developing the software, and
they were designated to handle the training for the 70 employees on
board at the time.

Our company was steadily growing and orienting the LWCC way
became another major training assignment. I submitted a proposal
for a new employee orientation to my boss, indicating what I thought
should be happening when new employees were hired. He discussed
this plan with the executive team, and they agreed that a new employee orientation would be a perfect setting in which to meet with
new employees. So we instituted a full-day orientation dedicated to
learning about LWCC. New employees spent a day learning about their
new employer and their role at the company and hearing presentations from a variety of staff, including the CEO and the payroll clerk.
Initially, I coordinated and facilitated this monthly session, which continues to be offered monthly.

Meanwhile, the employee market was becoming exhausted of available seasoned insurance professionals, and it was apparent that we
would eventually need to grow our own insurance professionals. The

vice president of claims was becoming concerned that we would not have adequate staff trained when the business started booming in his area. We had discussed informally the needs of the Claims Department, but it was not my number one priority. Because this was apparent to him, he began searching for a trainer for his division. His plan was to hire someone who would devote 100 percent of his or her time to claims training. The trainer would report to him, but because the person would work very closely with me, I was included in the interviewing process. His need was definitely a clue that I needed help. Training was about to become decentralized, and it was not my goal to be the person whose only role was to set up the equipment or schedule meeting rooms.

Reevaluating Training Priorities: The New Training Plan

With the growing need for claims training along with all the other training needs ranging from phone skills to management skills, I began to reevaluate training priorities and needs of the corporation. In January 1993, I went to my boss and screamed the indisputable, "I need help!" He said, "Prove it." So I did. I submitted a 17-page business plan to him, the CEO, and the chief operating officer that described the needs of the company. A summary of the document follows:

Training Plan Executive Summary

LWCC has made a commitment to restore the workers' compensation market to a stable and competitive industry. This commitment will be made a reality through LWCC's most valuable asset—competent and trained employees.

The Training Department of LWCC will play a vital and visible role in this commitment by providing training, education, and information to the employees of LWCC. A Training Department focused on the mission of the corporation and the educational needs of employees to fulfill the mission will enable them to achieve the corporation's objectives with the highest possible efficiency, effectiveness, and professionalism.

The fulfillment of this mission requires a staff that is focused on the education and training of LWCC employees. A training program that has a staff dedicated to its mission will do the following:
- Tie training to the corporate strategy.
- Make training concise and focused on the corporate need.
- Design high-quality courses.
- Tie training to the actual task of the job.

- Develop careers through training.
- Deliver training that does not waste time.
- Choose the best training materials.
- Respond to a changing workforce.
- Cultivate attitudes about change.

The plan outlined the following objectives, goals, and strategies of the Training Department:

Objective #1: The Education and Training Department of LWCC shall be responsive to the educational needs of all employees.

Goal: The Education and Training Department shall maintain channels of communications with senior management and department heads to ensure that training needs are fulfilled.

Strategies:
- The education and training manager will survey the needs of each department annually. The needs analysis may be conducted by an external source when appropriate.
- An Education Committee will meet quarterly to discuss needs and provide ways and means of prioritizing and meeting needs.
- The education and training manager shall use all available resources to communicate educational opportunities to all employees in an adequate and timely way.

Objective #2: The Education and Training Department shall provide education that is practical and effective in assisting departments to achieve their objectives.

Goal: The Education and Training Department shall design courses and course materials that will be useful in day-to-day operations.

Strategies:
- The Education and Training Department shall identify and emphasize areas of interest to employees of each department.
- The Education and Training Department will work with subject matter experts to ensure validity of course syllabus.
- The Education and Training Department will provide evaluation tools to measure course effectiveness.
- The education and training manager shall recruit consultants, vendors, and other experienced external sources with experience to share in education and training.
- The Education and Training Department shall design courses to provide a workshop environment, whereby participants can apply the course to their own experience and specific work environment.

Objective # 3: The Education and Training Department shall provide tools, information, and resources that will afford well-rounded professional education in all major areas of LWCC.

Goal: The Education and Training Department will coordinate and present courses and course materials in technical areas.

Strategies:

- The Education and Training Department will provide continuous training in the Workers' Compensation Insurance System (WCIS).
- Work with the Bayou Chapter of IIA to provide classroom instruction, independent study or group study for the corporation's major areas:
    —insurance principles
    —workers' compensation coverage
    —principles of premium auditing
    —loss prevention
    —underwriting basics.
- Develop working relationship with the medical community to provide seminars, workshops, and classroom instruction in the following areas:
    —medical cost containment
    —rehabilitation
- Solicit outside instructors for seminars, workshops and classrooms instruction in the following areas:
    —special investigation
    —marketing
    —information systems
    —Louisiana law and workers' compensation
    —records management.
- Provide ongoing software applications training to maximize employees' use of computers in their day-to-day work operations.

Objective #4: The Education and Training Department shall provide employees with computer-based training tools that will enhance their understanding of the workers' compensation industry.

Goal: The Education and Training Department will assist and coordinate with the Information Systems Department the development of a computer-based training program.

Strategies:

- Solicit the assistance of experts in the field of multimedia training.
- Confer with management on the advantages of having a computer-based training system.
- Utilize the technical in-house experts to develop the syllabus for this type of training.
- Provide ongoing training for existing and new users of the system.

Objective #5: The Education and Training Department shall develop and maintain a comprehensive program that will provide the external customer of LWCC (agents, insureds) with tools to promote, provide, and maintain a safe workplace.

Goal: The Education and Training Department shall coordinate or develop instructional materials, or both coordinate and develop them, to assist in the promotion and maintenance of a safe workplace.

Strategies:

- The Education and Training Department shall expand and improve curriculum materials and instruction for customers of LWCC.
- The education and training manager shall recruit and maintain the best instructors available to provide quality seminars, workshops, and classroom instruction.

Objective #6: The Education and Training Department shall serve as a resource center providing workers' compensation education, training, and information nationwide.

Goal: The Education and Training Department shall develop courses, workshops, and seminars that will provide a well-rounded education in workers' compensation.

Strategies:

- Develop programs that will educate in general knowledge of workers' compensation.
- Provide LWCC in-house classroom instruction, seminars, and workshops to educate employees of other companies.
- Provide education and training to other companies via teleconferencing, LWCC videos, and computer-based training.

Determining Training Needs and Staffing Requirements

To confirm and justify my business plan, I requested that we conduct a training needs survey. The most important thing I envisioned this survey to do would be determine the employees' needs and justify staff needed to do the training. My recommendation was approved, and I secured an external source to handle the survey.

The consultant had visited our corporation on other occasions in different capacities, but his conversation always seemed to come back to how we were addressing our training needs. I saw this as a challenge and an opportunity. Here was someone on the outside looking in. Perhaps he had another agenda, but his conversations with the CEO concerning ideas about training deserved my attention. We met and discussed what he could offer the corporation. During the meeting, I recognized the talent that he brought to the table. He could help with the survey and would bring objectivity to this project. We discussed price, and his was a market price, and besides he had been around enough to hit the ground running with my request.

The assessment consisted of a two-step process. There would be management personnel interviews, and information from these would be incorporated into a written survey for all employees. The consultant used the American Society for Training & Development's (ASTD's) Toolkit (Allen, 1990) in the development of the survey because it provided the information needed to design a training needs assessment that supported LWCC's mission more than a generic product would. The written assessment asked employees their perceptions of their skills and knowledge, their need to improve, the importance of the skill or knowledge to their job, and the managers' ideas about key changes that would have an impact on the business in the next few years. The written survey listed numerous job components and for each one it asked employees to assign a rating (very low, low, average, better-than-average, or high) for their current skill level or knowledge of it, their perceived need to improve the skill or knowledge level, and the importance of the skill or information to their performance. The survey covered the following general areas and job-related skills:

- client-related skills (such as interviewing policyholders and handling complaints)
- communication skills (writing memos and reports, resolving conflicts with others, and the like)
- computer skills
- co-worker interactional skills
- other skills like time management and stress management
- job-specific skills and knowledge (underwriting basics and negotiation, for example)
- managerial skills (such as setting objectives and motivating employees)
- legal issues (like workers' compensation and sexual harassment).

The survey also asked employees' views about training programs, their availability to attend programs, and where they thought there was need for training. To demonstrate senior management's support of the assessment, the survey included the following cover letter from Steve Cavanaugh, the president and CEO:

> As our Corporation grows, the need for corporate wide training strategies and long term planning become imperative; therefore, I am asking for your assistance in completing this questionnaire. I expect to get 100 percent participation in this project. Please return this survey by closing time Wednesday, March 24, 1993.
> I appreciate your support and interest in training.

In March 1993, the assessment was complete, the face-to-face interviews were done, and the assessment document was distributed.

The key assumption in the training needs assessment was that LWCC employees could make good judgments about the skills they needed to perform their job functions. The employees were the consumers of training plans and strategies, and they were critical to the mission of the company. Another key assumption was that training would be easier and appreciated more if the trainees wanted to learn. The survey's intent was to discover those areas in which employees felt they needed training. Once the employees completed the survey, they were instructed to drop them in a box designated for the consultant. At the time of the survey, we had 161 employees, and 144 responded, an exceptionally high response rate. This observation provided evidence that employees were interested in completing the survey, giving serious responses, and probably believed that their responses were respected.

We shared the results of the survey with the senior staff and published them in our corporate newsletter. The feedback from the survey was great. In the open-ended questions, employees overwhelmingly stated a needed for more computer training and training on the insurance software system. The management interviews discovered many ideas about the goals and priorities of training, although virtually everyone stressed a much larger role for training in the company's future. Respondents indicated that the following areas were important and they needed training in them:

- orienting insurance agents to LWCC services
- underwriting basics
- technical writing
- mediation techniques
- using the insurance software
- reporting details of investigation
- using laptop computers
- setting objectives
- using database tools
- asking the right questions
- using Windows
- team building
- using word-processing programs
- interviewing
- understanding insurance terminology
- performance appraisal
- stress management
- knowledge of workers' compensation
- negotiation

- overview of insurance industry
- medical aspect of claims
- medical cost containment
- introduction to claims
- lifesaving techniques
- investigative skills—claims
- workers' compensation law.

Increasing the Size of the Training Department

The needs assessment not only confirmed training needs, but also justified a Training Department to handle those needs—a department that would have its own budget and cost center. Because the Training Department was not producing widgets, which would show a profit or loss, it was vital to show how it spent the budgeted funds. It was important to produce a monthly report for the department head that would serve as a snapshot of monthly costs and year-to-date training expenses that represented the investment the company was making in developing its human assets. This year-to-date report would complement and explain the monthly report accounting produced, which presented no link to that human asset investment. Table 1 is a sample 1994 year-to-date training report.

An immediate result of the needs assessment survey was an addition to staff as well as my promotion to education and training manager in April 1993. The vice president of claims agreed that a divisional trainer for would no longer be necessary for the Claims Division, provided that someone would be assigned to handle the group's specific needs. I was impressed with the trainer the vice president had considered hiring, so I offered her the job of program development specialist (PDS). in the Training Department. Because she had interviewed with the vice president of claims, she had a clear idea of her first project as well as her customer's expectations.

Because of our concern that the market for seasoned claims adjusters would soon be dried up, we began recruiting for claims adjusters while the PDS began our first claims adjuster training program. A critical partnership of the employment manager, the PDS, the training manager, and the vice president of claims took shape during this project, as the colleagues met to discuss everyone's needs and expectations. By the meeting's end, several things were accomplished:
- We formed a rough draft of the course syllabus.
- Three subject matter experts (SMEs) were on loan to the Training Department to assist in the design of the program.

Table 1. 1994 year-to-date training report.

Month	Number of Classes	Total Attendance	Total Cost of Training (Includes Facilities and Development)	Total Investment per Employee	Total Training Hours
January	23	223	$2,173.57	$9.75	71
February	28	354	$3,669.47	$10.37	111
March	39	352	$7,043.36	$20.01	119.5
April	20	119	$6,937.50	$58.30	111.5
May	28	241	$6,789.00	$28.17	81
June	38	147	$6,625.00	$45.07	119
July	43	292	$2,832.72	$9.70	116
August	33	203	$5,783.01	$28.49	115
September	37	464	$11,637.76	$25.08	126
October	45	481	$8,272.15	$17.20	142
November	29	307	$5,627.44	$18.33	93
December	51	421	$2,972.60	$7.06	69
YTD totals	**414**	**3,604**	**$70,363.58**	**$19.52**	**1,274**

- The employment manager walked away with a job description for this new position.
- The vice president had good news to deliver to managers about the opportunity to interview and select candidates for the associate claims positions.

The partnership worked well. The trainer and the SMEs met daily to discuss and design the syllabus. The PDS and I met weekly to make sure everything was on schedule. This was our first big project and it had to go well—the credibility of the Training Department was on the line, and we had to prove that we brought something of value as training professionals. Although we were not insurance experts, we were the people who would ensure effective learning. The Claims Adjuster Training Program went exceptionally well, and we graduated 21 associate claims adjusters. A formal ceremony was planned with the CEO giving the commencement address and our chief operating officer playing a role in this exercise as well. Once again we were marketing training. Evidence of a job well done came in the form of a request to repeat this course for the next group of trainees that would be hired six months later.

While this project was under way, it became apparent that we needed to get our administrative house in order. We needed a training tracking system that could manage training information, quickly identify the training courses being offered, and update student transcripts. I began researching software packages to manage this information. After looking at several demonstrations, I chose the Gyrus' *Training Administrator* as the tracking package that would serve the department's needs and requests.

I enjoyed the administrative part of my job, but it was becoming overwhelming, and my management responsibilities required more of my time. Monthly reports, course manuals, and budget maintenance records, to name a few items, were piling up on my desk. My next hire was a training assistant. She took care of the clerical and some of the administrative tasks. She also took over the weekly orientation session. Being a recent college graduate and an ambitious and intelligent individual who immediately began working on her master's degree in education, she would be the perfect future candidate for a trainer. Under her wing, the orientation session grew to a full two days.

The heart of our business process was in the workers' compensation insurance software package. Our survey strongly indicated that training was needed on this system. It was evident that the training done earlier did not address all the needs and that changes to the insurance software were being done daily. My request for an instruction and development specialist (IDS) did not come as a surprise to my boss. The request was approved, and I began interviewing candidates for the position. The IDS came on board in September 1993, not a day too soon because the needs assessment indicated that she was needed six months earlier. On her first day with the company when I introduced her as the person who would handle all of the training for our insurance software, there was a sigh of relief from everyone. A month into the job, both of us knew that this job was bigger than the original job description had implied. With this job, a partnership with Information Systems (IS) was a must. Programmers were making changes everyday, which affected which courses would be taught. To handle this requirement, we mapped out a strategy that would guarantee that the end user was getting the right information and just-in-time training. Through a partnership with IS, the Training Department was kept informed of upcoming systems changes—the IDS was invited to meetings where systems changes were discussed in their just-a-request" stage. Because this software was the heart of our business, training was being designed and classes were being taught continuously.

Technical training was not the only need that stood out in the survey. Soft skills training also needed attention. Because the training staff had its plates full with current projects, I devoted half of my time to researching options for the soft-skills training. Because I had previously developed modules on management training, I took on the task of teaching some of the management courses. I outsourced most of the management training, however, because managing the budget, conducting performance evaluations, and the like were time-consuming. Also, time had to be planned for staff development. In my budget process, I included dollars to keep the Training Department abreast of issues in the profession. It was mandatory for the training staff to be members of the local chapter of ASTD. Other resources for us included my membership in ASTD National was a resource for us as well as other publications specific to the training profession.

Although it was evident from the survey that training was needed and that training was happening daily, opportunities for marketing training could not be missed. The PDS visited other managers outside of her assigned area to ensure that their needs were being met; this was also a cross-training adventure. We had monthly staff meetings, and the one standing agenda item was "what's happening on the floor." Other agenda items included planning the training calendar, corporate updates, departmental updates, and trends and issues in the training profession. In one of these meetings, we decided to market our courses through one more source—a course catalog. The course catalog would serve as a snapshot of all the courses that were developed and ready for delivery. Our course catalog grew from five to 45 courses within six months of its existence, and every manager had one. All of the courses were a result of the needs assessment, and over time, we began to receive requests for courses that appeared in the catalog.

We were growing our own insurance professionals and the PDS was assigned to that project. The insurance software package was changing every day, and there was a computer applications instructor assigned to that project to train the end user on the changes. But there were still soft-skills training needs that were not being addressed. Who could help? The training assistant was doing an exceptional job with the orientation and had undiscovered talent that could very well be the answer to our soft-skills training problem. She began to devote about 30 percent of her time to developing soft-skills training modules. Because part of our mission statement was to educate the policyholder, she began working on a presentation skills course that would prepare the presenters at our policyholder meetings. This program was a success and the need for this type of training demanded a full-time person. The training assistant was promoted to a PDS and because she did such a good job with orientation, kept that program. With orientation under the direction of the PDS, all that was left were strictly administrative duties. The training assistant's job went to someone who enjoyed clerical duties, found creativity in them, and who would not get bored easily by those tasks.

Lessons Learned

Managing a small training department is lifelong learning. The survival of this department five years later with four full-time employees and an approved budget for five full-time employees is the same prescription used in the beginning—a needs assessment and survey. It has been proved over and over in this small training department that the consumers have to need it and it's extra nice if they want it. My key learnings in this assignment are simple:

- *You have to prove the need for training.* If you do not have hard evidence that training is needed, you will have a hard time convincing those who control the purse strings. If you lack the budget for a formal survey, an in-house survey of employees is a good tool to show that trained employees will have an impact on the bottom line.

- *Pay attention to your surroundings and know your key players.* It is important to hear the unspoken message. When the head of a division makes a request, act upon it and follow up. Consultants who have senior management's ear may play a self-serving marketing game that may challenge your role. You can find a way to work with such people so that you have a win-win situation.
- *Learn about your company's product and business.* Although it is important to stay abreast of trends in the training profession, it is just as important to stay abreast of relevant business trends and your organization's products. You bring more to the table when you can show the need for training in the language of your business.

Questions for Discussion

1. How important is a needs assessment? Is there a time when it should not be used?
2. If given the opportunity to redesign the needs assessment, what would you change?
3. When is it safe not to play politics?
4. When should training be decentralized?
5. List some critical issues for proving the need for training.

The Author

Debra T. Taylor received her undergraduate degree in business education from Southern University A & M College in Baton Rouge, Louisiana. She formally began her training career in 1984 when she was promoted from branch manager to a statewide trainer of a Louisiana savings and loan association. She developed training programs and traveled throughout the state training employees. She spent 15 years in the banking industry, of which seven years were in the training profession. She moved on to the Resolution Trust Corporation (RTC) in 1991, still in the banking industry as a career development specialist. After being informed in March 1992 that the RTC would be closing its Baton Rouge office, she took on the responsibility of coordinating an outplacement center for its employees. Through that role she learned of the Louisiana Workers' Compensation Corporation (LWCC), a new insurance company whose corporate office would be in the Baton Rouge area. In July 1992, she came to LWCC as the training coordinator and in 1993 was promoted to education and training manager. She can be contacted at: Louisiana Workers' Compensation Corporation, 2237 South Acadian Thruway, Baton Rouge, LA 70808; phone: 504.231.0589; fax: 504.929.5626.

Reference

Allen, Edith L., editor (1990). *ASTD Trainer's Toolkit: Needs Assessment Instruments.* Alexandria, VA: American Society for Training & Development.

Time Management Training: Small Investment—Big Results

Logitech

Nancy G. Nunziati

This case demonstrates that a resourceful person with an interest in training can quickly learn the ropes and create an effective one-person training department. Nancy Nunziati shows how she listened to her internal customers and used an off-the-shelf time-management program to help change Logitech's company culture to one of increased accountability. Nunziati describes an effective process for selecting the best supplier for HRD programs as well as a process for demonstrating the impact of time management training.

Company and Training Background

Founded in 1981, Logitech designs, manufactures, and markets control devices and imaging solutions that enhance communication between people and computers. Logitech is the world's largest manufacturer of mice and trackballs and a market leader in hand-held and sheet-fed personal scanners. In addition to a broad variety of retail pointing devices, the company supplies mice for 18 of the top 20 systems manufacturers. In April 1996, Logitech shipped its 100 millionth mouse.

Logitech has over 2,500 employees worldwide. At the Fremont, California, headquarters, which is the subject of this chapter, the company has more than 350 employees. These employees are at all levels, including skilled labor in the distribution center, supervisors, managers, and executives. The primary functions at the Fremont site are product development, hardware and software engineering, sales, marketing,

This case was prepared to serve as a basis for discussion rather than to illustrate either effective or ineffective administrative and management practices.

distribution, finance, and administration. The company also has employees in Switzerland and Taiwan as well as a large manufacturing plant in China.

When Logitech celebrated its fifteenth anniversary last year, the training function was just over one year old. Logitech initiated its Training and Development Department as a result of an effort to improve employee retention. During a period of particularly high turnover, the Human Resources Department organized a series of meetings with employees to identify areas that needed improvement. The employees clearly identified career development and employee training as critical areas that had not received any significant attention since the company's founding. Because these were areas of interest for me, I "volunteered" my time to help with this effort and eventually transferred into a newly created position to manage the training function. This position, senior manager of training and development, reports directly to the site general manager.

Challenges and Opportunities

This new position was most appealing to me because it offered tremendous potential to have a positive impact on the organization. The company, still suffering from high turnover, desperately needed programs to help employees grow and develop, and the employees needed to know that Logitech was interested in providing these opportunities. Many employees, feeling that opportunities for growth did not exist within Logitech, had been leaving for better positions at other companies. Logitech needed quickly to give people the tools they needed to improve their own performance and the effectiveness and performance of the organization.

I was also ready for a change and was interested in the opportunity to broaden my own skills. To accelerate this personal development, before the position was even created, I enrolled in the University of California Berkeley Extension Training and Development Program. My background in product management, product marketing, and market research had given me a good business foundation, but I felt that I needed the technical skills that the course work—Introduction to Training and Development, Designing Training Programs, Presentation Skills, and so forth—would provide. It was very valuable to have the classroom learning and access to instructors and other students at the same time that I was establishing the training function. Overall, I was fortunate to have the opportunity to help the organization through this stage of growth and to create benefit for employees by providing appropriate learning opportunities, all while I learned skills that would be useful in any future career path I choose.

The opportunities were almost limitless. The potential for having a positive impact on the organization clearly existed, both from a company and an employee perspective. The first real challenge for the newly formed training and development department was to create visibility, establish value, and build credibility for the function. Because there was so much pent-up demand for training and the expectations had been set by the employees, it was important to get up and running as quickly as possible. The goal was to create the department and define the training plan all in a very short time frame.

Along with the challenge of creating something new came the excitement. The ability to create something where nothing previously existed was fun and exhilarating. And, being a one-person department was a great advantage because I could move very quickly through the definition phase and create the function as I thought it would best work.

There Must Be Something to Worry About

Throughout this exciting time of challenge and opportunity, I had two major concerns:

- *Gaining active management support.* I knew that management would support the training activities but wasn't sure to what extent the executives would participate. Training had the highest chance for success if they took a visible, active role in the training programs. I realized that much of my work would involve working with the management team to understand its needs and encourage each member to demonstrate support in active and visible ways.
- *Getting swallowed up by training logistics.* Even though I had never worked in training, I had a sense that there was a great deal of administrative support required. I knew that if I did not manage that properly, I would not have time to achieve my goals and objectives.

Overall, the opportunities and excitement by far outweighed my concerns. It was time to build the department.

Creating the Training and Development Department

The first step in establishing direction for the Training and Development Department was to define the charter. To do this, it was important to look to the company's corporate mission and values. One of our values states: "Logitech provides an environment that recognizes achievements and supports continuous learning to help employees grow, develop their skills and experience, and gain a sense of personal satisfaction." Using this as the guiding value, the department's charter became the following:

> The ultimate goal of Training and Development is to partner with members of the organization to maximize employee effectiveness and enable Logitech to achieve our corporate mission.

To address my concern about getting swallowed up by training logistics, one of my first goals was to get some administrative help. I knew this would be necessary if I were to run an efficient and effective department. I needed someone to help with registration, facilities, and training records. Because our site served only 350 people and we were just getting under way, a full-time person was not necessary. I defined the requirements for the position and was fortunate to secure an arrangement to share the services of an executive administrative assistant who spends less than 10 to 15 percent of her time supporting the training function. Having the administrative help has enabled me to focus more on understanding and meeting the training needs of the company and less on the event logistics.

Needs Assessment

Logitech had a relatively new senior management team at the time that the Training and Development Department was formed. The team had immediately identified the need to "grow the middle management team," and that became a key corporate objective for the year. This provided a clear focus and target audience for the training department—middle management. The challenge was to translate the broad corporate objective into specific business needs and training requirements of the target audience.

To do this, I held a training needs assessment meeting with the senior management team. The objectives of this meeting were
- to identify the qualities, skills, and knowledge that all Logitech managers should have
- to identify the qualities, skills, and knowledge required for specific organizations
- to define success in each of these areas
- to determine what we need to achieve success in each of these areas
- to identify where we currently are in each of these areas.

Prior to the meeting, I sent a message to the executives asking them to think about the following two questions and to come prepared to discuss their thoughts at the needs assessment meeting: What specific qualities, skills, and knowledge should be shared by *all managers* at Logitech? What specific qualities, skills, and knowledge *specific to your organization* need to be developed over the next 18 to 24 months?

At the meeting we used a brainstorming exercise to collect these ideas, then rated our current performance on each item on the list. Finally, the executives identified their own top three priorities and the skills that were necessary to achieve success in these areas. The training needs that were identified through this process included areas such as communication, team skills, goal setting, and problem solving. Based on these needs, I was able to develop the training plan for the year and quickly move into the implementation phase.

Program Development and Vendor Selection Process

A one-person training department would only have limited resources for developing and delivering training. The type of training our needs assessment showed we required was available off-the-shelf from many high-quality suppliers. The challenge was to select the best, most appropriate training to meet the need. During the first year, I adopted and refined a process that I now use to help me to manage this difficult task. The five steps are as follows:

1. Find all possible suppliers. References from other trainers and training managers are invaluable when looking for new suppliers. People in the training industry freely share information—what has worked for them, what has not worked, and why. I frequently contact colleagues and friends in other companies to find out what programs they are using and if they have any knowledge, experience, or references in the topics of interest. Other sources that I have used are the Internet, American Society for Training & Development references, trade shows, CD-ROMs that list available training, and the mountain of mail I get from training suppliers. I sort and save almost all training brochures, so that when the need arises, I have a file of potential suppliers for any given topic.

2. Narrow down the list of suppliers. The next step is to meet with the internal client, or person who has requested the training. If the training is corporate-wide and has no clear sponsor, I recruit one or two key managers to work with me as sponsors of the training. We meet to review information on potential suppliers and then select two or three who appear to be the best solution for the identified needs. Next, I schedule meetings with the suppliers and sponsors to further narrow the choices.

3. Preview the training. After meeting with the potential supplier, I try to preview the training either by attending a public seminar or by gaining permission to attend another company's training event. Ideally, a representative from the internal client group previews the training with me, so that we can be sure that the training would meet the needs of the target audience. If the supplier has multiple trainers, I try to preview the trainer who would deliver our in-house training. This way, I can be sure that there will be no surprises when the training is delivered at Logitech.

4. Make a go-no-go decision. Generally after the preview, we can decide to proceed or step back and look at other suppliers. This evaluation process can be laborious and time consuming. However, the payoff comes when the training programs are high quality and meet the needs of the participants and the company. Once the program has been selected, we move into the logistics phase. The first consideration is how the target audience would like to have the program delivered. For example, an eight-hour program may take place in a full-day or two half-day workshops or in a series of lunchtime workshops. Once the best format has been determined, I work with key managers to select the best day and time for the participants, turn the logistics over to the administrative assistant, and begin marketing the program.

To market the program, I generally begin by inviting the target audience in an e-mail message that describes the benefits of the training and what the participants will learn. Those interested in attending the training then register through e-mail with the training administrative assistant. Classes usually fill after the first announcement. If this is not the case, I follow up with posters and one or two more e-mails.

5. Develop in-house or select off the shelf. In the training department's first year, I used mostly off-the-shelf programs customized to meet the audience's needs and delivered by the outside suppliers or consultants. The lack of in-house resources and the small training audience did not justify the time and expense of training an internal trainer. Also, because I wanted the programs to be of the highest possible quality, it made sense to use professionals who were experienced in delivering the program.

Training Success Story
The Need

The original needs assessment indicated that senior management expected employees to be more accountable for their actions and to improve their ability to meet commitments. Logitech's company culture has always been informal and not highly structured. For example, no corporate standard defines how to conduct meetings or how to communicate action items or follow up on them. This loose approach was a contributing factor to senior management's frustration with the lack of accountability and follow through.

At the time we were to begin a training intervention to address these issues a few employees mentioned to me that they had recently attended a one-day TimeQuest® training workshop, from Franklin Covey Co. in Salt Lake City, and that it had made an enormous impact on their productivity and effectiveness. Because the employees were unanimously enthusiastic, I decided to preview the training. I was initially skeptical that a time-management training program could have that much impact. After all, all of us have calendars and to-do lists, and we make reasonable progress with these tools. What more could be there be to it? When I attended the training myself, I realized that this particular program could help our employees be more productive and also help change our culture to one of increased accountability.

The decision to bring the training in-house was easy. My only concern was how the employees would react to such a structured approach—how they would feel about everyone carrying around the same type of planners. Basically, my concern was the same one I had before I previewed the training. However, if the training were set up and marketed properly, we would overcome these objections, and employee enthusiasm would help us carry the message throughout the organization.

Finding the Right Trainer for Time Management

One critical element to the success of the training was the selection of the trainer. The trainer who had delivered the public seminar that I attended was excellent, but not a good match for our particular culture. I met with Sharon Pillsbury, our account representative from Franklin Covey, at our site, so she could get a feel for our culture, understand our particular issues, and recommend the best possible trainer for us. She identified Dave Green as the right trainer because he had done a great deal of work for high-technology companies and thoroughly understood our issues.

Plan for the Measurement and Implementation

Another important aspect of the training preparation was the measurement of results. It is always important to understand the impact of training, but it was particularly important in this case because we were trying to change the culture at the Fremont site by introducing a major portion of the staff to a new system for managing their work. Fortunately, Franklin Covey made it very easy for us. For a nominal fee, Franklin Covey would tabulate and analyze results of a pretest, administered before the training, and a posttest, administered 30 days after the training, to assess the change in skills, behavior, and attitude as a result of the TimeQuest Training.

We included this assessment in our contract, set up three training dates, and booked the training facility. The plan was to schedule enough Logitech and Franklin Covey training events to achieve critical mass and then to have new employees and late adopters attend the Franklin Covey™ public seminars. In terms of logistics, we hold most of our in-house training events off site because we currently do not have adequate training facilities at our site, and attendees are more focused if they are away from the office.

It was not possible for me to preview the trainer Dave Green before he delivered the program, so he and I had a telephone meeting to discuss our goals for the training and background information about the company and the participants. It was important for him to know, for example, that the audience would be international and diverse. And, like a typical high-tech company, we are used to a fast pace and have no time to waste. Once the details of the training were set, it was time to market the program.

Marketing the Program

As usual, we took a benefit-oriented approach to the marketing the program. I used a combination of e-mail bulletin board postings and small flyers posted throughout the building. The class was offered as an open enrollment, available to Logitech employees of all levels. Interested participants registered via e-mail with the training administrative assistant. Within just 24 hours of the initial announcement, our first class of 30 participants was full. Others were put on a waiting list for the next class. This overwhelming response confirmed that the subject was of great interest to our employees.

Training Effectiveness

The first training day began with an explanation of the purpose of the pretest and administration of the test. An excellent day of training followed, and the participants responded very well to the training and the new time management tool. The Level 1 evaluations came back overwhelmingly positive. The most meaningful results came 30 days later when we assembled the group for the posttest. My goal was to get 100 percent participation on the posttest to make the data as reliable as possible.

To improve the attendance and to make it useful and fun, we had a Franklin Covey brown-bag lunch in the company cafeteria during the lunch hour. Participants brought their lunches, and Logitech supplied desserts and soft drinks. We distributed the posttests as people came in. Once they were completed, Franklin Covey's account representative Pillsbury and I led a discussion on what was working and what was not working. This opening provided the opportunity for Pillsbury to give us additional information on using the Franklin Covey system and for the participants to exchange their own tips and tricks. It was a good opportunity to review the skills trained and refresh everyone's memory. After the discussion, we held a drawing for some Franklin Covey supplies. (I think that was the real reason people attended—to have a chance to win a leather binder!) No matter, the cost of the event and prizes was a small investment to get the data we needed to measure the effectiveness of the training.

A third party was to compile the posttest results for Franklin Covey, and we received them several weeks later. They showed that the participants in the TimeQuest Training reported saving an average of five hours per week, or 250 hours per year. The calculated return-on-investment was $7,000 per year, per employee, or 1,679 percent. Figure 1 shows the change in positive results. Results were outstanding in the areas we had set out to improve. Keeping commitments went from a 29 percent positive result before the training to 72 percent after the training, and follow-up, which received a 31 percent positive result before the training, skyrocketed to 91 percent after the training.

Here's a typical comment written in the open-ended section of the 30-day posttest: "In my opinion, the Franklin Planner system is a very effective tool for planning my daily activities. I have found that I'm getting more tasks done throughout the day and I am able to be more proactive in other activities. Thank you very much for offering this class/tool."

There are many daily signs of the program's success. At meetings, for example, everyone has their planners, enabling them to record action items, use calendars for planning, and set up future meetings quickly and easily. Also, when working on action items or following up with someone, people now use a common vocabulary, saying, "It's an A1, I'll get it done today." or "It's a B3; I'll have it for you Thursday."

Figure 1. Logitech before and after Franklin Covey TimeQuest®.

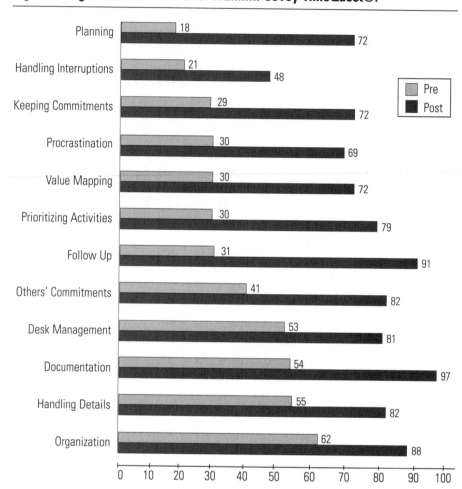

Finally, some managers have seen the positive impact on individuals who have been trained and now require everyone in their department to attend the training and use the system.

Key Success Factors

Overall, the Franklin Covey training was one of our most successful training interventions. Some of the reasons for its success follow:

• The need for the training was clear both from senior management objectives and the needs assessment. Simultaneously, there was a strong employee demand for the training.

- Franklin Covey's training was well designed and well executed. The content, pace, and delivery were all on target.
- An easy-to-use tool supported the training.
- Each participant received an audiotape for posttraining review or a refresher.
- We provided an opportunity for follow-up via the brown-bag lunches.
- The training had benefits for employees at all levels and functions.
- The training was exactly what our employees and company needed at the time.
- The results were easy to measure using Franklin Covey's pre- and posttest system.

Ongoing public seminars are readily available for new employees or employees who missed the original in-house sessions. This is of critical importance. Without these, we would have to wait until we have critical mass to put on an in-house session. Running in-house sessions worked very well to build momentum. Then we were able to maintain the program by using public seminars.

The Franklin Covey training was particularly satisfying because we achieved an important culture change, had measurable results, and realized an excellent return on our training investment. Our initial investment of less than $25,000 for the first three in-house sessions was small when compared to the efficiencies we gained by using the system. Another reason that I am enthusiastic about this training is that the benefit to the participants extended beyond the workplace. The Franklin Covey system encourages identification and focus on personal values and goals, and there is an emphasis on life balance and priorities. In addition to the obvious corporate benefits, it was a special bonus to know that the training had a positive impact on the whole person.

Lessons Learned

Over the past 18 months as a lone ranger in the training department, I have learned lessons beyond the key reasons for success of the Franklin Covey training. Here are some of the other lessons I have learned (mostly the hard way!):

- **Build credibility early.** Make your first program flawless and then you'll have no trouble selling future programs. Conversely, it takes a long time to recover from a miss. Take on a straightforward requirement—a sure hit—first.
- **It can't always be perfect for everyone.** This sounds contradictory to the first point, but it's not. You can plan and deliver a flawless

program that is on target, meets the training need, and fulfills the company's objectives. Twenty-nine people will give the program the highest possible rating, but one person will rate it satisfactory or below. The lesson here is that people have different needs and learn in different ways and at different paces. Follow up with the dissatisfied person so that you can learn why, but don't forget to celebrate that you succeeded with most of the participants.

- **Market, market, market.** Marketing and promotion are critical. Market and promote yourself and your programs. Remember to sell the benefits in all of your presentations, memos, and e-mails. Don't just tell the staff what training programs are coming, but also tell them what benefits they will derive by attending the programs. Use testimonials from key employees and demonstrate how the training ties to their objectives and the company's objectives.

- **Join forces.** Establish partnerships from the start. Just because you're a lone trainer, don't think you have to go it alone. When training needs arise, partner with key managers for the duration of the training development cycle. Make it a joint project. Don't develop programs in isolation.

- **Know your customers.** Remember that the key managers and trainees are your customers. The key to satisfying your customers is to understand their needs and deliver a product (the training, in this case) that satisfies these needs.

- **Stay in tune with the business.** Don't get too far removed from the business. Stay connected with managers, employees, and executives. Be visible around the organization. Talk regularly with employees from all areas. Ask them what's going on in their work areas and what challenges they face. This will make it much easier for you to understand the training needs and to develop or source the best programs.

- **Trust your instincts.** Sometimes all the information, data analysis, and referrals from others aren't a match for your own good instincts. If you stay close to the business and understand the corporate culture, you'll know what is right for your company and your culture. This doesn't mean you should skip the information-gathering and data-collection phase—you can't. Gather all the data and information you need to make a solid business decision. Just don't discount the value of your own intuition, especially when it relates to how well a particular training program or trainer will fit with your company's needs and culture.

Questions for Discussion

1. What other methods could Logitech have used initially to assess training needs? Would these methods have been more or less successful than the method used?
2. What do you think about Logitech's decision to outsource most of its training?
3. Under what circumstances should Logitech develop its own training programs or train its own internal trainer to deliver programs?
4. What are some other ways Logitech could have measured the success of the TimeQuest Training? What are the advantages and disadvantages of this method versus the one the company used?
5. What are some other ways that Logitech could have marketed its training programs? What impact would these other methods have on the success of the training programs?

The Author

Nancy Nunziati is the senior manager of training and development at Logitech, the world's leading manufacturer of products that enable communication between the physical and the digital world. She joined Logitech in 1988 and held positions in product management and product marketing before starting up several new departments, including customer marketing, customer satisfaction, and training and development. In addition to her work in training and development, Nunziati has worked to facilitate the revision and communication of Logitech's corporate vision, mission and values, as well as a variety of other internal communication and customer satisfaction projects. Prior to Logitech, Nunziati worked at GTE Sprint and Net-Express Systems where she gained international experience in telecommunications and hardware and software imaging systems. Nancy received her B.A. in organizational/industrial psychology from the University of California at Berkeley. She can be contacted at Logitech, 6505 Kaiser Drive, Fremont, CA 94555-3615; phone: 510.713.4530.

The Outsourced Director of Training and Development

STRATEGIES FOR THE 90's

Anne Monnin

This case provides a thoughtful discussion of what it is like to make the transition from being an external consultant to being a one-person training department inside a large metals manufacturer and then returning to being an external consultant. Monnin's case shows how one person can successfully direct training from either inside or outside of an organization. Readers gain insights into how to survive downsizing and then develop a profitable and fulfilling relationship with a former employer. This case highlights how Monnin provided a successful training intervention to support her former employer's quality initiative in pursuit of ISO certification.

Background

STRATEGIES FOR THE 90's was born in northern California with its first consulting contract in the spring of 1985. During its first eight years, the company became established, grew to two consultants, moved to North Carolina, existed on both coasts for a year, was trimmed to just the East Coast, and became established there.

As the principal consultant and trainer, by early 1993 I had been training for 20 years, boasting clients from diverse industries in 70 countries and 14 states. I had been on a two-year retainer with a three-state gas company and was just beginning a three-year retainer with the Charlotte Chamber of Commerce. In addition, I had taught or directed departments at 16 colleges and universities and in three M.B.A. programs and reviewed manuscripts for two major publishers.

My networking involved me in community and professional organizations. I was then serving as president of the my small town's chamber of com-

This case was prepared to serve as a basis for discussion rather than to illustrate either effective or ineffective administrative and management practices.

merce. Because our little chamber was part of a larger county chamber, I automatically served on its board of directors. The president of the larger chamber was senior vice president of operations for a large manufacturing firm located in a neighboring town. Through my civic connection with this chief officer, I was invited to interview for a vacant position as director of training and development.

Opportunities and Challenges

At the time, I knew nothing about this large manufacturer with five plants in four southeastern states, and I had no intention of leaving my own consulting firm. I agreed to meet with the vice president of human resources. What I thought would be a short chat became a full-day meeting with four top vice presidents, including lunch at the country club, a full plant tour, and a meeting with the human resources benefits specialist. I thought I had made it clear that I would be happy to work with them as an outside consultant but that I had no interest in being a trainer on the inside. After all, my company was growing, and I had some big contracts in motion. Before I knew it, however, I was being enticed into the organization.

When the company offered me the job, I took it. I realized that being the first female director in the history of this large corporation would thrill me and would round out my resume in the manufacturing arena. There was no way I could learn as much on the outside as I could on the inside of such an organization. I negotiated well and got everything that I wanted including permission to keep my company alive and time off to continue my work with all current contracted clients as long as I didn't market myself to others. I maintained my home office for STRATEGIES FOR THE 90's, and moved my daily activities to the plant's Training and Development Department.

Where I had headed a one-person training and development firm, now I also directed a one-person-plus-secretary training and development department with responsibilities for approximately 1,600 employees spread all over the world, including six domestic and three international sales offices. Within the first two months, I went through the office files of my deceased predecessor, and I facilitated a team-building retreat for the Human Resources team, of which I was now a part. I also designed and implemented a salaried employee orientation program, which I participated in myself.

The roles I played within the corporation varied between strategic planner, counselor, trainer, organizational development specialist, quality specialist, ISO 9002 Master Training Plan designer, training materials reviewer and developer, operator certifier, a Kepner-Tregoe-certified trainer, succession planner and personnel developer, Human Resources team member, and corporate "Mommy," among other duties. This list is similar to what many one-person training departments reflect, and it took more physical, mental, and emotional energy than I had at times. I was used to a more flexible schedule, but soon got used to the new one.

When the corporate president of 30-plus years had initially interviewed me, we had discussed what I thought was a shared vision of creating a "learning organization," becoming certified for ISO 9002, exceeding customer quality expectations, supporting a team environment throughout, and developing the workers through training and education. I was very enthusiastic at the time. As I grew to know this man, however, I realized that he would buy into the stylish trends that would impress customers, but that his personal authoritarian approach would never change. The vision that we discussed in that first meeting has been carried out as far as the ISO 9002 certification, some quality training that customers mandated, and some product work groups that call themselves teams. The other ideals seem to have gotten in the way of production, so they have been forgotten over the years.

Providing Value to the Organization: Assessing and Meeting Training Needs

While serving as director of training and development, I got to know the culture by interviewing people in all departments, at all levels. I was a different type of employee because I was the first real trainer that the corporation had ever hired who had not worked her way up from a technical or manufacturing position. My needs assessment consisted of questions concerning past training, what employees and managers felt could help them to do a better job, and how urgently they needed training support. I found the company needed general interpersonal as well as technical skills training. Also, with the transition to desk-top personal computers, there was much software training needed. I prioritized topics by group size and urgency of need, coordinating all training and development through my office. Departments conducted most technical training on the job. Later I would get more involved with these hands-on areas when I helped to create programmed learning packages for operator certification.

Problem solving and quality management were key skills that the company desired to build throughout the organization. As a result, I was certified by outside organizations to instruct several programs.

In July 1993, just before I became a full-time employee, the company sent me to attend a four-day certification program of Kepner-Tregoe, a consulting firm for problem solving and decision making in Princeton, New Jersey, to learn management-level training in problem-solving and decision-making techniques. This program included training in four modules—Situation Appraisal, Potential Problem Analysis, Problem Analysis, and Decision Analysis. I have used this training fairly frequently. Later in June 1994, the company sponsored my certification in the Kepner-Tregoe Project Management strategies.

The company also wanted me to learn a specific quality process, so it sponsored my attendance at a weeklong Quality Improvement Process Management College that Phillip Crosby & Associates presented at its headquarters near Orlando, Florida. Although I had already been trained and had experience in total quality management (TQM) processes, my new company had been indoctrinated by Crosby, so I followed the example of its top management and attended the college to fit better into the culture.

My intuition said that my time within the corporation might be limited, so I instituted a monthly Quality Leadership Training Program for all supervisors, managers, and directors, with vice presidents sometimes attending. My thought was that I could reach the hourly employees immediately by training their bosses. There had been little management training done in the past, and nothing recently, so I felt that would be a good first training series. I scheduled myself plus some skilled trainers, whom I knew through local networking, to design and implement the ongoing program. We created a series that covered many aspects of leadership, project management, problem solving, communication, team facilitation, train-the-trainer strategies among other topics. I chose trainers whose focus on one or more leadership issues would blend well with the program objectives and other trainers' topics. About 150 people attended one day every month in groups of 25 to 30 per class. A sign-up sheet allowed these participants to plan early and choose the one day within the five-day training week that best fit their schedules. The evaluation comments for these monthly programs were positive, and I felt that if we could get to this population, we could begin to make some cultural shifts.

When several departments or individuals requested the same training topic, I usually offered in-house sessions that I or another topic specialist taught. Occasionally individuals attended "public" seminars in cities close to their work location. Training requests went through my office for approval, and my budget of $200,000 paid for training costs plus travel expenses for trainers to come in-house and individuals to attend off-site training.

Top management realized before I was hired that the main plant needed a good training center with break-out rooms, so plans were made to remodel one section of a building at the plant to provide this. After about a year, we finally had an improved facility, and I had a new office nearby. One of the smaller break-out rooms became a computer software training lab, whereas the other, which I had earmarked for computer-based training, is still not being used. The new training center much improved the situation, but we still had to go outside to local motel meeting rooms for additional space.

Creating a Mission and a Training Plan

One of my main accomplishments as director of training and development was the development of a Master Training Plan for ISO 9002 certification. Companies that want this certification to support export to Unified Europe go through rigorous audits to meet and document set quality standards. One aspect of certification includes prevention strategies with a high emphasis on training for all employees. Certification requires the documentation of all projected training for each level of employee per year. The Master Training Plan for my company was an extended document that incorporated the company training mission and objectives, and assigned required and elective training topics to every category of employee throughout the company. The document, which was created to guide training and development into the future, required extensive research into the job classifications and training needs of employees.

I created the company's training mission based on past culture and ISO 9002 requirements. The company's culture is evident in terms like *ProfitableGrowth*, which appears twice in the mission statement. The statement, which was publicized, said the following:

> A Learning Organization demonstrates in continuous action a commitment to a long-range strategic plan through the development of all employees in a variety of ways.
>
> A vital tool of the Learning Organization is the Master Training Plan. This tool provides the practical steps to be taken to move closer to the vision of the Learning Organization.
>
> The purpose of our Master Training Plan is to involve all of the people of THE COMPANY in a process of continuous and relent-

less improvement that leads to personal evolution, creative decision-making, and ultimately to ProfitableGrowth.

As part of the CONGLOMERATE Federation of companies, we can utilize our inherent strengths in sharing our training programs, ideas, and resources across department and company boundaries. We move toward becoming a "virtual corporation" in association with our sister companies.

Our over-all goal is sustained ProfitableGrowth built on satisfying customers. Through the application of the attached Master Training Plan, THE COMPANY will demonstrate its commitment and dedication to its employees and customers through its evolution as a unique learning organization.

Ethical behavior is our hallmark and continues to guide our business activities as we pursue our goal, by providing a working environment which encourages both individuals and teams to excel and evolve.

The Master Training Plan objectives stated the following:

These are some of the specific goals of THE COMPANY which can be achieved through the Master Training Plan. (This list evolves as the Learning Organization itself evolves.)

1. To improve Customer Service
2. To improve Quality
   —in our products
   —in our people
   —in our work environment
3. To improve Cycle Time in all processes
4. To reduce cost
5. To improve productivity by removing barriers
6. To support effective teamwork
7. To manage change
8. To reduce and prevent accidents
9. To operate ethically
10. To allow the individual and the organization to develop

Changing Direction

Although the company had visionary ideas and the company leaders were intrigued by Peter Senge's concept of a learning organization (Senge, 1990), enacting it was a challenge, given the company culture. The Master Training Plan was achievable, but top management commitment was not there. I found this out dramatically when all training was postponed in the late summer of 1994. My role was limited to coaching the product teams in the throes of "storming" during team building. Then in October, my position was eliminated.

I had met the goals set in my hiring agreement and the company had been doing well, but now production became the main priority. I had weathered two waves of mid- and upper-level management layoffs before downsizing finally hit my position. Because of my short tenure, I was given no severance. I would simply return to my own business full-time. After all, the firm was still alive, and I had some clients. Although I had not actively marketed myself during the past 20 months, I felt sure that I would be up and running quickly.

I was given three weeks to pack and wind down my position. I was able to conduct previously scheduled team training and meet individually with several employees whom I had been helping with career counseling. I knew not to burn my bridges if I wanted any consulting business from the company. Even on my last day, Halloween, I facilitated my last team training as director of training and development. Then I retired to STRATEGIES FOR THE 90's full-time.

On the Outside Looking in

Many people who are laid off consider the entrepreneurial road as a good next alternative. It is not as easy as it might seem. I was out of the loop after 20 months, and it took time getting reestablished. My existing contracts kept me fiscally afloat, but consulting life was quite different from receiving a guaranteed paycheck. After COBRA, the continued health benefits, ran out, I was able to rejoin a reasonably priced group health insurance plan through the Charlotte Chamber of Commerce. I fell behind in paying certain bills and relied on credit cards, knowing that I might not be able to pay off debts in full immediately. Computing, declaring, and paying my quarterly taxes in addition to double FICA as a self-employed person was a hassle I had not missed. My paradigm had shifted again—I had to work back up to financial security on my own. I got out and networked, reconnected with past clients, and started to land some small consulting and training contracts.

Five months after my departure, I contracted with the company for my first outside project—helping the safety director put together an orientation videotape. This was fun, as this individual and I had been good buddies and neighbors at the plant. I was able to use my creative juices, coach him, direct the video, support some hourly actors, and manage the project for him, saving him a lot of extra hassle.

My next assignment was to work with the Finishing Department superintendent to develop programmed learning packages for training new employees and for certifying cross-trained employees on new job skills. Because I was out in the plant, I learned the work processes as I shared my training expertise with others. I enjoyed being in the plant and doing hands-on work, and I wished that I had insisted that the vice presidents supported me in pushing for learning packages when I had been there full-time. During my time as director, I had discussed working on such a program, but there had been no buy-in from top management. Now ISO 9002 requirements as well as customers were calling for job process documentation and for standardized skill training for each process. I was very happy wearing my jeans to work and bypassing all management as I headed directly to the plant and its workers. I got the program going, and then other less expensive consultants and internal resources followed through, taking the concept to other departments.

About this time, another plant manager invited me to facilitate some Kepner-Tregoe problem-solving and decision-making strategies training for his management staff. I was more than happy to comply, and enjoyed the trip out of state. What surprised me was how the people at this plant welcomed me back with open arms. This was the only union plant in the company, and the employees were used to regular layoffs followed by rehirings. Now I was not only one of them as a layoff victim, but also no longer a member of upper management. The trip was quite successful, and I was glad to see old friends again.

My next project was to help design an environmental regulation awareness program for all employees of the company that would cost under $20,000, including my consulting charges. The parent company required the training to commence in less than four months, and the environmental manager was swamped with other compliance issues. This project was both challenging and educational for me. I sent out a call for bids from environmental consulting groups, connected with a state environmental resource center that created customized training programs, and learned much about regulations and the legal ramifications of noncompliance. I collected, reviewed, and recommended proposals and then helped two groups design two different training programs: a large program for company employees and a shorter program for managers.

The larger program involved creating a video to be used at all company locations for all nonmanagement employees. This program successfully met the requirements of educating approximately

1,500 people worldwide. However, the more expensive program, a half-day training for managers, was not as good as we had hoped. The consulting company that designed the program had just gone through reengineering, and one of its consulting partners had left the company two weeks before the training. As a result, a new colleague who was an ineffective trainer handled part of the program, and the principal consultant had to instruct the training with a terrible cold. Having helped to hire this company, I felt bad that the program was mediocre. Just as I had shouldered responsibility for outside trainers in the past, I still was partially responsible in this new position.

As year-end approached, another company asked me to propose a consulting arrangement wherein I would serve as its "outsourced director of training and development." I realized that this was actually what I was doing for my former employer, even though I was not on a formal retainer.

Successful Training Intervention

By January 1996, I began creating an ongoing quality training program for all employees at my former company. This project was the biggest consulting job in the company's history. The project included designing and implementing two levels of quality training that would meet the program objectives that I drew up and on which management would agree. My objectives were as follows:

- THE COMPANY's ongoing Quality training requirements will be met per the Master Training Plan.
- New employees will be introduced to the specifics of the Quality culture of THE COMPANY.
- ISO 9002 training requirements will be met and the COMPANY Quality Policy will be applied by all employees.
- Employees will review specific quality concepts and tools.
- Employees will learn and apply new quality concepts and tools.
- Real work processes, problems, plans, decisions will be analyzed for results.
- Cross-functional groups will workshop on shared issues during training sessions.
- A local facilitator, familiar with THE COMPANY culture, will offer the sessions during all three shifts for the convenience of employees.
- Training sessions will be held quarterly for short 2.5 hour time segments so that production will not be negatively impacted.
- Supervisors will provide input concerning issues and cross-functional groups relating to these issues.

Management and I decided to focus on two groups of employees with different levels of quality training background. Group A, consisting of employees hired since 1991, would receive their initial quality orientation. In this series of five modules, I would incorporate all past quality concepts and strategies and bring these employees up to speed, so that by the end of the year all employees would have received training on the TQM tools and principles that the company wanted everyone to be able to apply. Group B, which had received quality training some time between 1980 and 1991 but had had no reinforcement training since then, would receive a review of quality training and continue to the next level. In all, I would facilitate approximately 130 classes on seven different quality modules. An overview of the training appears in table 1.

Table 1. Overview of quality training.

Module	Topics and Focus	Number of Sessions
Program A	*New employees since 1991 (approximately 400 employees)*	
A-1	Orientation and history of total quality management initiatives and philosophy at the company	16
A-2	Philip Crosby quality concepts, corporate quality acronyms, Kepner-Tregoe potential problem analysis	16
A-3	Prevention vs. reaction, process improvement, total cycle time analysis, cause and effect diagram	16
A-4	Process flow diagrams, Kepner-Tregoe situation appraisal process, continuous improvement cycle and analysis	16
A-5	Statistical process control, control charts, Kepner-Tregoe decision analysis process, program summary and recommendations	
Program B	*Review for seasoned employees (approximately 600 employees)*	
B-1	Review of quality initiatives, emphasis on company quality policy, continuous improvement focus, the supplier-customer relationship	25
B-2	Company quality acronyms, prevention vs. reaction, review of total cycle time analysis, process improvement strategies, Kepner-Tregoe potential problem analysis, cause and effect diagram	25

Building Sponsorship for the Project

I had to build ownership in the program to make sure that upper- and midmanagement supported it well and that we would make it through the year's duration of the contract. While I had been a director, I could market my own programs and even mandate training. Now on the outside, I had no clout whatsoever. I had to depend on my internal champions—the vice president of quality (the man who had first introduced me to the company) and the vice president of Human Resources (my former boss)—who were in charge of the program. I urged them to sell the program to others. I also requested that all manufacturing division superintendents help me to identify specific topics to cover in each training. If these people had buy-in, they would feel better about allowing their people to leave production to attend the training. Prior to development, I called a meeting of these top managers, and we reviewed what had been trained, what specific practical application needs each department had, and how to introduce topics to keep all levels of employees interested.

Implementation Challenges

In the minds of some of the manufacturing managers, the purpose of my training was to briefly review or introduce a topic, strategy, or TQM tool to the employees so that it could be applied later in a departmental meeting with the right people focusing on a real work issue. Others expected me to provide relevant workshops so that their people could apply the concepts during the training session. Because of scheduling difficulties, each of the approximately 130 classes that I taught in the two programs was made up of people from various levels and departments, rather than a homogenous group that could focus on specific issues.

As a result of the heterogeneous audience, I was limited to using general examples or companywide problems in the cross-functional classes. I applied generic videos and specific diagrams and strategies that had already become part of the corporate culture, and I incorporated examples from personal life as well as from work for application and better learning. What I taught had to pique the interest of the hourly people as well as the engineers, accountants, managers, and other salaried employees. I often had people break into smaller groups of departmental colleagues, but usually there were one or two individuals who had no teammates in that class and had to work alone. Individuals and groups were asked to describe processes to each other, apply cycle time analysis to their specific work tasks, address problems, plan for prevention, and work cross-functionally on suggesting improvements to each other.

Many new employees found this discussion across departments to be informative because it helped them to see the big picture of the process flow and supplier-customer relationships throughout the company system. Interactions between the hourly operators and the salaried planners and support people led to productive discussions that many employees in both groups enjoyed. Other employees wanted to meet with their teams to apply the tools more practically and claimed that sharing with "strangers" seemed like a waste of their time.

The scheduling would have been more practical if training sessions had been offered by department and spread out over a longer period of time. It would have been easier for me as an inside salaried employee to offer such an ongoing program. Because top management had not supported my previous attempts to do this, the company would have to live with a less-than-perfect situation. It appeared that management just wanted the training to be taken care of so it could check off the requirement on the Master Training Plan.

As an outside consultant who had formerly directed the training function, I ran into another challenge relating to the scheduling problems. The direct customer I had to do business with was my past secretary who was now in charge of coordinating all training. She had the authority to manipulate my training schedule as well as my pay schedule. She knew exactly how much money I was making and what hours I was keeping. Because she summarized all of my evaluation sheets following each training session, she sometimes knew the outcomes before I did. This was a very strange and awkward situation, but we tried to make the best of it. Had I not maintained a good previous relationship with this individual, I never would have made it through the project.

During this yearlong training contract, I trained each group of employees during its normal shift. Some weeks were quite tiring when classes were scheduled for first, second, and third shifts. To maintain my sanity and energy level, I limited myself to a maximum of three 2.5 hour classes per 24 hours, and usually trained three to four days per week. I was able to travel to the two northern plants five times each. I enjoyed my time at the union plant and managed to schedule a day of skiing at a nearby resort during two of my winter trips. (Consultant schedules can be wonderful!)

Evaluating Results and Success

My 1996 Quality Training Project with my previous employer was a success. I met all of the originally proposed objectives of the program on schedule and provided company orientation to over 400 employees hired since 1991. This supported the culture as well as the quality initiative. The employees who participated in the sessions felt and demonstrated a greater sense of "team," and they became more familiar cross-functionally with others in the corporation, understanding various processes and positions in the overall plan. We maintained flexibility in the program design throughout the year, and this enabled employees and managers to provide input that could be carried out immediately in the subsequent session. Throughout the year, changes in policies and procedures were often announced through these training sessions.

The Level 1 evaluations also indicated that the program was a success. With a heterogeneous population of 800 to 1,000 people who actually attended, there were mixed attitudes about the courses, but more than 80 percent of the evaluations were positive. While I was a director, I had designed a course evaluation sheet, which appears in figure 1, that helped to determine the effectiveness of a trainer and the course content. This helped to maintain quality control in using external or internal resources. Because I was well known and accepted as the trainer for this year-long program, after several sessions I redesigned the after-class evaluation sheet to try to evaluate the employee interest and commitment to the quality concepts. (See figure 2.) My goal was for employees to apply the concepts that they learned immediately on the job and to see value in doing so. Many of them did this, but others claimed that their busy work schedules, standard procedures, or managers wouldn't allow for them to vary from their daily routines. I realized that a bell curve success ratio was to be expected from this population that could not be scheduled for the most effective results.

In addition to the planned objectives, I also created a set of short videos on each main topic for use with new employee orientation, 1997 spot training, and introduction of TQM tools prior to departmental meetings where the concepts would be applied. I designed graphics using Microsoft PowerPoint, hired the local university radio and TV department film professor to shoot and edit the videos, set up a studio in my living room, and created nine short videos. At $300 per 15 minutes of finished product, plus my time, the videos

Figure 1. Training evaluation form.

Please take a moment to give us your comments and evaluation about this training. This will help us to ensure quality in future sessions.

TAQ SESSION: _____ DATE:_____ PLANT:_____

FACILITATOR: Anne Monnin, Ph.D./Strategies for the 90's

Please circle the appropriate response to each of the following:

		Poor	Fair	Good	Very Good	Excellent
1.	To what extent did the subject matter meet your needs and interest?	1	2	3	4	5
2.	How was the ratio of lecture to discussion?	1	2	3	4	5
3.	How well were the objectives stated?	1	2	3	4	5
4.	How well was the program kept alive and interesting?	1	2	3	4	5
5.	How well were charts, chalkboards, audio-visuals, books used?	1	2	3	4	5
6.	How well did the leader summarize the program?	1	2	3	4	5
7.	How well did the leader maintain a friendly and helpful manner?	1	2	3	4	5
8.	How well were points illustrated and clarified?	1	2	3	4	5
9.	What is your overall rating of the leader?	1	2	3	4	5
10.	What is your overall rating of the training program?	1	2	3	4	5

What are specific ways that this training will assist you in your work?

Specifics that may assist others in your department or companywide:

WHO: WHAT:

Additional comments about this training experience.

PLEASE RETURN THIS FORM TO THE FACILITATOR FOLLOWING THE SEMINAR.

Figure 2. Revised training evaluation form.

Please take a moment to give us your evaluation and comments about this training. This will help us to ensure quality in the sessions.

TAQ SESSION: _____   DATE: _____   PLANT: _____

FACILITATOR: <u>Anne Monnin, Ph.D./Strategies for the 90's</u>

Please circle the appropriate response to each of the following:

	Strongly Disagree	Disagree	Neutral	Agree	Strongly Agree
1. I was interested in the topics covered.	1	2	3	4	5
2. I got information from this session that I can use immediately in my job.	1	2	3	4	5
3. This session taught me more about the company and culture here.	1	2	3	4	5
4. The session was well designed. (pacing, time for Q&A, and so forth)	1	2	3	4	5
5. The speaker used good presentation skills.	1	2	3	4	5
6. The speaker appropriately involved participants in discussion.	1	2	3	4	5
7. The seminar met my expectations.	1	2	3	4	5
8. I will take the next steps to apply what I have learned here.	1	2	3	4	5
9. I look forward to the next quality training session.	1	2	3	4	5
10. This session was valuable and I would recommend it to others.	1	2	3	4	5

What did you like best about the session? What can you apply most to your job?

What changes would you suggest to make the seminar more effective?

PLEASE RETURN THIS FORM TO THE FACILITATOR FOLLOWING THE SEMINAR.

were a good deal. Although they aren't exciting, the videos cover each topic adequately, provide some culture-specific examples of application, and include a written workbook and reference manual. In my opinion, the videos would have been better if they included quizzes at the end, but the vice presidents who commissioned the work could not agree on this, so they were left off.

Key Success Factors

The 1996 quality project was successful for a number of reasons. In an environment where TQM training had not been emphasized for five years, permitting over 1,000 employees at five plants in four states to attend a series of training sessions was a coup in itself. Both the manufacturing environment at the time and the senior management helped to support the program. I already knew the culture, processes, and key players, so this familiarity helped to ensure a better program for all involved. As an outside provider, I was flexible and could build the schedules of other clients around this, my biggest client. I practiced what I preached: The customer comes first. I was willing to make last-minute schedule changes and train at any hour of the day or night, depending on my audience and the shift during which they worked. I designed the training that the company wanted even though at times I would have preferred introducing different approaches and strategies. The important point was to provide what the customer wanted, what fit best with its training history, and what matched its past and present cultures.

Lessons Learned From Being an Outside and Inside Training Director

Because I have had the benefit of looking at training and development from both the inside and outside, I have learned quite a bit about the trade-offs involved with each. Personally, I enjoy being an outside consultant better than being an internal trainer. I enjoy my solitude and the peace and comfort of my home office, which is much better outfitted than a company office. I no longer fear that any of my books will disappear or that my computer files will be disturbed because my clients do not come to my office—I go to theirs.

During 1996 and 1997, I have picked up two other long-term clients who openly refer to me as their outside director of training and development and who treat me with great respect as an unbiased expert. I am invited to top-management strategy sessions, most of which I facilitate, and I coach all levels of employees. I am currently helping one big steel manufacturer to reorganize into manufacturing "channels" similar to "focused factories." I am leading both this and the other health and safety equipment manufacturer through extensive team building and TQM training for all levels of employees. Although I am informed about what is going on, I do not need to be involved with inside politics. This unemotional involvement is more comfortable and less stressful for me. As a result, I feel that I can be even more effective as an outside coach and provider of new ideas than I could on the inside.

Years of experience on the outside have taught me how to quickly get to know an organization's culture and its key players so that I can best serve its needs. I find that building a strong relationship with several top decision makers helps ensure that I receive ongoing support. Just as I had the benefit of two vice presidents on my side during 1996 with my past employer's contract, I have built strategic relationships with these two new companies, which promise to extend two-year retainers out to 1999 and beyond. In one company, I strategize directly with the president, plant manager, and human resources manager. With the other company, I have strong support from the vice president of sales and marketing, the local plant manager, and the human resources manager. In both cases, I have trained all levels of employees including managers, technical salaried employees, and hourly operators. Each group sees me differently because of the varied courses I teach, and each offers me a sense of camaraderie that I did not ever experience on the inside with my past employer. My course evaluations have reflected excellent ratings for all levels of training.

I know now that those companies that have a stronger buy-in to the concepts of employee empowerment and personnel development are easier for me to work with. Managers who believe in helping their subordinates to grow are much more open to me as an outside resource. Those companies that are not ready for new paradigm management concepts either don't hire me, or might try me out and then not extend the contract. My experience tells me not to take this personally because groups like this are just not ready for what I have to offer. I try not to waste my time trying to convince this type of organization to use my services, but instead, go find those that are ready and waiting for me to appear.

As an outside consultant, I do not threaten managers or any level employee. They can accept or not accept my ideas. I do not take up a space in their protected head count, and I provide my own clerical services and office equipment. Although they pay me nice fees (which I adjust based on long-term relationships), I handle all of my own benefits and taxes, so the accounting is easier for them.

My time is spent more efficiently now than when I shared an office with others at the plant. I have fewer interruptions because there are no walk-ins. I can screen my voice mail. Memos don't swamp me because the only mail or faxes that are sent to me pertain directly to what I am doing with a client. I use my time according to my energy level. When I am creative, I either design the next training session or write my book. When I am tired, I check out and take a nap. Each day is different, and every week varies in schedule, but on Wednesday mornings I have an important meeting with the tennis court next door, and usually I can schedule my clients around that. Exercise helps me to think better and to have more energy to share with my clients.

As a self-starter and an overachiever, I find my one-person training office a fun challenge for me, but this life wouldn't be good for everyone. In addition to the rigors of self-direction, one must have expertise in marketing, accounting, and negotiation to make the business work. If it weren't for my 25 years in the field, I wouldn't be qualified to do what I do now. (I often tell this to young people still in school who send their resumes to me and want to become my consulting associate.)

There are still obstacles and misconceptions to overcome in being a consultant and independent trainer. Because outsiders earn more on an hourly basis than our counterparts on a guaranteed salary with set benefits, there may be some resentment. Some people consider consultants to be people who are in career transition who hang out a shingle because they don't know what else to do. Most good consultants are skilled professionals who have proved themselves on the inside before striking out on their own. Many people feel that those who work out of their homes should find a real job. My home office is better than the one I had at the plant. And finally, there is still a bias against us from our own colleagues in internal training positions who often feel threatened by us. As in most professions, there are some consultants that give the rest of us a bad name. I am finding, however, that my services greatly benefit reengineered companies where the human resources personnel have requirements that they can't meet. As partners, with their goals in mind, we both win.

Questions for Discussion

1. What are the benefits to your organization in using external training and development specialists?

2. Are you a good candidate for going outside as an external specialist? Why or why not?

3. What outside resources do you currently use or could you use to your organization's benefit?

4. Why have you or would you choose these specialists?

5. Is there a chance that you might find yourself downsized out of your position? Why or why not? Are you in denial?

6. What would you need to learn to be an effective specialist on the outside?

7. Who are your mentors or champions? How would these people support you in becoming an external consultant?

The Author

Anne Monnin brings over 20 years of training and consulting experience to her firm, STRATEGIES FOR THE 90's, founded in 1985. She was founding director of the first U.S. international training institute sponsored by a consortium of academic and corporate members (1980–1984), and director of training and development for a large metals manufacturer located in the Southeast (1993–1994). She has taught or directed programs for 17 colleges or universities, served clients in 16 states and 70 countries, taught in three M.B.A. programs, and reviewed manuscripts for two major publishers. Monnin writes a weekly newspaper business column and is currently writing a book on downsizing. She can be contacted at: STRATEGIES FOR THE 90's, Box 459, Waxhaw, NC 28173; phone: 704.843.4020; fax: 704.843.2264.

Reference

Senge, P.M. (1990). *The Fifth Discipline: The Art & Practice of the Learning Organization.* New York: Doubleday and Currency.

Streamlining Technical Training in a Multifunctional Manufacturing Facility: How to Do It With a Small Staff

Monsanto

Michael J. Gettle

This case is an excellent illustration of how to introduce performance-based training into an organization to increase the efficiency of training. Gettle describes his training system, which involved the use of job aids, on-the-job training, and technicians as trainers at Monsanto's plant in Muscatine, Iowa. To gain buy-in for the new approach to training, Gettle created strong partnerships with all levels of employees, especially the technicians who delivered the training and helped with its development. The case describes the challenges and requirements for building training skills of nontrainers to implement such an approach.

Introduction

Three years ago, I accepted a job offer to become the training coordinator for Monsanto's plant in Muscatine, Iowa. During the interviews, I was told the position had only three responsibilities: compliance training, technical skills training, and professional development. Procedure development and improvement were added later. Although these goals may seem like a daunting task, they can be and are carried out. This chapter is a case study in how a small training staff provides technical training at the Muscatine plant and how we introduced a performance-based training approach that created an ongoing learning environment.

This case was prepared to serve as a basis for discussion rather than to illustrate either effective or ineffective administrative and management practices.

Organizational Background

In 1901, John F. Queeny formed the company of Monsanto Chemical Works in St. Louis, naming the company for his wife's maiden name. The company's first product was saccharin. From this small start, an organization developed that produces chemicals, fibers, pharmaceuticals, herbicides, and disease-resistant and pest-resistant crops. Monsanto's products focus on the company's goals of manufacturing and marketing products that are a benefit to society. In 1964, the company changed its name to Monsanto Company to better reflect the diversity of its products (Forestall, 1977.) Today, Monsanto is a global life-science company that employs more than 20,000 people worldwide.

Monsanto competes with numerous chemical companies. In a few years, Monsanto will lose patent protection for its main herbicide product in the United States, which will increase competition for our product. Continued success depends on driving manufacturing costs down, while maintaining and improving product quality. A key strategy is providing employees with the necessary skills and knowledge that allow them to provide valuable input resulting in better business decisions.

Monsanto's Muscatine Plant began operations in December 1961. Over the years, the plant continued to add facilities to produce additional products. The 550 Muscatine Plant employees produce several products for two markets—agricultural chemicals and plastics. The plant is divided into nine different operational areas, including several support areas. An area leader heads each area and is responsible for its operation. Area leaders report to one of seven business unit leaders, who along with the plant manager, comprise the plant management team, called the plant business team (PBT). The function of the PBT is to provide the plant with a strategic direction to meet the company's manufacturing needs.

The Muscatine Plant has a reputation for producing a quality, low-cost product. Employees generally have a can-do attitude that is evident in their excellent work ethic and conscious efforts to do the right things correctly and quickly. The workforce is well educated with an extensive experience base. On average, production technicians have 18 years of experience and maintenance technicians have 21 years. Most technicians are from the local area, which is an advantage from an educational aspect because the local educational system is excellent. The experience of most of the people, however, is limited to the Muscatine Plant and area, and this sometimes limits the acceptability of new ideas from outside the plant. One must keep on guard for the not-invented-here mindset, which turned out to be one of the greatest barriers to implementing change and the source of many sessions in which I asked myself "How do I?"

The Training Function

The plant's training function has four responsibilities: compliance training, technical training, professional development, and procedure development and maintenance. The staff of three includes a training coordinator, a maintenance training coordinator, and a training clerk. The training coordinator is responsible for coordinating compliance training, technical training, and professional development, whereas the maintenance training coordinator is responsible for implementing and improving the maintenance training programs. The training clerk provides support by tracking training efforts and assisting with developing training materials. In addition to these responsibilities, the training staff also became internal consultants on how to train, which turned out to be critical in the implementation of improved training.

Challenges and Opportunities

As recently as six years ago, Monsanto's Muscatine plant was seeking consistent guidance on human performance and training issues. Employee training was effective, but not necessarily efficient. Qualification programs were usually content based and difficult to correlate with actual job performance. Training effectiveness was measured subjectively. Training occurred, but a strategic human development plan did not exist. The lack of a shared, systematic approach to training prevented the plant from taking advantage of shared training resources between units as well as from approaching human performance issues using a common process. Several attempts by outside groups to introduce new training systems into the plant had had minimal success in improving training. There was little employee ownership of these new programs because many employees did not have input into new programs. Employees viewed new efforts with suspicion—wondering was this going to be another flavor-of-the-month program?

The plant had taken steps to increase its competitiveness by increasing its workforce's skills and knowledge. Increasing skills and knowledge filled two needs. First, it ensured that new employees were provided with the necessary training to succeed on the job. Second, it enabled current employees to maintain skills and knowledge and to upgrade their skills on new or modified equipment. These efforts to increase employees' knowledge and skill were fragmented because there was no systematic approach that would allow training to be attached to the organization's and plant's goals.

The Muscatine plant's history was a significant challenge to implementing such a systematic approach to training. We had to determine how to introduce up-to-date training systems in the plant when there were bad memories from previous attempts to do so. To gain acceptance for any system we introduced, we had to build on what was in place—it had to be more of an evolution than a revolution.

Providing Value: Assessing Training Needs

Being new to both the Muscatine plant and the chemical industry provided me with an opportunity and a challenge to learn about the plants' needs. My past experience gave me an advantage. I had spent the last 20 years analyzing, designing, developing, implementing, and especially evaluating technical training programs for utility generating plants. This experience afforded me a technical background to complement my training background, and provided me with a base to learn the new processes and a common language link with the technicians.

The first step in analyzing needs was to assess the current status of training in all areas of the plant. This may sound simple; however, the plant consisted of numerous autonomous units, and each unit's training was as different as the units themselves. The status of each of the training programs was further complicated because several of the units fell under the Process Safety Management (PSM) rules of the Occupational Safety and Health Administration, although others did not. The PSM rules called for training programs as well as requalification programs—something that should be in all training programs for the maintenance and improvement of all employees' knowledge and skills.

These PSM requirements pointed out which programs to work on first. We had to get the PSM programs done first because this was a "right to operate" issue. Although it gave us a starting point, developing the PSM training for these programs would be a headache because we needed to develop the test before upgrading the training. The solution was to define the tasks for the jobs and then develop the tests based on the task list. Although awkward, this process provided us a beginning point (the task list) and an end point (the tests) for these programs. This headache proved to be a blessing in disguise because it showed plant employees that training systems could work for them. Each area had a training program in place and, generally, it was relatively easy for areas to develop these requalification programs.

The needs analysis had to give an accurate description of the status training. Data collection consisted of a detailed review of all of the plant's training programs as well as the implementation procedures for the programs. Interviews with the trainers, training participants, area leaders, and plant management followed this review. Input from the Production Training Team and Safety Committees as well as a review of the materials from the plant's previous false starts at training systems provided a lot of useful information. This assessment process took approximately four months. I was a bit nervous about how long it took to gather enough information to move forward. To the credit of plant management, they told me to take as long as was needed: They wanted it done right.

As a result of this effort, we realized the need to develop a systematic approach that each area could use to identify its specific training needs and to streamline training to meet these needs. Our approach involved developing a task list for each of the jobs. Once the task list was identified, we were able to develop a bank of test questions for the requalification test. This process defined the job and also identified if there were gaps in the programs or if there were any unnecessary training programs being conducted. Our review indicated that training was typically content based and that the on-the-job training (OJT) portion was unstructured, consisting of time-in-grade, that is the particular time in a grade before moving on. We referred to this type of training as FMA for "follow me around."

The Challenge and the Mission

The need for a systematic and consistent training approach became more evident as a result of this training review. It would require additional effort to further revise the training into streamlined, performance-based programs. From a business perspective, it was necessary for our programs to train a competent person as quickly as possible because time in training costs money as well as lost productivity. The challenge at the plant was to switch from previous training methods that were effective, but not necessarily efficient. We needed a way to make sure the training met the areas' needs without having any gaps. The mission of the training coordinator was to develop performance-based training programs that provided skilled and knowledgeable technicians in the shortest time possible.

Critical Populations

Although the area leaders had the overall responsibility for training, the technicians were both the end users and the providers of the training. The technicians and the area training coordinator (usually a technician) were the key players in implementing the training. To succeed, the training system had to have value to the technicians, that is, it had to be easy to develop and useful to both new and experienced technicians. A major strategy was to develop "champions" at all levels to implement the new training system and make sure that they succeeded. The key players in developing and implementing performance-based training programs at the Muscatine plant were as follows:

- Area training coordinators (ATCs). The ATC function was usually filled by a technician who also had production responsibilities and training accountabilities. The ATCs were technically qualified, but not necessarily knowledgeable about training. As a whole, technicians had the technical skills to conduct performance-based training, but they needed to learn training skills for this system to work. Their need for training skills posed a set of problems: What skills to provide and when were key questions.

- Production training team. This team consisted of ATCs who represented each of the plant business units and the training coordinator. The team's function was to provide a vision of what training should look like and how it would best fit into the current practices at the plant. The team gave critical input to the training coordinator about whether a particular tactic would work or not, and also served as an excellent test bed for training methods and a communication means for the rest of the plant.

- Area leaders (ALs). The ALs were responsible for all aspects of their production unit including their area's training programs, and they were critical to implementing the changes in training. Being responsible for production and cost control, ALs needed to see how any intervention would be of value to their area. Previously, the ALs had developed content-based training specifically for their unit's technicians. Because most ALs had engineering backgrounds and were unfamiliar with human performance issues and interventions, it proved to be a great challenge to provide them with the knowledge to deal with human performance efforts.

- Plant Business Team (PBT). The PBT, comprised of the plant manager and the business unit leaders, provided strategic guidance in all aspects of the plant's business. The training coordinator, through the human resource business leader, provided input and received direction on strategic human resource development initiatives. This group provided strategic leverage to introduce the process of improving human performance via improved training and a learning environment.

Development of Systematic, Flexible Approach to Training

The training system developed for the Muscatine plant was a derivative of the instructional systems design (ISD) approach used in training the military. The basic five steps of ISD—analyze, design, develop, implement, and evaluate—were modified to best meet the needs in this plant. The ISD system was simplified to enable people unfamiliar with training to use it easily. Also, wherever possible, we translated training jargon into terms that made sense to the technicians and provided them with in-depth explanations and examples. Although our training system was developed along the lines of well-known technical training processes and models, the training process had to be flexible so it would meet specific area needs and be incorporated into the current plant systems and culture with employee buy-in. The content and methods and who implemented the program could change, but the requirement that training be performance based could not be compromised.

The great thing about training models is that they can be modified to meet an organization's evolving needs. The flexible character of our training system allowed it to meet our organization's needs and set the stage for training champions to succeed. This was a win-win-win scenario. If the technicians, trainers, and area leaders had a system, it would be valuable to all. A training system was developed with the concepts in mind that training should be based on job requirements, it should be performance based, and technicians should develop and implement it.

The training coordinator's role was to develop the training system, to provide the ATCs and technicians with the skills to develop and implement the training programs, and to monitor program development and implementation. Figure 1 illustrates the basic components of the training system.

Job Definition

The first step in implementing the system was to have the technicians define the job using a job analysis. I learned quickly not to use the term *job analysis*. What worked better was to approach this from the angle of defining the job. *Define the job—define the training*

Figure 1. Components of the training system.

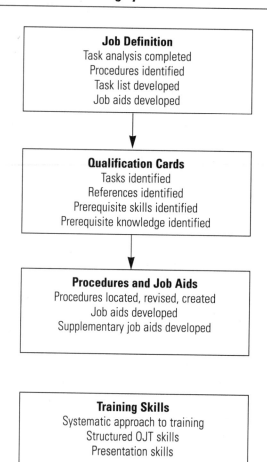

became a well-known phrase in the plant. Also, we planned training as one would an engineering project, starting by defining and specifying the project parameters. This approach was extremely helpful in selling the concept of training systems to the technicians and engineers. Once the job was defined, training could be defined from what was needed on the job. The job analysis provided the area with a list of tasks, which became the most critical tool for program development. This task listing formed the basis for the performance-based training programs, served as the main development tool for the qualification card, which includes the task list and required skills, and also identified the procedures and job aids that needed to be in place. The tasks were collected on a task listing form similar to the one in table 1.

The task listing described the job. Almost every task on the task listing would be on the qualification card for the initial training program. The reference information was useful in identifying the procedures and technical manuals that formed the basis for the training materials. The comments section included additional information that might be used later. Other information involving rating the difficulty, importance, and frequency of each task was not always collected. This rating information would be useful in determining tasks to include in refresher training, but it would not be as useful at the beginning of this process. Ignoring the rating scales was not a major issue because it could be gathered later.

One difficulty we encountered in developing the training was changing the technicians' and managers' thinking from how they were taught to the new approach—training new employees to *perform tasks*. Typically these people had received content, or knowledge-based, instruction, which was usually developed by committees based on the best guess of what was needed on the job. The concept of making trainees demonstrate that they could do tasks was new. Based on their experiences, the technicians usually wanted to identify topics to be taught first. In contrast, the best way to develop performance-based training is to identify the result (the tasks) first and then the knowledge and skills. Determining the tasks before the topics confused the technicians as well as plant management. One way we kept design sessions on track was to ask the technicians what work (task) the topics supported. This approach usually focused the discussions back to the tasks.

Table 1. Sample task listing.

Task	References	Comments
Start up the incinerator.	SOP—41A Incinerator	Done one/year
Unload/load tank cars.	SOP—32 Material Handling	DOT requirements
Monitor Provox parameters.	Provox procedures	Multiple procedures
Line up the cooling system.	SOP—1 Start-up	
Line up the holding vessel.	SOP—1 Start-up	Difficult, safety considerations

The next step was determining the necessary steps and knowledge for each task as well as the procedures and resources used in accomplishing the tasks. This step was critical in identifying procedures that could serve as training documentation as well as identifying procedures that needed to be upgraded. As a result of this process there was a significant improvement in operating procedures for some areas. The process for conducting this task analysis is shown in figure 2.

Each task was broken into the steps needed to complete the task. Because these steps are analogous to procedure steps, we often used the procedure steps to identify task steps. This simplified the process and also showed the technicians that the training system related directly to area operations. Knowledge needed was identified from the task itself and the task steps. This again showed that the training skill and knowledge related directly to the job. Information gathered in this phase often led to improved procedures or to an opportunity for job aids. In one case, job procedures were completely rewritten based on the skill and knowledge information gathered. When revisions to procedures were necessary, the development of job aids was encouraged.

Figure 2. Process for conducting the task analysis.

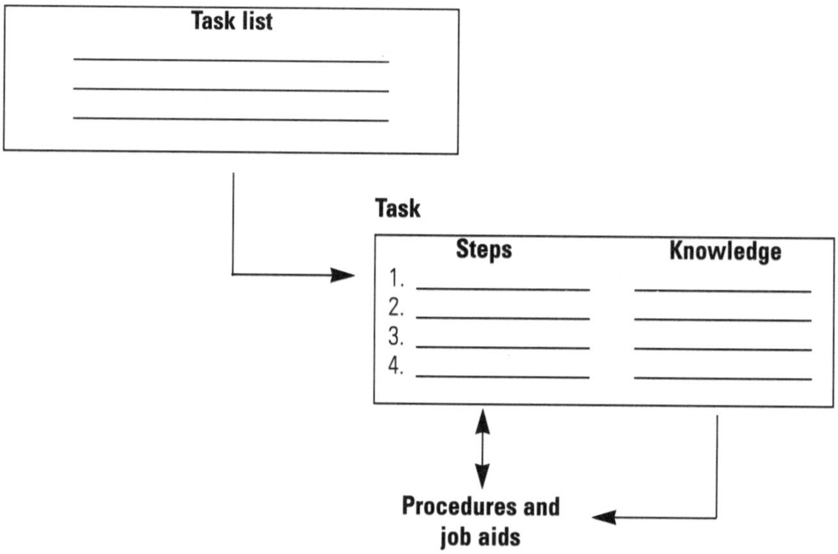

Qualification Cards

From the task list, a qualification card was generated. The card is a rather lengthy document, containing the task listing along with the required references, skills, and knowledge and other information (such as tools and equipment) necessary for a particular task. Table 2 shows a simplified example of a task taken from a qualification card.

The qualification card served two purposes: It provided trainees with information needed to prepare to learn the task, and it provided trainers with an aid for giving consistent training. The card clarified what trainees were expected to learn to do. There was no need for a learning objective because performing the task was the objective. The trainee used the qualification card to prepare for training. Having prepared, the trainee contacted a qualified technician to receive structured training. After completing training, the trainee contacted another qualified technician to demonstrate that the trainee could perform the task unassisted, safely, and successfully. If the trainee could not perform the task, the qualified technician reverted to a training mode. There was no stigma attached to being retrained; it was simply a step in learning the process.

Table 2. Line up the CAC cooling system.

TASK: Line up the CAC cooling system.		Trained: _____ Evaluated: _____	Date: _____ Date: _____
References:	SOP 0134 CAC Cooling System Operation EFD Drawing 0134-D CAC Cooling System Technical Manual on CAC systems Job Aid CAC-0134		
Tools and equipment:	Standard PPE Gloves Valve wrench		
Knowledge needed:	Use of hand tools Locations of references Safety information on valve manipulation		
Prerequisites:	Task qualified on CAC cooling system normal operation		

Procedures and Job Aids

The key to developing training in the areas was to integrate training with existing systems. This meant using procedures and job aids that were the primary training tools and documentation in area operations. The procedures provided the content for the training of tasks. Using materials the technicians developed and used in daily operations fostered ownership and also integrated training into the way things were already done. It minimized the number of training manuals that often sit on shelves collecting dust, and it also allowed technicians to use familiar materials when delivering training. In some instances, job aids were developed that assisted in the operation of the equipment and the delivery of training. In addition to the procedures and job aids used on the job, supplementary job aids were planned to cover topics that were prerequisite to the accomplishment of a task or a set of tasks. This documentation might be called "lesson plans." Incorporating this information into job aids forced the instruction to be job related and performance based.

The benefits of using the procedures and job aids for the main training tools were twofold. First, it tied the training documentation directly to the job. Second, the training documentation was automatically kept current with operating practices. There were several problems to overcome with the use of procedures for training. The foremost problem was the quality of the procedures, which varied from one area to the next as well as from one procedure to the next in the same area. The job and task analysis identified problems with procedures—in some cases procedures did not exist, and in other cases procedures existed for tasks that were no longer done. The most bothersome problem was a procedure that contained incorrect data. Fortunately, the job and task analysis enabled us to correct these types of problems.

During the revision and development of procedures, one question kept popping up: At what level do we write the procedure? The answer depended on who needed the information most. We wrote the procedures to a level that would help a newly qualified technician complete a task successfully and safely. Also, a procedure at this level would help experienced technicians refresh their knowledge about an infrequent or complex task. This guidance enabled technicians to write procedures that both new and experienced technicians could use.

Prerequisite Training

Not all training was OJT—there was prerequisite training as well. We did not want technicians to be just valve turners: We wanted operators to know and be able to apply the underlying principles of the processes they ran, and to be able to anticipate the system responses to their actions. The prerequisite training came from the requirements for the tasks and was incorporated into training courses that were conducted prior to OJT. This system provided another level of safety to the plant processes.

Program Implementation

Program implementation had three main components—the qualification cards, the procedures and job aids, and the trainers—and all three needed to be in place for maximum benefit. During implementation, I found that I was explaining the structure to numerous people. There appeared to be a symmetry to the system. From giving these explanations, I developed the model depicted in figure 3.

The following sections describe how the three components work together.

OJT Models and Qualification Cards

One implementation issue that influenced our training approach was the plant's work schedule. The plant operated 24 hours a day, and each area operated using a different shift schedule. These shifts made the use of OJT a necessity. Any training for groups of people would have had to have been scheduled multiple times—not a pleasant thought and not efficient or timely either.

Qualified technicians were trained to conduct structured OJT using the Expert OJT Workshop designed by Jeff Nelson (1996), an out-

Figure 3. The training system.

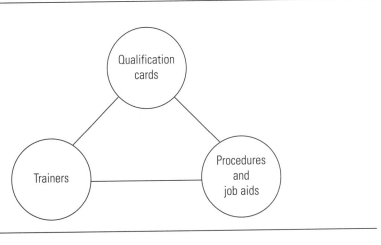

side consultant. This workshop provided the technicians with the skills to conduct structured OJT in a manner that gets results as well as with the skills to develop job aids to support training and operations. The skills taught in this workshop had been used with success at one of our sister plants.

The OJT implementation method started with the use of the qualification card, which communicated the training expectations to each trainee and resulted in trainees taking ownership of their training. Trainees used their qualification cards to prepare for the training prior to asking for the OJT sessions, and proceeded through the training program at their own pace within certain guidelines.

During program implementation, the ATC issued the qualification cards to the trainees and provided them with information on how to use the cards as well as how to submit ideas for improving the cards. The ATC then monitored the input to improve the qualification cards and procedures, which was the next step in controlling the training process. Qualification cards allowed trainees to track their own progress and allowed the area trainer and area leader to track each individual trainee's progress in the training program.

The qualification card concept worked better than anyone expected. In one area, technicians in the training program were given the cards as they came in on their shifts. The ATC was deluged with requests for cards from people who were not in the training program and did not receive the cards. Qualified technicians asked, "Where were these cards when we were in the training program?" We are still receiving positive feedback. The main comment is that the card provides clear expectations and direction on what is expected of the trainees.

Procedures and Job Aids

For years, Joe Harless (1978) promoted the use of job aids as a viable human performance intervention. Our approach relied heavily on job aids as tools that would help people perform consistently with a minimum of training. The expected result was employees who were trained to use the job aids or procedures to perform a task successfully.

To apply the job aid concepts to improve procedures and focus training on job performance, we used the documentation process and format of Information Mapping®, developed by Robert E. Horn of Information Mapping® Inc. (1994). This documentation process complemented concepts taught in the Expert OJT Workshop and blended well with existing procedure efforts, including QS9002 certification, a stringent certification and quality control process. Of more importance, the technicians viewed this a straightforward method that would help improve their procedures.

In our system the procedures became the main training documentation. There were no three-ring binders collecting dust. By using on-the-job procedures, the level of fidelity between the training and job was the same. How did we know that we had won? When we went into an area and saw that OJT conducted with job aids or procedures and that the documents were dirty, dog-eared, and stained with coffee cup rings, we knew the training documents were being used.

Trainers

A critical need we identified early on was that the people assigned to carry out training did not have the training skills to implement it. Also, each area had different content needs. Each ATC was provided with training in the systematic approach to training, structured OJT methods as well as presentation skills. Technicians received training in developing job aids and procedures and in developing and conducting structured OJT. As a result, technicians could update and improve the training program as they learned improved ways to run the plant processes. Our thinking was if the technicians know how the program works and have ownership of the program, then they will sustain it. Training provided to improve the technicians' training skills included the following courses:

- Training Systems (a Muscatine Plant course)
- Presentation Skills (conducted by various vendors)
- Procedure and Job Aid Writing (conducted by Information Mapping)
- Structured On-the-Job Training (conducted by Expert OJT)

Technicians received these courses as needed. They were the minimum items for an ATC to function. For other training competencies, the ATCs could call on the training coordinator.

The Information Mapping courses and the Expert OJT course reinforced the use of job aids and procedures as a means of job and training documentation. The Expert OJT course also taught the technicians how to conduct on-the-job training using on-the-job-materials (procedures and job aids). The feedback from the technicians has been mostly positive. One technician was "volunteered" to attend the training. After the training, the technician was one of the area's strongest advocates of OJT and developing procedures in the job aid format.

One lesson learned in developing the technicians as trainers was not to provide a lot of theory—they wanted the nuts and bolts of what they needed to get results. Just as the average person doesn't need to know how the telephone works, the trainer doesn't need the underlying theory for all the training tools. Besides, that's why the plant has a professional trainer—to make systems so they can work in the organization's environment.

Program Status and Results

Area training programs are still evolving. The dollar expenditure for this training has been minimal, but there has been a large investment in program development time. What has been the payoff? One goal was to increase the efficiency of training. Previously, the time to complete training programs was not monitored except that someone needed to be in the job a minimum amount of time. Under the new training system, plant training programs now have a maximum amount of time a person should be in the training, with little restriction on how fast a person can progress through the qualification process. Although not all the results are in, where the new training system has been employed, there appears to be a reduction in the amount of time it takes to train a competent person. In one case, there has been a 50 percent reduction for a new program that typically would have taken over two years. Also, training costs for areas employing the new training system tend to be below that of other areas. We are not sure if this is a direct effect of the training system, or a secondary effect of area management looking more closely at training.

The main result of our approach is that training is tied to the job, and excessive training is avoided. Gaps in training programs have been identified and filled. Our programs are not only effective, but also efficient. The trainees using the new training programs have provided positive feedback. They now know what is expected of them. Technicians have also provided feedback that they wished the training program and expectations were in place when they started. Also, the trainees are not tied to an artificial time-in-grade.

Our new training system produced several positive outcomes relating to business, safety, and quality. First, we had a business impact by increasing efficiency through performance-based training. Second, the training program resulted in the safe performance of tasks. There was no confusion about performing a task safely because the correct way was the safe way. The trainer reinforced safety by instructing the trainee to perform the task safely, and the procedures and job aids were written to perform the task safely. Finally, our training approach encouraged producing a consistent, high-quality product. Quality was redundant with safety—the safe way to do a task was also the way to produce a consistent, quality product.

Contributions to Success

What has helped the new training system to succeed? The key has been reducing the time to train a competent person, which has reduced our costs. By its very nature, the training system has been integrated with operations. Scheduling of training has not been an issue—with technicians delivering training, it could be done on shift, as needed.

A key success factor was overcoming resistance by building involvement. The training coordinator and training staff were charged with switching from content-based training programs, followed by time-in-grade, to performance-based training. The obstacles of introducing this system to the plant centered around changing the culture, the status quo, and the approach to innovation. Resistance was especially strong because of several previous false starts in implementing training systems. We were able to reduce resistance by using the current culture as a starting point and by incorporating input from plant personnel to develop the training. The key to change was having one area implement the program successfully, then using that program as a springboard to other plant areas.

Ownership of the programs was a powerful tool in implementing new programs. The Production Training Team provided a valuable reality check by being a test bed for the new processes. Their input, although harsh at times, provided information needed to revise the process to best fit the needs of the technicians. This input and the subsequent revisions set the stage for the ATCs, the real champions of the training system, to better accept the new system. In discussions about the new training methodology with each ATC, we received information about how the system could work in their area. The system was again revised, based on their input. Once the area input was collected and the system revised, we gave an overview of the training system to the area leaders and the PBT, who approved the process. This approach—starting from the bottom and working up—may seem a bit odd, but without the ownership of the technicians who developed and implemented the training, our new training system would have been doomed. This is not to say that we kept management in the dark—management was kept up-to-date by periodic briefings on the development of the system—but the system had to belong to the technicians.

Lessons Learned

There were three main components of success in this effort; technician ownership and buy-in, integration with current operations and plant beliefs, and alignment with plant and business goals. We did not always follow the letter of the system—technicians and the training coordinator sometimes changed the system to meet the specific needs of an area. Once the flexibility of the system became known, the technicians found that they could develop a training program to fit their area. The lesson learned here was that you could have it your own way as long as we ended with the correct result—a consistent quality product safely made.

The technicians' buy-in of the program was closely related to the second component, integration with current plant operations. In the best of worlds, training would occur in the area and no one would know that the training happened. The third component, business alignment, was critical. The trainer in an organization must first think as a businessperson and then as a trainer. Our plant is in the business of making chemicals that benefit farmers and food production; we are not in the training business. Once the trainer has the business goals in mind and aligns the human performance efforts to those goals, support for those efforts comes from all sides.

The recommendation to the trainer facing a task such as outlined in this chapter is to make the system and organization work to your advantage. The following recommendations may help you in your efforts:

- Develop a training system that is workable for the plant personnel.
- Train key plant personnel on how to use the training system, especially the means of defining the job.
- Train area personnel in the skills of developing procedures and job aids.
- Train area personnel in the conduct of structured OJT.
- Provide support in the development and implementation of the training programs.

The Lone Trainer

You will note that I was not alone. The support from the technicians, the area trainers, and plant management was there as long as the efforts fit the plant and aligned with business goals. In fact as a lone trainer my role was to provide guidance, training, and internal consulting to the employees that did the bulk of the actual development work.

Learning Assignment

There are several ways to approach implementing training systems. Part of this case study was to provide a means of generating new ideas of methods to use in similar circumstances. Below are information and questions that can be used to generate discussion and better ideas for the implementation of training systems that a small staff oversees. Your assignment is to develop a training system that will upgrade current training to performance-based training using the following resources:

- Training staff: two people, yourself and a training clerk.
- Resources: expendable budget of $20,000 per year.
- Target population: 400 technicians working in eight different plant areas.
- Current training programs: content-based training programs in place at the different areas. Each program is implemented differently and is in a different stage of revision.
- Area training coordinators: Some areas have training coordinators, some don't. Training coordinators are technicians who handle the training activities in addition to their other duties.

Questions for Discussion

1. What systems would ensure that training is job related and necessary?
2. What techniques could overcome the cultural barriers to change?
3. What training competencies should a technical person have?
4. How would you persuade the key players to switch to performance-based training?
5. What items would you consider in a needs analysis?
6. What other approaches could be used to deliver the training given the resource constraints?
7. For prerequisite training, how would you implement the courses for the different areas of the plant?
8. How could you coordinate the courses to spend the minimum amount of resources necessary?
9. What other training competencies would you provide the technicians?

The Author

Michael J. Gettle is the training coordinator at Monsanto's Muscatine Plant. He has over 20 years in the field of industrial training. He spent 17 years analyzing performance issues, developing and implementing training solutions, and evaluating power-plant training programs in the utility industry. Gettle spent the last three years at Monsanto's Muscatine Plant designing and developing a human development strategy for the plant employees. He has a B.S. in education from Millersville State College and an M.Ed. in adult education program management from Georgia State University. He has also received extensive technical training while with the utility industry. He can be contacted at Monsanto, Box 473, Muscatine, Iowa 52761; phone: 319.262.7126.

References

Forestall, Dan J. (1977). *Faith, Hope & $5,000: The Story of Monsanto.* New York: Simon & Schuster.

Harless, Joe. (1978). *Job Aids Workshop.* Newnan, GA: Harless Performance Guild.

Information Mapping®. (1994). *Mapping ISO Documentation.* Waltham, MA: Author.

Nelson, Jeff. (1996). *Expert OJT Workshop.* Newport News, VA: Expert OJT.

Managing the Training Function Through Employee Participation and Involvement

Navistar—The Springfield Assembly Plant

Raquel Fornoles Arnold

This case provides an excellent illustration of building credibility and shared ownership through a training advisory board. Raquel Arnold, the lone trainer for Navistar's Springfield, Ohio, Plant, created a "Progressive Education Council," consisting of both management and union employees, that helped her to set direction and ultimately improve the effectiveness of Springfield's Interactive Learning Center. By conducting a thorough needs assessment and working closely with this advisory board, Arnold was able to shift her role from coordinator to problem solver and human resource development strategist.

Company Background

Navistar International Corporation manufactures and markets International® brand medium- to heavy-duty trucks, school buses, and midrange diesel engines in North America and selected export markets. In 1995, sales were $6 billion. With 15,000 employees worldwide, it competes in six businesses: heavy truck, medium trucks, school buses, parts, truck financing, and engines. Besides the corporate offices in Chicago, Navistar has 10 manufacturing facilities, two engineering and technical centers, eight parts distribution centers, 13 used truck centers, five export sales offices, and various other Navistar branches. Two manufacturing facilities are in Springfield, Ohio. The Springfield Assembly Plant, the subject of this case, has approximately 4,500

This case was prepared to serve as a basis for discussion rather than to illustrate either effective or ineffective administrative and management practices.

employees, 80 percent of whom are members of United Auto Workers (UAW) locals 402 and 658.

As a result of a major downsizing in the early 1980s and a hiring trend that started in 1994, the plant has a unique culture. In 1994, for the first time in approximately 25 years, Navistar started hiring new workers, including more women and minorities. This move had a significant impact on the composition of the current workforce. Prior to 1994, most employees in the plant had been with Navistar for at least 35 years, and as with most companies in the automobile industry, they perceived employment with Navistar as a lifelong proposition and they planned to leave upon retirement. Also, there had been a lot of struggle between union and management in the past, resulting in an obvious lack of trust in each other.

The Training Function at the Springfield Plant

In the 1980s, there had been little training activity because of all the restructuring in the company, and an employee in human resources (HR) was responsible for training as well as for compensation and wages. A resurgence of interest in training for both union and nonunion employees occurred in 1990, and the company hired its first full-time training coordinator. The intention was for training and development to be this coordinator's focus and not an additional responsibility of another HR staff member. This position reported to the HR manager with support from corporate headquarters. The corporate headquarters' Human Resources Development Department provided the plant with training for nonunion and management employees through the core curriculum. The training coordinator arranged corporate-initiated training, such as programs based on W. Edwards Deming's philosophies and teachings and programs about statistical process control. When the training coordinator left Navistar two years later, training became the responsibility of the HR manager.

When I was hired in 1994, no one had held the position of full-time training coordinator for more than two years. My primary responsibilities were planning, developing, implementing, and evaluating a plantwide training program as well as managing the Training Center and the Interactive Learning Center. As training coordinator, I was the only full-time employee in the department, but the task before me could not be done alone. Students from local universities provided able assistance on many of the training projects. For instance, a local undergraduate student in computer science helped develop a training database, and a graduate student in training and development provided assistance in planning, developing, and conducting a needs assessment survey. I also found help by building an internal support network for training, which was instrumental in garnering support throughout the company for the training initiative.

Initial Opportunities and Challenges

In late 1993, the plant manager, Larry Clement, and the manufacturing operations manager, Ann Wiseman, decided to focus on training and development for the entire organization. They had skilled in-house workers renovate part of the plant for a state-of-the-art training facility, consisting of four classrooms equipped with TVs and VCRs, whiteboards, overhead projectors, and other audiovisual equipment.

When I came to the company as training coordinator the next year, I was excited about working in a large manufacturing organization with a union—a drastic change from my last job. I felt that I could benefit professionally and personally from being part of a large manufacturing organization and was excited about helping to build the training function from the ground up.

My first task as training coordinator was to host an open house of the Training Center and one of my challenges was to meet the expectations that came with the new facility. Although the center symbolized management's commitment to training, the prolonged absence of a training professional had created a perception that training was not a critical function. There was also a perception that a training coordinator's function was primarily to schedule classes and maintain the Training Center. Although various departments and individuals offered a variety of training, no one was held accountable for connecting all these fragmented efforts into a comprehensive plan. Thus, there was an opportunity to integrate all these initiatives in a plan that truly addressed performance gaps. Building the credibility of the training function to both union and management would be a great challenge.

Building Credibility—Initial Steps

Having the support of Clement and Wiseman, I was able to meet the challenge of establishing my credibility head-on. My first step was to identify potential supporters who could become advocates for training. It was necessary to involve people throughout the plant if training were to have an impact on this organization of close to 5,000 employees. In discussions with senior managers, I inquired about their vision of the organization and how they thought training and development could help in achieving it. These discussions led to the development of a plantwide advisory group. Although hiring outside consultants was an option, we needed a strong internal support system—the training advisory group—that would help advocate for training and development ideologies and would provide willing minds and hands. These discussions also helped me to sell the idea and to learn about other people in the organization who could support this function.

Through observing committee meetings, consulting with senior managers, facilitating a business planning session for the manufacturing operations, and in other aspects of my work, I concentrated on getting to know my target audience and helping them learn about training. In our discussions about performance issues, I stressed the importance of determining the specific performance problem that this audience wanted to address and of identifying various interventions that might include training. If there were training needs, the manager and a representative of his or her organization was involved in developing the training intervention. If we determined a need for other interventions besides training, we strategized ways to address these issues.

At the same time, I worked on establishing a positive image for the Training Center. It became an accessible place that could address the varied needs of our diversified workforce. It was marketed as an information center where employees could find college and university brochures, professional organization packets, and HR-related forms such as education reimbursement forms and 401K material.

Providing Value to the Organization—Creating a Training Advisory Group

To provide the relevant training, it was necessary to determine the business needs and related training needs. The initial step was to conduct informal discussions with senior managers, who were also the department heads of the company's various organizations (such as production, accounting/finance, environmental and safety). Before these meetings, I reviewed their departmental business plans, which were available online and gave me information that was critical for these discussions. I also gathered data from such various sources as career guides and focus groups. I formulated a list of eight possible training areas, such as product knowledge (for example, industry trends, truck assembly, and Navistar business), manufacturing operations and processes (business planning, audit training, and so forth), and safety and environmental awareness. On a matrix, I listed each area, who might need training, whether training was a high, medium, or low priority, and the expected outcome. An example appears in table 1.

On a separate matrix, senior management and union officials rated the priority of each area for the different groups of employees in the organization.

In spite of my wish for informal discussions, the early sessions with senior managers were very formal. Some managers were taken aback by my request for an interview, perhaps because they perceived the training function more as coordination than "thought leadership." The process was an opportunity for my customers and me to get to know each other and for me to sell and market training. These exchanges produced a lot of important information that helped in developing the training plan. For example, senior managers identified individuals from their own organizations who could best represent their interests in an advisory group. From their suggestions, I recruited individuals from different departments and levels of the organization.

In 1994, the training advisory group came into being. The group consisted of frontline supervisors, a business team leader, a staff-level manager, an exempt employee, hourly workers, and union representatives. At monthly meetings, the group reported and reviewed training issues, analyzed corporate-initiated training, and assisted in change management efforts such as improving culture and communications. We spent most of our initial meetings formulating our mission statement and coming up with a name for our group—the Progressive Education Council (PEC).

The Progressive Education Council's Mission and Plan

The PEC's mission is to facilitate the training and educational development of all Navistar employees to deliver high-quality products to satisfy our customers. To accomplish this mission, the PEC's goals are to do the following:

- monitor the use of training resources
- increase employee awareness
- enhance skills development and the ability to work together more effectively
- serve constituents by gathering and disseminating training-related information
- increase the awareness of the role training plays at Navistar and assist in motivating employees to take advantage of training opportunities
- make recommendations that will address current, short-term, and long-term training needs to union and nonunion leadership.

Table 1. Training Matrix for Springfield Assembly Plant.

Training Area	Who Needs to Be Trained (Check items that apply.)						Priority High Medium Low	Expected Outcome (Check or provide information to items that apply.)		
	M	BTL	RL	TL	402	658		Awareness of Concepts Principles, and Trends?	Learn NewSkills (please specify)	Mastery of Skills (please specify)
1. Product knowledge										
—Industry tends										
—Navistar business										
—Truck assembly										
—How truck works										
—Conversion of specs										
—New product structure integration										
2. Manufacturing operations and processes										
—Lean manufacturing/enterprise										
—Business planning										
—Accounting 101										
—Shaware										
—MOST appreciation										
—AIS										
—Audit training										
—Activity-based costing										
—Budgeting										
—DFMA										
—Labor contract										
—Windows software package										

Based on our mission, we created a short-term action plan. This plan helped us to focus and enabled us to identify the critical steps necessary for achieving our goals. To collect the data we needed, we developed a process and a tool, a written multiple-choice survey for assessing both the union and nonunion employees anonymously. The survey asked employees to rate their current level of knowledge, skills, and abilities—no, basic, intermediate, or strong—in performing specific tasks and to rate the level they thought was needed for those tasks. The survey covered the following training areas:

- mission and business planning (knowledge of Navistar Business Plan; the planning process)
- management and leadership (ability to generate ideas for continuous improvement; motivate and build commitment)
- Navistar business (product line, customers, profitability, and industry trends)
- labor contract
- current issues (workplace issues such as sexual harassment and diversity)
- safety awareness
- workplace skills
- total quality/problem solving
- handling conflict and change.

The items in the survey were based on information from the initial interviews with the senior managers. Given our unique working environment, we decided that we could conduct the survey most effectively if we provided participants with a specific place and time for completing it. Survey participants were randomly selected and scheduled to report to the Training Center where they were given space and 15 to 20 minutes to complete the survey. The survey population consisted of 12.9 percent of all union employees and 34.7 percent of all nonunion employees. The data gathered were statistically analyzed at a local university. The key findings suggested that there were significant gaps in the knowledge, skills, and abilities in most of the training areas covered. It further indicated that the gap in employees' basic workplace skills tended to increase with length of service. Based on the results, the PEC developed a training plan that we presented to senior management for review and approval.

Avoiding Pitfalls in Working With an Advisory Group

A plantwide training advisory group can only be effective if empowered to be so. A pitfall to avoid when organizing such a committee would be dictating what the members can and cannot do. Giving them too many limits on how they can effectively support the training function could lead to disappointments, frustrations, and disillusionment. Our committee was a diverse group from various departments, so it was important from the beginning that everyone participate and express their expectations. Although it was natural for each participant to be concerned only about issues relevant to his or her organization, we had to focus on issues that concerned all of us if we were to succeed in developing interventions that truly addressed our common goals. We accomplished this by creating a mission statement at the outset and by brainstorming immediate goals where we had agreement. We also recognized early on that our involvement in a plantwide training advisory group was an opportunity to grow and learn by discovering new things. Members of the group also felt very strongly about setting an example of how a labor and management committee could work toward achieving a common goal.

A well-structured selection process is critical to the success of a training advisory group. This process is especially important when an organization does not perceive training as a strategic business tool and does not give much thought to who serves on a training advisory group. Membership may then consist of some ill-suited individuals who have been forced to be part of the group. Normally those individuals are weeded out as the group matures, but why wait until then when something can be done early? One way to guide the selection process and choose the best possible members is to develop a list of core characteristics and competencies. Also, you need to be willing to stand up for your selection requirements. I was elated when union officials allowed the people I had requested to become part of the PEC.

The composition of the PEC and the support of management have helped contribute to its effectiveness. Having representation from both labor and management in the committee made it more competent and made involvement a way of life rather than a statement on a poster. The continued support of management has also been critical, especially when they released people for meetings while under the constant pressure to keep building trucks. Their understanding that these meetings are as important as building trucks keeps the PEC afloat. And then there has been the commitment from each and every PEC member. We've lost some members as a result of job transfers and organizational changes, but the group has kept the faith that we do make a difference.

Having clear and constant goals can be important in maintaining momentum and helping to demonstrate success. At this time, it is difficult to evaluate the success of the PEC based on any given standards. Although we have had goals in the past, organizational changes have kept us from zeroing in on a specific target. Instead we have found ourselves focusing on an ever-moving target that has caused group members some disgruntlement and dissatisfaction. Despite this state of mind, we have made a difference in our organization simply by our very existence. We have learned to work together as Navistar employees—not as union or management representatives—with shared goals and dreams for the company.

Adding Value Through Training
Program Development

Training programs are developed in a variety of ways. The Corporate Training Department has established a personal development program for the nonunion and management group that is required to obtain 40 hours of training credit every fiscal year. The *Personal Development Catalog,* a consolidated, internal training resource of courses, assists employees in managing their own development. These programs are off-the-shelf courses that are available in various locations and use both internal corporate trainers and consultants from whom they've purchased the programs. Companies like Development Dimensions International, Kepner-Tregoe, and Franklin Covey Co. offer these courses. Nonunion employees can take advantage of off-site training for technical and other professional training needs that are not available in-house.

Specific training involving computer software applications, environmental and safety, quality, and other training areas are offered in-house using subject matter experts (SMEs) as both developers and trainers. Some programs, such as Business 101, have been designed and developed by a consulting firm through a joint, negotiated agreement between the UAW and the company. This kind of program uses the train-the-trainer approach whereby employees train both management and union on business aspects of the company.

My role in program development varies. For the development of the core curriculum, I participated in discussions to determine the best way to address our supervisors' training needs. We made decisions about whether to develop the training internally or purchase off-the-shelf training programs. Once that decision was made, we reviewed materials and processes from various vendors and selected our provider. For the assembly plant training, I take a lead role in determining how identified training needs can be best addressed (customized or off-the-shelf) by working closely with the department manager who owns the performance issue. After resources have been selected, I have continued to manage the project. For off-site training, I have reviewed proposed programs on a case-by-case basis and have recommended or rejected them based on given criteria.

Program Delivery

Typically, only the nonunion group has the opportunity to receive corporate-initiated training, which is given locally by internal trainers or external consultants. In-house SMEs train for local compliance training, such as safety and hazardous materials, as well as other process-related topics. In addition to instructor-led classroom training, we also provide video, self-study, and multimedia as options for training delivery in our on-site Interactive Learning Center (ILC) described in the next section. Initially, I selected and purchased the courseware with the assistance of our information organization. Later in the process, an ad hoc committee from the PEC helped to manage the ILC, including the selection of vendors for both equipment and courseware.

Program Evaluation and Tracking

All on-site and off-site classes as well as self-study materials (video, audio, and computer-based training) are tracked on a companywide training database (On-Track for Training). Evaluation continues to be a paper-and-pencil effort and is currently limited to participants' reaction to the training, Level 1 of Kirkpatrick's (1994) four-level evaluation model.

Success Story—The Interactive Learning Center

Like most manufacturing operations, the Springfield Assembly Plant is expected to produce a certain number of trucks and buses a day at an accepted quality ("First Time Quality"). The environment is such that frontline supervisors and middle management are expected to facilitate this process with a lot of help from the hourly workers. The pressure to do it right the first time is urgent and critical. To make this happen, on-the-job training is a top priority for everyone. But who has time to train?

Requirements for an Interactive Learning Center

Training is critical to the operation and, therefore, has to be available at all times. It should be flexible and relevant to the special needs of our aging population, be appealing to younger workers, and be adapted to an employee's level of knowledge and skills. Given these criteria, instructor-led training failed to address our urgent training needs effectively. Instead, we established the Interactive Learning Center (ILC) to provide us with the capability of delivering just-in-time training (that is, training when it is needed, not when it is convenient for trainers). Critical components were timing, flexibility of use, and a variety of options that addressed the differing training needs of a diverse group. To succeed, the ILC had to

- address the needs of most of the workforce
- be perceived as a fun way of learning a skill
- show measurable results
- be cost-effective.

Our on-site ILC, which is available to both union and nonunion employees, consists of five stand-alone computers with CD-ROM capability. The ILC provides the employees with a variety of courses such as Microsoft Office Suite, Windows 95, Spanish, keyboarding, time management, Quality Tools, QS 9000, electrical safety, and lockout/tagout.

Problems and Challenges

The idea of establishing an interactive learning center existed before I joined the company, but no one knew what the technology would be like or how it could be used effectively. CD-ROM courses had just been introduced at that time, but they were expensive and complicated to manage. A lot of research was needed to understand the hardware requirements. Our lack of knowledge and experience with interactive learning centers led to a mismatch in what we needed and what our Information Organization had provided. After we installed our newly purchased software, we had one big problem— we could not run it on our new computers. We needed to step back and review what had just happened.

Finding a Solution

The problems with the Interactive Learning Center provided the PEC with an opportunity to become a hands-on group, not just an advisory group. An ad hoc committee from the PEC looked into the issue of the ILC. Ray Starr and Tom McNicol, both from Department 65, and Arnel Manalo, a Wright State University student, banded together with me to study the hardware system that our internal Information Organization had set up earlier. The ad hoc committee met and decided to hire an outside consultant who gave us an objective analysis of our system and provided us with various solutions to our problem. After some research, we discovered that the video card in the hardware would not run the video in our multimedia courseware. Having learned from our earlier experience, the ad hoc committee became involved in reviewing the specifications for the equipment and in purchasing courseware.

Together with the consultant we hired, we were able to formulate a plan. As a first step, the technical support person assigned to the project evaluated all our current courseware to determine the systems requirements. Next, he created a list specification and sent it to the hardware group in another location whose expertise was building a system. He also shipped all of our software there for testing. When this process was done, the technical support person installed the software in our PCs. The subcommittee of the PEC made decisions about what to purchase in terms of training topics and areas, and we decided to lease some of our courseware, because it made more financial sense to do so.

When establishing a technology-driven facility like an Interactive Learning Center, an organization should have realistic expectations about how such new technology might be received by the intended user. As with any other change in the way an organization does things, new technology is likely to be met with initial skepticism and doubts. We needed to educate everyone—end users and decision makers—about the power of technology and how our organization could benefit from it.

Marketing the Learning Center

Through educational efforts like open houses, we were able to dispel the doubts, and then the Interactive Learning Center was not difficult to market. Most employees were interested in trying it out. Hourly workers, who would otherwise shun typical classroom training, have been very eager to use the ILC. Their interest stems from a growing interest in technology and a recognition that all of us need to adapt to this ever-changing environment. Many people have personal computers for home use and wanted to learn more about the technology. To publicize the ILC, we published articles about it in the weekly newsletter and sent managers e-mail messages about the opening of the ILC, which they passed on to their respective organizations. Another key reason for the ILC's popularity has been the support from the PEC. Members of the PEC became the ILC's leading advocates by spreading the word to their respective organizations. The face-to-face interaction turned out to be the most effective marketing tool.

Evaluating Success

The Interactive Learning Center's success has been easy to observe. The ILC gave us the ability to offer an alternative method for learning. It addressed our need for just-in-time training and our workforce's need to learn a skill set on its own, at its own pace and time. Currently, 75 percent of the employees who use the ILC do so to learn computer basics and the specific skills in Microsoft Office Suite. Another 10 percent uses QS 9000, Spanish, and Quality Tools. The ILC serves as a testimony to effective training using technology. It challenges people's paradigm of training and is a way of introducing our workforce to the future. Our success lies in the people who use the ILC. More and more employees are seeking us out, realizing their need to learn specific skills. They now recognize that the ILC enables them to manage their own learning.

Lessons Learned

The key to my success as a lone trainer has been the involvement of the right people—getting them engaged so that they own the solution and are accountable for results. When I came to Navistar, I had expertise in training and development but knew nothing about the company's operations. Success was only possible by asking a lot of questions—about people's vision, where they wanted to take the facility in the next few years, and whether they would participate—in order for me to understand the organization and the issues that training might be able to address. Through listening, observing, and being objective, it was possible to understand the people and the processes and to establish an honest, open relationship.

Technology helps to keep the communication open. Our voice mail system reminds participants of scheduled classes, the network common drive posts class schedules, and e-mail sends messages about training. Various forms and templates enable employees to send information about training via the network, fax, or e-mail. The ILC is the best example of providing our employees with just-in-time technology-based training.

My experience as a lone trainer has been significant and profound, adding substance and value to my once academic view of training and development. Over time, I have learned to draw upon internal and external resources, to establish partnerships with various organizations, individuals, and my professional organization, and to keep a database of internal and external SMEs.

What would I do differently in the future? I would establish more structure to the training advisory group to allow them access to both union and management leadership. I would schedule dialogues between PEC and the plant leadership to make the PEC more visible so it could support organizational goals more effectively. Although communication is imperative among the members of the committee, it is even more important for them to communicate with the people we want to serve.

Questions for Discussion

1. What challenges did the training coordinator face as a lone trainer?
2. What steps did the training coordinator take to overcome those challenges?
3. Describe the needs assessment approach.
4. What are the pitfalls to avoid when organizing a training advisory group?
5. How could an Interactive Learning Center benefit your organization?

The Author

Raquel Fornoles Arnold is currently the training coordinator of Navistar's Springfield Assembly Plant. She received her B.A. from the University of the Philippines in sociology and completed her M.A. in training and development from Wright State University in Dayton, Ohio. She has almost 12 years of full-time professional work experience in training and development in public and private sectors. Arnold is a member of the American Society for Training & Development and the International Society for Performance Instruction. She came to the United States to join her husband, a former Peace Corps volunteer in the Philippines, 12 years ago. More recently, she worked at Mead Data Central (now Lexis Nexis) and NCR as an intern and as a training specialist at YUSA Corporation, a Tier One supplier of Honda of America Manufacturing. She can be contacted at 6128 Sonia Circle, Dayton, Ohio 45449; phone: 937.438.1735; e-mail: Storm78@worldnet.att.net.

Reference

Kirkpatrick, D.L. (1994). *Evaluating Training Programs*. San Francisco: Berrett-Koehler.

Zen and the Art of Motorcycle Technician Training

Millar Farewell

This case is a good example of how a small training shop provides techni-cal training to a widely dispersed target audience of Honda Motorcycle deal-er technicians. Farewell explains how training at American Honda has evolved over time. In its heyday the department had over 14 training resources, but now it has to provide value-added training with a staff of three people. The case reveals how Farewell worked with an outside consultant to provide deal-er technicians with training to help them solve the challenging, though in-frequent, electrical problems that they must resolve to keep customers happy.

Company Background

American Honda Motor Company is a wholly owned distribution subsidiary of Honda Motor Company. Started in 1959 in Los Ange-les, the company grew rapidly through the 1960s and 1970s as Amer-ica fell in love with motorcycles. In the 1970s, the expansion of power equipment sales and the introduction of the Civic, Accord, and oth-er automobile models fueled even more growth. Today American Hon-da has 4,770 employees in 30 locations. The Motorcycle Division has over 1,100 motorcycle dealers nationally with 3,300 employees work-ing in service-related activities. A sister company, Honda of Ameri-ca Manufacturing, has 11,500 associates in six different factory locations in Ohio and has announced construction of a new all-ter-rain vehicle (ATV) factory in South Carolina in June 1996.

This case was prepared to serve as a basis for discussion rather than to illustrate either effective or in-effective administrative and management practices.

Growth has not always been steady. During the 1980s, the motorcycle market shrank to 30 percent of its previous size as a result of the availability of other leisure products, such as personal watercraft, and a weakened dollar against the Japanese yen, which increased prices. This drastic decrease in sales caused management to downsize the Motorcycle Division, including the Motorcycle Service Training Department when 10 of its 12 instructors were redeployed, as were its full-time instructional designers. This case examines how this three person Training Department provides technical training to Honda motorcycle dealer technicians.

Mission of Motorcycle Technical Training

The purpose of the Motorcycle Technical Training Department is to train dealership technicians in the maintenance, repair, and diagnosis of Honda motorcycle products in order to provide our customers with enjoyable, trouble-free operation of their Hondas. Our students are employees of franchised Honda motorcycle, ATV, and scooter dealers. Our training courses cover all aspects of service and repair of our products. To understand how we operate today, it is helpful to understand a bit of the history of motorcycle technical training at American Honda.

Training Department Historical Overview

As far back as the mid-1960s, American Honda was conducting technical training for its motorcycle dealer technicians. The original driving force for training dealer technicians was to reduce warranty costs by improving dealership technicians' skills at repairing customers' motorcycles. The training conducted in Training Centers was hands-on with a focus on developing critical skills in the technician workforce. In one-day Update Clinics held in large cities for dealer technicians in those area, they received information-based training about new technology for new models. The training department developed and delivered training for use in the dealerships through filmstrip and cassette programs that were supplied to dealers on a subscription basis. These were later moved to videotaped programs. The training at that time was based on the motorcycle line up with classes related to single-, twin-, and four-cylinder models. As a result, training changed quickly as models changed.

During the late 1970s, training was changed to a subject-based format with two weeks of training on routine maintenance followed by one-week courses on each of five advanced subjects: chassis and suspension service, electrical service, engine service, fuel and induction service, and machine shop techniques. Subject-based training provided a structure that accommodated changes in technology without necessitating changing a complete course. In the early 1980s, we began to change the curriculum to a modular format based on performance objectives.

Training's Evolution in the 1980s and 1990s

I arrived at American Honda on June 1, 1982, as an instructional designer, having left my previous job with Honda Canada the day before. My background was rooted in Honda motorcycles and everything technical to do with them. I have worked at three different Honda distributors in Canada and the United States. Having taught my first technical class in 1969, I came to American Honda as a subject matter expert with some training experience. I was amazed at the immensity of American Honda. Here entire departments performed the work that one or two people would have done part-time at Honda Canada. In my new job, I worked full-time developing training materials, whereas previously I had done this type of work one or two months of the year.

When I joined the company, the Motorcycle Section of the Training Department had 12 instructors, two instructional designers, and a training administrator who managed the in-dealership training program. Classes were taught in six Training Centers that were located at regional parts warehouses or in the same building as regional offices for motorcycle field service staff. The instructors in each Training Center reported to the regional service manager as did the district service managers. All of the instructional staff were part of the Motorcycle Field Service Department. The instructional designers and program administrator were part of the Service Communications Department in the national headquarters at Gardena, California. A similar field structure existed in the Automobile Division.

During the mid-1980s, we discovered and embraced the criterion-referenced instruction methodology of Robert Mager (1992, 1997). We modularized our entire curriculum in both motorcycle and auto technician training and named our new training method Individualized Skills Training. American Honda built seven new Training Centers that were designed to accommodate our new competency-based training methods. Each center included a centrally located student resource room with windows that allowed an instructor in any of the three learning areas to observe students in the resource room. This resource room contained individual stations where students could watch videotaped lectures and demonstrations.

By 1992, after a 70 percent drop in sales and significant reductions in staff, the Motorcycle Training Department consisted of two instructors, a program administrator (who develops the video-based training), and a supervisor. Training was conducted in five locations—California, Texas, Georgia, New Jersey, and Ohio—by the two remaining instructors and myself, now the assistant manager of motorcycle service training. (See figure 1.) The West Coast instructor was based in Torrance, California, and the East Coast instructor was in Atlanta. In addition to teaching at their base Training Centers, the two instructors flew into unstaffed Training Centers and taught for two-week periods.

Today, technician training is individualized with videotaped information and demonstration segments and with a modular format that allows us to track student progress by module. Computerized training records provide employment and training records for all dealer employees. The training season starts in September and ends in March with one-week sessions that are self-paced and open-ended. The summer, a peak sales period, is used to revise and develop training materials.

Challenges and Opportunities

Since my arrival at American Honda, I have studied and learned the craft of instructional design. As an instructional designer, I started out by working on Full-Cycle filmstrip programs, a series of programs used in dealership training. I learned to read scripts, including

Figure 1. Organization of motorcycle service training.

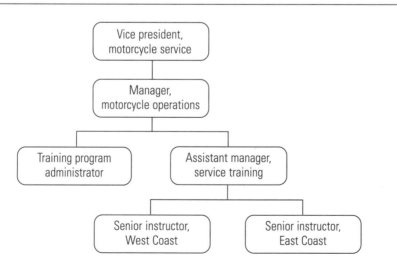

the visuals, and edit for correct technical and learning content. Since then, I have developed two of the courses in our curriculum and edited much of a third. I have taught all of the subjects related to motorcycle service, and I enjoy teaching the electrical subject the most. Many technicians don't initially get involved with the subject of electrical systems. Most are hands-on people who can figure out the mechanical parts of the motorcycle, but get intimidated by the electrical systems. After learning about electrical systems, I found great joy in teaching the subject to others. Watching a class of technicians move from being quiet, fearful, and nervous to being excited and confident provides great satisfaction.

When I was a new instructional designer, I was surprised to find that the materials students received during training to be motorcycle technicians were worksheets that instructors developed together with photocopied pages out of manuals and bulletins. The materials were not consistent from one Training Center to the next because instructors received outlines that they each fleshed out as they saw fit.

In 1983, I started work on developing a new standardized chassis and suspension course. I traveled to different Training Centers, where I watched, listened, and obtained copies of various student materials. In the office, I sifted through the material looking for content common to all areas. I developed a new course with separate modules for each of the skills needed to perform the tasks that we had identified from a repair order analysis completed a few years previously. The new course had 20 modules in six sections. It included an instructor's outline with overhead transparencies and a presenter's guide. The instructor would lecture for one or two hours each morning, and then the students would practice and learn the activities during the rest of the day. The instructor would coach and advise students as needed. When each student had completed the module, the instructor would ask questions to confirm that the student had learned what was intended. There were no written tests for the simple reason that we wanted technicians who could do the hands-on work, not write an essay. Because our instructors were not used to lecturing from someone else's notes, I had to cajole them and revise the presentation until all of the instructors were comfortable using it. As a result, we had our first self-paced, competency-based modular course—chassis and suspension.

In 1988, I was promoted to assistant manager of motorcycle service training. Our last full-time instructional designer left the department in the spring of 1991. By 1992, our curriculum had become outdated in some areas; it was the victim of too many projects, too little time, and a shrinking staff. Most modules had been written many years before, and in some cases referenced motorcycles that were no longer even in production. Presenting courses consumed most of our time and energies. Our department had only five months during each spring and summer to revise and develop training materials. During this time, our management understood that three people could provide only a minimal training presence. We had many modules to improve and little time in which to do it. We prioritized each module by the severity of revisions needed and listed them. From this we determined that our Electrical Service course was the first choice for revision.

Needs Assessment and Program Development

In the past we have assessed training needs in the following ways: We have surveyed technicians, service managers, district service managers, and dealers for information about which skills to include in training. We have reviewed the type of questions our Technical Help Desk received from dealers and the quantity of warranty claims received for the subject being researched. We have also reviewed repair orders in dealerships to determine what tasks are being performed by technicians. As a former motorcycle technician, I use my own experience to evaluate the data collected.

Our program development is split into two parts—initial development and maintenance. The initial development was done in the early and mid-1980s when we changed our basic curriculum structure from lecture and group-paced training to modular self-paced training. All of our training curriculum development was done in-house with vendor assistance for production of final printed materials and production of video support materials. Maintenance of that curriculum has occupied our time since then. As new technology is added to the products, such as computerized fuel injection, the Training Department reviews it for new maintenance and repair skills. When new skills are identified, the Training Department evaluates the existing training to see if the new skills can be taught by revising an existing module or by writing a new one. The shift from analog to digital multimeter, for example, led to a new module. In some cases, we have revised an entire subject course. The Electrical Service course is a good example of this.

Program Delivery

There is minimal classroom training in delivery of technical training. Instructors serve as coaches who provide individualized guidance and evaluation. As mentioned above, all of our training is self-paced and modular. Training sessions are conducted in one-week periods because a typical student can complete each topic in that time. Students who complete all of the material in less then a week can either continue with modules from another subject or leave early. Those who do not complete all of the material in a week can return and complete the remaining modules during a later training session. Because we track completion by module, we can measure student progress by module completion rather then by course completion.

Students learn by reading student notes in each module, watching videotaped information, and practicing repairs on real motorcycles with standard problems. Where a demonstration or lecture is needed, they are recorded on videotape. Students simply walk across the hall to the Resource Center, find the appropriate tape, and watch it at one of the viewing carrels. In a few situations where video support has not yet been developed, instructors present one- to two-hour lectures in the morning. After this, students work at the workstations set up around the learning area. It is normal to see 10 students all working on different modules during a session. This has a significant benefit because we can teach a session without having to provide 10 of each part, engine or motorcycle.

A typical session starts on Monday morning, with introductions, an overview, and walk-around explanation of the learning area taking the first two hours. We then assign students a starting module, and they begin by reading the module and watching a video segment before proceeding to the workstation and starting the practice activity. During practice, students call the instructor to check their progress whenever a progress check is indicated. At the completion of the module, the instructor reviews any written answers to questions and asks a few questions to confirm that the student has understood the material and completed the activity correctly. The instructor then initials the student's course map, and the student proceeds to the next available module.

Success Story
Business Need

Let's look at the development of one program, our Electrical Service course, which met a critical business need. General industry perception is that electrical troubleshooting is complicated and not generally done well by the technicians in dealerships. Our needs analysis confirmed this. Poor electrical troubleshooting skills can cause the dealers' service department lost profits from incorrect repairs, lost credibility, and lost customers. To be successful this course had to change nonperforming technicians into successful electrical troubleshooters who could repair electrical problems correctly the first time. Their successful performance would be evident to the technicians, their supervisors, and their employers. Comments from these people would be reported by our field staff of district service managers to our management. Comments in quarterly reports from district service managers who have taken the course would also communicate the success of this training to management.

The Electrical Service course was a continuing sore point for instructors and students alike. It did not build the skills and knowledge of students in a smooth process. The modules had dense pages of text that were hard to read, and an audience with poor reading skills found them difficult to understand. Some explanations were unclear, and the modules were not smoothly integrated. After a detailed review of our curriculum in 1992, we decided to revise the course. It was obvious that we would need outside help to accomplish what we wanted to do.

I found the help we needed when I attended a three-day workshop titled Training Applications for Cognitive Psychology that Ruth Clark presented in the summer of 1992. I was impressed both with the workshop and with Clark who had just started a consulting company, Clark Training and Consulting. (See Clark, 1995, for more on her approach to technical training.) We discussed a project to conduct a needs analysis for a new electrical service course. Within a few days of returning home, I met with Steve Hayward of Clark Training and Consulting, and we ironed out a few more of the details. I was heartened and reassured to learn that he had ridden a motorcycle in his youth because some knowledge of motorcycles would be helpful in developing our training. The needs analysis proceeded well and was completed in two months. A second project followed to develop the training from the needs analysis.

Assessing the Need for Training

In the needs analysis, Steve Hayward and I looked at data from our dealer technical help-desk records. As part of our needs assessment for the course in electrical troubleshooting, we evaluated repair orders at dealerships and reviewed technical help-desk records for the quantity and content of phone calls related to electrical questions from dealer technicians. From a survey we sent to dealer service managers a few years earlier, we knew that they were very interested in improving their technicians' electrical troubleshooting skills. We found that even though all electrical repairs totaled only 7 percent of the total repair orders written, electrical problems represented 15 percent of the total help-desk call load.

The findings confirmed a long-held hunch that electrical problems were infrequent, minimizing the opportunities to practice troubleshooting skills. When electrical repairs were needed, technicians frequently had difficulty finding the cause of the problem and repairing it. This assessment was born out by our field service staff who dealt with this kind of problem every day in their visits to dealers. Further study showed that technicians had difficulty troubleshooting the charging, ignition, lighting, and accessory systems. From our interviews with technicians, we also uncovered some misconceptions and misinformation about the basics of how electricity works.

We also conducted one videotaped protocol analysis with a technician who had recently completed the existing course. In this analysis, we had the technician troubleshoot a motorcycle with an electrical problem. We asked the technician to think out loud as he went through the process of troubleshooting. We videotaped the process with questions to draw out how he was thinking whenever he stopped talking. This helped to pinpoint some of the cognitive strategies used during troubleshooting.

Program Development and Delivery

Steve Hayward wrote the Electrical Troubleshooting course with input from both of our instructors and me. To make the materials readable and easy to use, he used Information Mapping®, a structured-writing process devised by the company of the same name in Waltham, Massachusetts. The instructors and I reviewed the drafts. Together with the student materials, Hayward developed and tested support materials. Revisions were made and retried in course materials and support materials.

In February 1993, I tested an early version of the new Electrical Troubleshooting course at our Training Center in Irving, Texas. Our formative evaluation after that test found several areas that needed improvement. Hayward made the improvements and delivered the course to us in the summer of 1993. As our fall training season approached, we prepared to test the new course in several of our Training Centers with myself and both of the instructors as facilitators. Our first class in Troy, Ohio, went well. The students learned the material easily, and many of them left the class excited at their newfound talents. Student reviews were good, and we began to feel that the course was out of the woods.

We continued to present the course in other locations. Ken Watts, our East Coast instructor, observed a class at our Moorestown, New Jersey, Training Center, where several weaknesses in the materials became clear. We reviewed the materials and looked for ways to improve them. During the Christmas holiday, I revised many of the modules in the course to improve their performance. We tested again and found that it still wasn't right, although many of the problems had been corrected. We continued to present the course, each time learning valuable new ways to make the materials work more smoothly and with greater success. The following summer, we created three video segments to replace some of the class lectures. Additional video segments will be produced to complement the remainder of the course.

Marketing and Program Evaluation

Our training in general is marketed through a printed training schedule that is sent to the dealers in midsummer before the start of the winter training season. We gave the Electrical Service course a new name and identified it as a new course to bring its revised status to the attention of our training customers. Word-of-mouth advertising from our district service managers who had attended the course and promoted it to their dealers helped to boost attendance.

We evaluated the course through postsession Level 1 evaluations. We surveyed the students for their comments on the applicability of the material learned to on-the-job performance, difficulty of material, and overall rating of the course. In a separate evaluation, the students rated their instructors.

Our district service managers reported that students and service managers praised the course and the value of the skills learned. Returning students described their experiences of using the skills they learned in the class to diagnose electrical system failures on the job. They talked about making more money by working smarter rather then harder. In the fall of 1993, I was observing a class and asked one of my former electrical troubleshooting students how his training had worked for him. He responded: "Well, when I got home, I practiced some of the things we learned in class like you suggested, and this summer I pretty much cut my troubleshooting time in half." Here was an experienced technician with 10 years in the trade who had come to Honda school to get certified and in the process learned how to do the job better. I was very pleased.

Key Success Factors

Ruth Clark and Steve Hayward brought a fresh objective viewpoint and good research skills to the needs analysis. Their careful analysis of the needs analysis material resulted in accurate objectives. Their strong instructional design talents produced training that leads the student through the material smoothly and easily. The use of information mapping structure in the written materials helped to improve the readability of the material. A strong relationship among our instructors, Steve Hayward, and me resulted in clear communication and faster development. Our tireless team of instructors who were willing to validate, review, and revise materials was a major factor in our success.

In this course, we changed the way students received feedback on their performance. Instead of having the instructor review each question in the module for a correct answer, we made up feedback sheets that contained the answers to most of the questions. The instructor checked the answers to the last few questions. This system reduced the instructor's interaction time for all sign-off interviews, thereby reducing the amount of time students had to wait and giving more time for individual coaching of students who needed it.

Lessons Learned

This project has taught me that small teams with the right combination of talents can complete major projects. It takes time and dedication, but it can be done. I would undertake similar projects in the future with more awareness that they are large and will take time. I would expect that other projects and duties would intrude constantly and cause the pace of development to be slower then I would like. To handle the work better, I would build a plan with many small segments and would revise the plan when other projects or activities cause delays.

Following are some of my insights based on this project:
- Vendors can amplify your talents and time. Find a good vendor with the right skills who will listen carefully and change what needs to be changed when you ask. When choosing a vendor, look at the experiences of individuals as well as the costs. Trust your instincts about whom you can work well with.

- Build a dedicated team with a common vision that is willing to keep at it even when the end is not in sight.
- Validate, revise, revalidate, and revise again. Keep doing this until it works.
- Find ways to celebrate finished segments and keep the project moving toward completion.

Questions for Discussion

1. Given a technician population of 3,000 to 3,500 people at 1,200 dealerships located throughout the United States, how would you train them if each of the dealerships has a video player available? How would you train them if each dealership has a video player and a computer connected to a Honda intranet?
2. How would you have chosen and prioritized the training for revision?
3. What criteria would you have used and why?
4. If you were the outside vendor, how would you approach this project?
5. If you worked in this department, how would you increase management's support for the department's work?

The Author

Millar Farewell first started working for a Honda-related company in 1967 in Vancouver, Canada. He has worked as a technician, district service manager, instructor and instructional designer in addition to his present position as assistant manager of the Motorcycle Service Education Department at American Honda Motor Company. He has worked in the Training Department at American Honda for 16 years. During this time, he has developed numerous training programs in print, filmstrip, and video. Farewell has a B.S. in business administration from National University and an M.S. in instructional technology from Rochester Institute of Technology. He rides a motorcycle everyday. He can be contacted at 6009 Pearce Avenue, Lakewood, CA 90712-1308; phone: 562.866.5613.

References

Clark, Ruth C. (1995). *Developing Technical Training*. Phoenix, AZ: Performance Technology Press.

Mager, Robert F. (1992). *Troubleshooting the Troubleshooting Course*. Belmont, CA: Pitman Learning.

Mager, Robert F. (1997). *Making Instruction Work*. Atlanta: Center for Effective Performance.

The Technical Trainer: Organizational Effectiveness Through Partnership and Learning

Nortel Corporation

Randy Maxwell and Karen L. Jost

This case is an excellent example of using partnerships with external consultants and with internal suppliers in a high-tech company to develop and deliver a solution to meet the training need to keep up with emerging technologies in telecommunications. The case illustrates the use of a variety of needs assessment techniques and alternative delivery methods, and it evaluates the impact of training at several different levels. Randy Maxwell, who is now with Nortel's Learning Institute in Alpharetta, Georgia, was the senior technical training specialist at Nortel's Atlanta Broadband Research and Development Lab at the time of this case. He continues to enjoy a professional relationship with his former dissertation advisor, Karen Jost, by jointly authoring papers.

Industry and Organizational Background

Telecommunications is rapidly becoming a deregulated, multi-vendor, competitive industry, in sharp contrast to the traditional monopoly network model that prevailed during Nortel's first century. Recently the industry has experienced major changes as a result of new emerging technologies, deregulation, and global competition. New forms of communications technologies and increased marketplace demand have fueled organizational and technological changes and have altered the missions of telecommunications companies. Over time, the industry's role has shifted and grown from being a suppli-

This case was prepared to serve as a basis for discussion rather than to illustrate either effective or ineffective administrative and management practices.

er of equipment to being a provider of network solutions to global customers. This communications environment could be described as a World of Networks.

With headquarters near Toronto, Canada, Nortel is a global telecommunications corporation with an internal network connecting more than 200 locations. The company has over 68,000 employees worldwide with key locations in Canada, the United States, and the United Kingdom. Nortel's mission is to develop market leadership in telecommunications through customer satisfaction, superior value, and product excellence. Success in this environment requires a network of dispersed management teams and operations. This network allows workers to exchange files, to have conferences with colleagues worldwide, and to access tools, databases, and other global resources, by supporting the exchange of voice, data, and video images. John Roth, the current CEO, has set collaboration as a major business objective, and the company culture emphasizes collaboration and empowerment. Collaboration occurs internally with departments and sites and externally as joint ventures with other companies.

Nortel is organized into four units—Broadband Networks, Enterprise Networks, Public Carrier Networks, and Wireless Networks—with the following focuses:

- Broadband Networks focus on products that transport voice, data, image, and video between locations within cities or between cities, countries, and continents.
- Enterprise Networks focus primarily on private digital switching systems, usually located in the customer's premises, which permit voice, data, or multimedia terminals to communicate with each other.
- Public Carrier Networks focus on products that telecommunications operating companies use to interconnect access lines and transmission facilities to provide local or long distance services.
- Wireless Networks focus on products that service providers use to address the mobile and fixed-wireless communications markets.

Broadband business units are located in Atlanta; in Richardson, Texas; and in Ottawa and Montreal, Canada. This case focuses on technical training for the Atlanta Broadband Business Unit, specifically its Research and Development Unit ("the lab"), which consists of 350 people. At the time of this case, the culture of Atlanta's lab was shifting—it was starting to focus on people development and employee satisfaction in addition to achieving business goals. This was a period of tremendous change in addressing different customers. For example, part of the Atlanta lab formed a joint venture with a cable distributor during this time.

Technical Training at Nortel

Nortel's major training functions include corporate human resource development, customer technical education, sales and marketing, and internal technical training for the research and development locations. At the corporate level is Nortel's Learning Institute, a global organization composed of approximately 60 people worldwide, which focuses on human resource development and organizational development and provides performance consulting for the business units. Training departments within the business units provide most of the technical training locally. Technical Training, an autonomous group within the Broadband Business Unit, is part of a network of internal technical training groups.

Atlanta Broadband Technical Training, which has responsibility for both technical training and human resource development, has been in existence since the lab's formation about eight years before this case study. Training is part of the Strategic Information Development Department, which also includes the Learning Resource Center and WEB Development. These areas are grouped to efficiently provide technical information, such as technical specifications, product knowledge, and competitive analysis information, as needed.

The manager of the Strategic Information Development Department allocates half of her time to training and assists with budgets, decision making, and course delivery. An administrative specialist, who takes care of training registration and logistics, is shared by the Training Department and the Information Resource Center. The only full-time employee in the Training Department is the senior technical training specialist whose duties include project management, analysis, instructional design, evaluation, and course delivery. In the Atlanta Broadband Research and Development Unit, this position receives support from the Strategic Information Development Department, the Nortel Learning Institute, and a technical training network and its subgroups (for example, the interactive distance learning team).

The entire Strategic Information Development Department developed the department's mission, which said, "To increase organizational and individual effectiveness by providing customer focused and cost effective learning environments and information services in a continuously changing, competitive business."

The department members decided that it was important to specify the link between services and organizational effectiveness and to use the term learning environments. Over time, the technical training specialist's job evolved to facilitating the design of environments where learning can take place.

Challenges and Opportunities

As with all small training departments, the major challenges were the limited resources in budget and dedicated staff. Another major challenge involved a change in the role of training from coordination to performance improvement. Traditionally at Nortel, support functions, such as information technology, purchasing, quality assurance, and training, had been budgeted and classified as overhead. Organizational changes led to a new emphasis throughout the company on proving the value-added contributions of all support functions. In addition, competitive pressures led to a need for shortened product cycle times, which created an associated demand for improved employee performance. To help meet this need, the role of training evolved to performance improvement.

The training priorities involved both technical training and human resource development. The recent shift to wireless technologies and Internet applications created an urgent demand for employees to understand emerging technologies and how to adapt Nortel's current product portfolio to fit these new market applications. In terms of human resource development, workers needed to be able to excel independently and also be able to work together interdependently in cross-functional teams. The idea of networking applied to the products the employees developed as well as to how they accomplished these networked solutions. The department also faced challenges of relatively low employee satisfaction and high turnover. Employee attitudinal surveys indicated that employees were only moderately satisfied with training and that they were dissatisfied if they were not being kept technically current with their jobs. Training had to address these areas by ensuring that employees' knowledge was kept current and by providing learning environments to address employee satisfaction and performance issues.

Although there were challenges associated with being the lone trainer, the position also brought excitement. The training specialist relied on his experience base in engineering and project management in the company to accomplish the Training Department's goals. Being the lone trainer brought a large degree of autonomy, which made the job more exciting than being a specialist in a large department. As some of the performance and employee satisfaction goals were accomplished, the feelings and perceptions of both the trainers and their clients changed. As part of that change, they developed more trust in each other.

Providing Value to the Organization—Approach to Needs Assessment

Several techniques, both formal and informal, were used to determine business needs, related training needs, priorities, and deliverables. First, the Training Department established a Training Advisory Board, consisting of senior managers in the lab, representing software and hardware engineering, and Human Resources. Its initial focus was to prioritize training needs. Second, the training specialist attended managers' staff meetings to identify training needs, and possible instructional delivery approaches. Third, employees throughout the company communicated their training via the company's internal e-mail system.

A fourth approach in assessing needs involved the development and analysis of training profiles. ISO 9001 quality-initiative compliance required that there be job-profile development plans for each employee, with a training plan for accomplishing that development. The Training Department created a template on which each functional group described its jobs, and then the department summarized the training profiles for each group. The department used these data to identify training needs and develop an overall training plan for the year. As the identified training was implemented, a partnership between training and line managers began to develop. As new projects began, managers learned to communicate performance needs, and the Training Department gradually gained credibility as training helped to improve job performance. Finally, the training specialist found that facilitating classes provided an effective informal way to assess training needs. As a facilitator, he could interact with others in the lab, identify training needs, and record ideas for training in a notebook during classes.

Program Development

Program development involved a variety of approaches depending on an assessment of the specific business need and including internal experts as well as external consultants. Program development methods included a tutor program, mentoring and on-the-job training, and the use of suppliers and outside consultants.

The tutor program was one of the most successful and cost-effective methods for sharing technical knowledge on software tools and organizational procedures. This program used 25 internal subject matter experts who were willing to conduct classes internally. The content of these courses included UNIX applications, C-programming, programming library systems, software tracking tools for product development, and courses in the developed products emphasizing newly developed features and systems interfaces. The lab director rewarded and recognized the tutors quarterly. The training specialist's role in the tutor process was to identify subject matter experts who matched performance needs of the business unit, to encourage them to participate in the program, and to work with them in designing the course.

Mentoring and on-the-job training were additional approaches to provide training in these content areas. New employees were often paired with mentors to provide them with the necessary initial training to become proficient. The technical training specialist identified mentors and subject matter experts.

Suppliers, both internal and external to the corporation, developed both technical and human resource development programs, which were not merely purchased off-the-shelf but were often customized for the lab. A key strategy was developing effective partnerships. For example, the training specialist worked together with the lab's Purchasing Department to select programs, and they worked closely with suppliers to customize content and delivery, while negotiating a cost-effective solution. They examined all cost factors to determine if the training specialist could use his skills to reduce certain cost elements. The training specialist played a vital role in customization to transform learning events into effective performance interventions. An important step in this process was to identify business and individual needs proactively as well as reactively. Often, suppliers' typical courses did not meet urgent needs, and customization was required to develop in-house versions of these courses. A good example of this was the redesign of an emerging telecommunications course to include content that was relevant to product development in the broadband group. In another instance, the training specialist worked with a supplier to put together a project management course that was customized to address specific Broadband Business Unit development processes.

Because training by suppliers and outside consultants is costly, the training specialist worked closely with employees and their managers to determine the right participants for training. The main determining factor in identifying participants for training was whether training was essential to their job performance; secondary factors were employee development and satisfaction. To spread the newly acquired knowledge and achieve a degree of organizational learning, course participants often took part in "lunch-and-learns" and developed their own internal tutor-led courses. This approach reinforced their learning, enhanced their development, and resulted in more effective use of training dollars and resources.

In program development, the training specialist acted as a broker and created learning environments for knowledge to be shared. Being a broker is an essential role for any lone trainer and partnership and collaboration are key to its success. This role involved bringing together all the necessary players and providing the interaction required to optimize the contribution of each function. The training specialist's design expertise was also put to use with suppliers and consultants in customizing both content and delivery of courses. The combination of program development techniques provided a savings of $400,000 over the cost of off-the-shelf training. As the training specialist's credibility grew, all levels of the organization consulted him for job-related and individual-development training.

Program Delivery—Taking Advantage of Technology

Nortel uses a variety of delivery methods including traditional classroom training and alternative delivery methods. The Training Department based its delivery decisions for the Broadband Research and Development Unit on a combination of factors. First, once performance issues were translated into training goals, it designed programs to use delivery methods that met the type of learning that needed to occur. A second determining factor was the technological capability of the learning environment, including what was possible through partnering with other areas. The third factor was cost.

The high-tech environment and culture of this telecommunications company contributed to a willingness of employees to try alternative forms of instructional delivery. The delivery formats included self-paced instruction books, video- and audiotaped programs, interactive distance learning, computer-based training, and Web-based instruction. Participant feedback indicated that most people preferred a combination of traditional instructor-led approaches with hands-on methods. The Information Resource Center provided alternative self-directed learning in the form of paper-based tutorials, video- and audiotapes, and computer-based training (CBT). To minimize class time, some of the technical product overview courses used a combination of self-directed instruction books, CBT, and instructor-led training. At times, the instructor-led training incorporated seminar and action learning instructional strategies.

As a telecommunications company, Nortel is well positioned to make use of technology to support training. Most of Nortel's sites possess videoconferencing equipment. Nortel's trainers from across all lines of business are part of a technical training network. The technical training specialist was a member of this network as well as of the interactive distance learning (IDL) team, a subgroup of this technical training network. The training specialist's participation in this network helped to form relationships that allowed the lab to take advantage of interactive distance learning and global computer-based training initiatives. The team developed ways to add satellite equipment with tandem arrangements to other sites to minimize equipment costs. Through the IDL team, the training specialist brought in programs that were broadcast to most of the Nortel sites, in areas such as emerging technologies and software programming languages.

A parallel corporate team existed for global agreements on computer-based training. The team developed technical methods to deliver CBT to the desktop using a variety of hardware platforms. An example of a method involved using the computing network and conversion software to emulate Windows interfaces on UNIX platforms. The CBT courses were also delivered by laptop computers that were available on loan from the Information Resource Center.

The company's intranet became an instructional medium by which to deliver learning products to employees because of the different types of computer hardware and software systems in use. Nortel's intranet has been used as a repository of information, similar to an electronic encyclopedia. One application to training has been to provide a vehicle for course descriptions and registration. An additional and more recent application has been in providing training curriculum tracking for individual development to meet ISO 9001 compliance. This application led to using the Web to gather needs assessment data. Future applications will include using the Web to provide instruction via distributed course delivery, with participants using the intranet for dialogues and problem solving.

Program Evaluation and Tracking

Determining training effectiveness was a major objective for the Strategic Information Development Department. It viewed evaluation as an important component of performance improvement and served several important functions. Evaluation provided the means to communicate to senior management the business impact of training. It helped to determine the priority focus for training and identify areas for continuous improvement. Also, it served as a critical tool to market future programs and build sponsorship for training.

The evaluation model followed the Kirkpatrick (1994) model, in which Level 1 was participant reaction; Level 2, learning; Level 3, behavior; and Level 4, business results. The Training Department adapted the evaluation model to include the Phillips' (1991) Level 5, return-on-investment (ROI) calculation, which takes into account program costs in addition to benefits. The ROI calculation proved especially useful in communicating training effectiveness to senior management. It converted benefits into a language they understood. Evaluation of training, particularly to Level 5, was time intensive and therefore costly. Consequently, the strategy to implement the evaluation model was to evaluate 100 percent of the training at Level 1; 20 percent of the training at Level 2; and 5 percent of the training at Levels 3, 4, and 5. Evaluation at Levels 3 to 5 included the high-dollar course interventions. This implementation strategy focused on providing feedback for continuous improvement and communicating the business impact for most of the training dollars spent, while optimizing the limited resources in collecting data.

The Training Department used a variety of methods to measure the Levels 3 to 5 evaluations. The training specialist conducted brief interviews with participants 30 days after a training intervention. He asked them if they had received the information they needed, if they had used the knowledge gained from the training, and how they had applied it to their jobs. The answers were stated in terms of the time it would normally take them to develop the skill or knowledge by research on their own without the training. He then converted the time to dollars using loaded financial labor rates, which give the cost per person including salary, benefits, and infrastructure. The interview responses were placed on a spreadsheet and benefits were calculated. Other methods that the training specialist used to calculate benefits included recorded development cycle time, software defects, and test yields on resulting hardware development. Data for these measurements were captured from online databases in the corporation. The key in these types of calculations was to determine a percentage contribution that was the result of the training.

At training advisory review meetings involving senior management, the Training Department communicated the evaluation results, and priorities and commitments to training programs were established. Senior management also obtained a clear view of the Training Department's contribution, which allowed it to move forward. The evaluation strategy served as a marketing tool for the training function.

Success Story
Business Need and Challenge

One of the most successful training interventions of the Broadband Technical Training Group was training in emerging telecommunications technologies through a series of mini-interventions implemented throughout the year. Because Nortel had evolved from a company providing product solutions to one providing network solutions, the emphasis on evolving telecommunications technology was critical. The customer base had changed from telephone companies set up with a cable infrastructure to include cable companies planning to provide telephone service. Before the training intervention, surveys had indicated low employee satisfaction with Nortel and low satisfaction with training because technical employees could not keep up-to-date with the latest information in their fields of engineering. In terms of job performance, employees were initially required to research these emerging technologies in order to design and test product designs, using equipment that was new to them. This research time increased product development cycle times, which were too slow to meet market demands for a steady stream of new products.

The training in emerging technologies was driven by individual development and performance needs in addition to organizational needs, which were identified by senior managers and the Training Advisory Board. The overall training goal was for the engineers to be able to redesign and evolve current products to meet the needs of new telecommunications markets. The audience for this intervention included hardware and software engineers who were either members of the scientific staff or managers.

Forming Partnerships

The training specialist formed critical business partnerships with the purchasing function, external suppliers, various development line managers, and the Technical Training Network. Partnering also occurred with different functions, such as marketing and finance. The partnerships helped to provide a more comprehensive needs assessment by including the people who were in touch with the real performance issues. The critical goals were to increase employee satisfaction with training and reduce product development cycle time. These factors influenced other organizational success criteria such as increased revenue and reduced development costs.

Funding the training as well as communicating with the different functions and levels of management in the company were problematic issues. The cost of the needed training exceeded the amount in the training budget, which was approximately $500,000. Finance and line managers worked with the Training Department to find creative ways to fund the programs through project budgets. It was important to obtain management's view of training needs and sponsorship, and at the same time to determine the needs of the people actually doing the job as to how and when the training should be implemented. Through a collaborative effort, training and management selected consultants on the basis of cost, technical expertise, quality, and service. Partnering with purchasing and suppliers led to customized content and delivery that was cost-effective. The technical training specialist acted as a broker in the process in addition to his role of performance analyst and instructional designer.

Marketing the Training

The Training Department marketed training interventions to the lab population primarily though the internal e-mail system. Other means of communication were one-to-one contact with the training specialist and announcements at management staff meetings. By the end of the year, with the addition of a Web Master, an Internet expert, the company intranet had evolved to become a more central means of communication, with participants using it to learn about and register for courses. The training specialist created the designs for the Web pages and documents.

Creating and Implementing an Evolving Training Solution

The initial training consisted of instructor-led classes on emerging technologies designed by an outside consultant and delivered in the work site. As a result of these initial sessions, the participants gained a view of the industry market demands for emerging technologies. The sessions also identified the need to determine the company market drivers and how current products fit in with these demands. To meet this need, we offered a learning session with a panel, made up of senior development managers and marketing, to provide a more direct view of critical technologies and our changing customer base.

The initial sessions were only a start to improving employee satisfaction. The lab population wanted more specific technical information concerning these new technologies. The Training Advisory Board and participants in the initial course offerings identified specific topics. The Training Department conducted research to identify people who were experts in these areas. The training specialist designed a two-day training intervention in emerging technologies with a selected international consultant who was an expert in this area. The interest in this intervention and satisfaction with it were overwhelming.

Later in the year, the training specialist designed another intervention with a supplier. The course was designed for people who tested the final designs of new product development and included hands-on training on network equipment. The demand for these courses was enormous. The training specialist worked with line managers to prioritize who participated in these sessions, linking attendance to project-related activity. Alternative forms of delivery were attempted to provide wider coverage with lower costs. Interactive distance learning was one technology that was piloted. The training specialist worked out an arrangement with another location, with satellite capability, to provide a tandem hookup to this site in order to provide a broadcast in emerging technologies to the broadband lab. The broadcast reached over 100 sites worldwide, and interaction was achieved through faxes and telephone. The pilot for this form of delivery was successful, but achieved a 20 percent lower satisfaction evaluation than the conventional method with an on-site instructor-led class. This was acceptable for piloting the instructional use of new technology. Satisfaction could possibly be increased through the use of more interaction techniques, but the results indicated that participants preferred an instructor in the classroom.

Evaluating Success

To keep track of whether the department was on target to meet these improvement goals, the training specialist developed an evaluation strategy, designed the evaluation instruments, collected and analyzed the data, and reported findings to management. The technical training specialist developed Level 1 feedback forms to measure training satisfaction and reported the evaluation results in a weekly operations report. To keep track of meeting performance improvements, the Training Advisory Board met quarterly to obtain feedback on training needs. The technical training specialist also met with line departments in their staff meetings, and received feedback on an individual basis through internal e-mail, phone calls, and one-on-one meetings.

The course interventions in emerging technologies were very successful. The Level 1 evaluations were in the 85 percent to 95 percent range. The overall training program, of which the emerging technologies interventions were a part, increased training satisfaction from approximately 50 percent to 80 percent. Through interviews with participants who had attended the more specific technical courses, the training specialist determined how the courses helped them on the job. Although the courses did not benefit everyone who attended, well-timed course interventions helped several people with their current work projects. For example, one engineer who was developing the packaging for a particular customer application, found that the training information on protocols saved him a week of research time and helped him to finish a proposal on schedule. The hands-on intervention saved several of the participants months of working through manuals of test equipment.

An examination of the hard data revealed a return-on-investment (ROI) of 106 percent and 176 percent for two of the most successful courses. The ROI calculation accounted for the costs for the course (instructor, administration, design), materials, and the participants' time in attending the course (using a daily loaded labor rate). The technical training specialist obtained the information needed to calculate savings through interviews with participants (time saved to accomplish job performance) and verified it with project and quality records. Presenting the results of these successful interventions increased senior management's awareness of the impact that training could have on their business.

Lessons Learned

The success of the emerging technology training program was primarily a result of the clear link between the identified training need and the future competitive success of the business unit. As a result of this link, there was buy-in from upper management, a high demand from the intended audience, and ultimately greater interest and satisfaction from the participants.

Partnering was also a key to the success of this training intervention. Collaborating with other experts is essential to the role of the lone trainer. To achieve business results, the Training Department had to partner with functions within the business unit, with other groups within the broader corporation, and with outside suppliers that provided training services. This partnering allowed each function to contribute in ways in which it added value and helped to avoid duplication of effort. It was essential in setting up the learning environments as well as in providing cost-effective solutions.

As a lone trainer, you can be very effective and make a real difference when you function as a performance technologist. One of the keys to the department's success was the identification of performance needs through a needs assessment. By developing relationships with the managers and end users, the trainer's role was able to evolve from training coordinator to a performance technologist. In this role, one must recognize the importance of the end users in clarifying real training needs and the best way to offer training. In the future, the Training Department plans to do a more thorough instructional analysis, particularly in terms of assessing the learners' needs and the context for learning.

Because of the urgency to achieve visibility and improve training satisfaction, there was pressure to develop more frequent interventions. In order to improve its effectiveness in the future, the Training Department will concentrate more on focused interventions that have an impact on the business unit and on the instructional design process in creating the interventions.

Training evaluation was a key in building the credibility of the Training Department. Evaluation was an important tool to convince senior management of the benefit and contribution of training to the business unit's bottom line. Management was especially appreciative of quantitative ROI evaluation data that showed that training had a desirable return-on-investment. Evaluation also provided formative information to the Training Department to help improve future decisions and training.

In summary, the role of lone trainer is an exciting and demanding one. There are high pressures and high rewards. Being a lone trainer allows more independence than being a member of a large department. Another advantage of the role is the reduced amount of filtering in determining organizational needs. The rewards are greatest once you've demonstrated you can contribute to the business, and your role shifts from coordinating programs to consulting on ways to improve business performance by improving employee performance.

Questions for Discussion

1. What is the role of the performance technologist in today's globally competitive organization?
2. What are the techniques to identify business needs at Nortel, and how do they compare with techniques you use in your own organization?
3. What would be an effective role for a lone trainer given the constraints and resources of an organization such as the Broadband Business Unit?
4. How would you compare the program development methods that the Training Department used?
5. How did the Training Department make delivery decisions?

6. Describe the role of evaluation and the model the training specialist used. How was evaluation accomplished in a cost-effective way?
7. How was partnering used to support training efforts in Nortel and how is it used in your organization?

The Authors

Randy Maxwell, is a human resource development manager with Nortel's Learning Institute. His chief responsibility is the design of learning and organizational development initiatives. His current accountabilities include developing a project management curriculum, being the "global prime" for Nortel's New Employee Program, and working on various alternative delivery projects such as interactive distance learning and Web-based instruction. His experience with Nortel includes training and development, project management, and engineering. Prior to his experience with Nortel, he was an industrial engineering consultant. He holds a master's degree in industrial and systems engineering from Georgia Institute of Technology and a Ph.D. in education, majoring in instructional technology, from Georgia State University. He can be contacted at the Nortel Learning Institute, 5555 Windward Parkway, Suite B, Alpharetta, GA 30201; phone: 770.661.4735.

Karen L. Jost, is an assistant professor of instructional technology at California State University, Chico, in the Department of Communication Design. Her responsibilities include teaching a course in performance analysis in the instructional technology program and graduate courses within the College of Communications and Education. She holds both master's and Ph.D. degrees in instructional design, development, and evaluation from Syracuse University. Her research and consulting experiences have included problem-based learning, distance learning, and the instructional use of technology. She can be contacted at the Department of Communication Design, California State University, Chico, 95929-0504; phone: 916.898.5028.

References

Kirkpatrick, D.L. (1994). *Evaluating Training Programs.* San Francisco, CA: Berrett-Koehler.

Phillips J. (1991). *Handbook of Training, Evaluation, and Measurement Methods.* Woodstock, NY: Gulf Publishing.

Creating a Successful Sales Campaign for a Mutual Savings Bank

Norway Savings Bank

Barbara "Bobbi" J. Buisman

This chapter demonstrates the vital role that a one-person human resource development (HRD) unit can play in a small organization, where HRD is enmeshed among many other functions. Buisman describes how she established the role and value of HRD in a mutual savings bank with long-standing roots in a New England community. Her case illustrates how she created and implemented a series of educational and motivational interventions to support a successful sales campaign that promoted a new debit card.

Background

This case study is based on experience and observations during eight years with a successful mutual savings bank headquartered in rural western Maine. Over 130 years in operation, Norway Savings Bank now maintains 110 employees (give or take a few seasonally) in seven locations. With assets of $305 million, it is no longer in the official category of small banks. Within its market area, Norway Savings has approximately 50 percent of banking customers. Growth goals are focused in two branch areas: one area is a new rural market for the bank, and the other is a relatively cosmopolitan and competitive market.

Management wants to continue to project the bank's personal, hometown flavor while rising to the advances in technology and the changing nature of competition. There is a strong traditional market to serve, particularly with the older, conservative segment of the

This case was prepared to serve as a basis for discussion rather than to illustrate either effective or ineffective administrative and management practices.

population. Management also recognizes the sophisticated younger generations with their needs and wants often resulting from their familiarity and comfort with technology. Management's understanding of the market area is enhanced by the managers' own histories—three top-level executives have been at the bank since they were tellers, and several high-level managers and their families have been living in the area for generations.

The sales approach is strictly based on customers' needs, with a vision of every customer having every bank product and service he or she needs at this bank. All employees, including back-office employees, are trained, coached, and encouraged to listen for clues in conversations that may lead to selling and referrals and to maintain a helpful, problem-solving attitude. The bank includes all employees in this goal because in this small community, anyone could have a opportunity for this type of conversation. Many people are related by blood or marriage, and the population is so small that most people know each other. Because of the types of conversations and questions that occur in social situations, the bank expects everyone to have product knowledge.

The HRD Function and Mission

Because of the bank's growth in asset size, branch network, and personnel, eight years ago, it established the Human Resource Development (HRD) department. Management had reached the point where it wanted to keep up with training demands by having someone design and implement the overall HRD function of the bank. I was recruited from my position as director of education for the Portland chapter of the American Institute of Banking to create a one-person HRD department. Because my responsibilities covered all functions of the bank, I reported directly to its president. The entrepreneurial nature of the position appealed to me; I have had the opportunity to become progressively involved in many bank functions, the variety and challenges of which I enjoy immensely.

As assistant vice president for training and development, my function began with straightforward job-skills training and supervisory and leadership development. My mission was to develop customer service excellence through employee processes and training such as coaching, counseling, creative problem solving, communications, and technical job skills. I now provide leadership for many projects and facilitate employee involvement and empowerment.

Some of my responsibilities involve general human resources functions. The bank doesn't have a formal human resource (HR) department, but develops those responsibilities within various other functions. For the most part, an assistant treasurer who is in charge of personnel, payroll, compensation, and benefits and I split the HR function. I developed the hiring function for nonofficer-level positions. Employees often come to me for career and job counseling and for help in solving work-related problems in general. I'll coach them to see things objectively, to take steps to solve their own problems, and to take control of their own career growth.

At Norway Savings Bank, the HRD function is enmeshed among many of the bank's other functions. The organization's size is one of the reasons for this arrangement: With only slightly over 100 employees in seven locations, it is easy for the functions to work closely together. Another reason relates to our people and our intimate work environment. There exists genuine concern for each other and an eagerness for each other's ideas. In our culture, collaboration of functions is integral to operations.

I have close working relationships with all the departments. As a member of most of the working committees within the bank, I stay involved, motivated, and up-to-date with changes and the general focus of business operations. Being on committees allows me to be influential and gives me the critical information I need for effective planning. Some of the committees I'm involved with include operations, lending, sales and marketing, and safety and health. I'm often the leader of, or a participant in, projects that emerge from committee discussions or my own recommendations. At one time, I organized a career development committee that created a plan and made recommendations to senior management that would increase the proportion of internal promotions over external hires.

My primary form of assistance on the job is a personal computer with word processing and desktop publishing capabilities. I receive administrative help from the president's executive secretary for tasks such as photocopying, assembling course materials, mass distributions, and miscellaneous tasks.

Challenges and Opportunities

As with many new training functions, there were differing expectations of my position. Although some people appreciated my nonbanker perspective, others believed that I was a technical bank trainer who was supposed to teach technical banking subjects, with no background and no depth of experience. It was difficult to get buy-in to the idea of subject matter experts (SMEs) as trainers—taking people off their normal jobs to train others in technical areas. One problem with that approach is that coverage decreases when employees with customer contact attend training, and it decreases even more by taking resource people off the job. It's a legitimate concern, and I must plan carefully to minimize the light coverage problem.

The informal culture can present challenges as well as opportunities. As a small organization, communications have remained informal and minimal. So many people in the bank are interconnected in their roles that it's sometimes hard to separate who does what. Ideas start somewhere and often end up as the group's ideas. We have a close-knit management team, and we have frequent discussions about what we're doing and how we're doing it. We spend a great deal of time in meetings, a major source of communication for us. Because we may make decisions in a committee meeting or while we're passing in the hall, it is difficult to keep communications functioning appropriately.

In our close-knit environment, people are enthusiastic about their jobs, and it's easy to implement ideas and processes. Although it's easy to take action, we sometimes plan too many things simultaneously and get overwhelmed, so we must take care to plan projects realistically. Fortunately, the organization is beginning to recognize the need for more planned communications processes as well as the need to start communications at the top, especially in managing change. This transition to more planned communications will be a great asset to my work.

Another challenge has been planning for training without a specific predetermined training budget. If an initiative has a high price tag, I discuss it with the appropriate person and proceed accordingly. There is no explicit determinant for this budgeting process; it's primarily a judgment call on my part. Generally, purchasing books, manuals, videotapes, and audiotaped programs doesn't require anyone else's approval. Employees' courses and seminars outside of the bank also fall into that category as long as the courses relate to their career goals and they get their supervisors' approval. However, an executive vice president must approve external courses that take employees away from their jobs.

The programs I recommend are usually well received and accepted as long as the training relates to our goals, the training resources have excellent credentials and references, and the decision makers are involved so that they understand the interventions. For example, management approved my recommendation that all supervisors and managers with supervisory roles participate in a coaching program because it supported our business goals. This program involved about 40 employees at $300 per person and required that supervisors be away from their jobs for two-plus days of training and individual consulting. In another instance, senior management approved my recommendation to contract with an external vendor to set up a sales culture program, which has not yet begun, and will involve all employees in activities over one year and will cost approximately $35,000 to $40,000.

Providing Value to the Organization
Assessing and Responding to Training Needs

I have used a variety of formal and informal techniques for bankwide needs assessment. My first step in organizing the training function was to establish a training steering committee, which comprised senior managers and department heads, to provide me with business direction. This group met quarterly to discuss direction and progress. I wanted this group to exist also as a way of building awareness of training issues and gaining management buy-in for the overall training program. Another early action was to develop an anonymous needs assessment form that potentially everyone in the bank could submit. I received 100 percent response to this assessment form. From that response, I realized how strong a desire there was for a better internal communications process. Many people came to me personally to talk things over. In addition, I visited all the branches to talk with every employee one-on-one to get a sense of their needs.

As time went on, the needs assessment has become less formal because of the personal nature of the bank. I talk to people and listen well, and they don't hesitate to tell me what they need. For example, they'll tell me in person, over the phone, by memo, in one-on-one conversations, or in group meetings that they're eager for ongoing product knowledge and for continuing reinforcement of sales skills. In response to these expressed needs, I continually create, revise, and distribute product fact sheets so people can keep up-to-date. In addition, together with other management personnel, I have developed a system of self-training for the branches; and we have internal and external resources developing our sales staff's coaching skills so that managers can provide continual reinforcement of sales skills.

Because the most urgent need from the needs assessment was to improve internal communications, I quickly established and edited our first in-house newsletter, the *Insider*, as an early step. The newsletter was participative in that it invited everyone in the bank to contribute to it, and many people did. It was a huge hit, especially with branch employees who felt a newfound sense of connection with the bank. At the newsletter's seven-and-a-half-year mark, the executive secretary took over as editor, adding her special flair to the established format. I continue to submit training-oriented articles.

Program Development and Delivery

Some training priorities came from information in the needs assessment as well as input from the steering committee. Because many of these priorities are specific to the bank and technical, I rely heavily on SMEs as resources in my work. Virtually all employees who are good in their positions have opportunities to participate in ways that are comfortable for them. Some prefer to provide background and technical information for a program, and some prefer to be presenters. Their involvement is both a valuable resource for me and a way for employees to grow in their jobs, which can be a motivational factor because turnover is minimal and advancement is limited.

A few of the basic banking programs were already available, having come to Norway Savings from the Financial Institutions Services Corporation (FISC). This was a company owned by several smaller banks, including Norway Savings, that needed services, such as training, that were too costly or weren't practical to have in-house. Eventually FISC discontinued its training function, and it gave the bank many of its manuals and other training products for use in classes such as teller training; customer relations, product knowledge and cross-selling, and other introductory and technical programs. For the most part, I deliver those programs, although I also rely on some SMEs because of their depth of experience.

Much of our federally mandated compliance training is outsourced to a contracted compliance consultant, and our internal compliance officer coordinates the dates. We also use vendors for some areas for which we want special emphasis. Examples of this have been coaching, performance leadership, and customer relations and needs-based sales. Vendors are a more infrequent source, and they are selected carefully largely on the basis of their willingness and ability to be responsive to our specific needs.

Other resources I use include some bank-specific off-the-shelf programs available through rental audio-video libraries and through two organizations in the state that exist as multifaceted resources to banks. I do a lot of program development myself for more nontechnical programs, such as customer relations, sales, communications skills, and problem solving.

There are some off-the-shelf resources available to banks that are very specific. A company called Sheshunoff, in Austin, Texas, for example, offers a Model Teller Training Manual with a computer disk that allows users to customize programs and handouts. I've used it to update the FISC teller-training program. Sheshunoff recently came out with the same type of manual for customer service representatives. Also, the Institute of Financial Education, in Chicago, offers many excellent resources in the form of seminars, self-paced learning, books, and workbooks on topics such as compliance, regulations, and many other bank-specific areas.

A variety of books in my office library provides program ideas in general. University Associates, in San Diego, publishes an *Encyclopedia of Group Activities* and an *Encyclopedia of Ice Breakers*. The book lists that come from the American Society for Training & Development and the Society for Human Resource Management, both of which are in Alexandria, Virginia, have excellent selections and keep me informed of what's new in the field. I also maintain a sizable collection of audiotapes that I listen to regularly while commuting and offer to all employees for their self-development. By subscribing to a couple of bank-specific video libraries, I've located videotapes for my use in training programs and for supervisors' use in their staff meetings. The publisher Business One Irwin offers many authoritative, concise, fast-paced books on key business topics such as supervision, telephone skills, teamwork, and hiring that I use and also distribute to supervisors as self-study resources. In addition, my file cabinets overflow with newspaper and magazine clippings and useful information I receive from newsletter subscription and other sources.

As often as possible, I guide employees in taking charge of their own learning and development. For example, the supervisors were discontented with performance review forms, with the review process, and with the whole performance management process. Early on, supervisors told me that their greatest need was learning about "the disciplinary process." What a world of opportunity that presented! Through training and discussion groups, we started with effective performance management basics and eventually progressed to review form, once a deeper understanding of the overall process was formed. Now there's an ad hoc committee of a few supervisors to review and revise the review form on the basis of input from their staffs. Upper management will review the revised form before it's approved for use.

Evaluation

Program evaluation methods vary. Participants of classroom training programs compare their learning with the program's learning objectives as well as with their own learning objectives at the end of a program. For a longer term assessment of program effectiveness, I depend on supervisors' feedback with regard to on-the-job performance. For soft-skills evaluation, I consult one-on-one with trainees, staying in touch with them and coaching them as appropriate. Coaching employees is an aspect of my job I find very rewarding, and I appreciate that the bank is small enough that I'm able to do that.

Success Story

This story illustrates how training was mixed with many other functions to facilitate a fun and successful sales promotion for our OneCard. The campaign was the first of its kind for the bank because employees normally used a suggestive, or needs-based, sales approach. This time employees were asked to promote a specific product, a debit card, which had very broad application. Because employees needed to project a positive attitude to customers, they had to be comfortable with promoting the product and excited about it. There were several activities planned to get motivation going: two employee contests with cash awards, training activities, newsletters, food, and festivities.

Business Need and Goals

Early in 1996, the bank implemented this campaign as a follow-up to the previous fall's introduction of the debit function of an automated teller machine (ATM) card. Management found that we had 5,000 existing checking accounts with no debit cards attached. Our goal was to sell an additional 2,000 cards. Projecting a low average of two transactions a month per card, the bank saw the potential to increase its income by $26,000 per year. Another goal was to increase usage because slightly less than 50 percent of existing cardholders were actually using their cards for debit transactions.

The bank's overall goal was to generate $5,000 per year in debit card income. The cards would not only generate income, but also cut costs associated with check clearing, imaging, and returns at a projected savings of $3,000 to $4,000 per year. Other reasons for encouraging use of debit cards had to do with technology and competition. Other banks were closing branches and forcing the use of electronic banking, and by doing so, they were lowering their operating costs. As competitors' costs went down, so would their fees, and we needed to be able to compete for depositors.

The OneCard Promotion Committee

For the special promotion, we formed a OneCard committee including the executive vice president and treasurer, senior vice president of operations, vice president of HRD (myself), assistant treasurer and deposit supervisor, a teller supervisor, a customer service representative, and the executive secretary. On the committee were representatives of most bank functions that would be affected by the changes and promotion. The members had great potential for thorough planning and success throughout the system. In addition, the major decision makers were involved, which helped to facilitate our plans for the four-month program.

Training and Implementation Issues

My part in the process was to train employees on how to use and sell the cards, and also to set the stage for employees to project a high level of enthusiasm during the promotion period and afterward. Some challenges we wanted to overcome immediately were resistance to change and fear of the unknown. We thought that getting employees to use the cards on a trial basis would help us to work the kinks out of the new system and that by involving employees and relying on them, it would help them work through their concerns about the change and their fear.

Another objective was to get all our operational systems synchronized for the promotion to go smoothly. When the employees received the cards, they were counted on as guinea pigs to test the cards and report problems to the person in charge of bank operations. We needed card usage to be as free of problems as possible for the employees and eventually for the customers.

The Motivational and Training Campaign

With our creative juices flowing, the committee decided to achieve two goals with one start-up activity—a contest to name and design the new card. This activity would accomplish some introductory training and also generate some excitement. Marketing and communication took many forms. The contest winner was eligible for "$50 in

COLD HARD CASH!" This was the attention-getter at the top of the introductory flier. The flier gave details of the contest along with an explanation of the card's functions and how it would differ from the existing card. This was also the beginning of the training process. The employees needed and wanted to know just enough information to come up with some name and design ideas.

The contest generated a great deal of excitement as well as 57 names and 29 design concepts out of just over 100 employees. A few employees also submitted some unsolicited marketing ideas. Response was better than expected, and I found myself constantly being asked to clarify points about the card—a trainer's dream to actually be asked for information! We set ourselves up for an easy training process for the duration of the program. The $50 in cold hard cash contest was the first of two employee contests.

Other activities were to include a second employee contest and mystery teams and goals based on sales of debit cards. There would also be a customer contest, lobby signs and ads, direct mailings, and preapproval of certain customers. All of these activities required the employees to be prepared and responsive. Everyone on the OneCard committee had a big part in making this happen. In preparing for training, I depended on the operational people to give me the background and information employees needed to follow through with terminal transactions and to explain the process from a customer's applying for the card through receipt of the card.

For the next part of the training process, I wrote and issued a special edition of the newsletter in preparation for a training meeting. The newsletter covered all the basics: the business benefits of the card; the special promotion and the reasons for having it, including the bottom line; the change in issuing the cards; an explanation of promotional methods, the customer contest and the second employee contest, and the concept of Mystery Teams; and the benefits and objections of the OneCard from the customers' point of view.

About a week after distribution of the newsletter, I held an evening training meeting to introduce the concepts of the Pot of Gold program to about 80 employees. This was a required meeting for all employees, and the committee made it festive with pizza and soft drinks for everyone. Hourly employees received compensation for the time. Using some overheads, I reviewed the newsletter in detail and showed marketing tools so that employees would understand to what they would need to be responsive. I explained the Pot of Gold employee and customer contests, whereby winners were eligible to reach into a large fishbowl of cash and pull out as much cash as they could hold. By offering employees the same reward as the customers, we hoped to create enthusiasm that they could project to customers. The contest objectives were different for each group because we wanted employees to sell the cards, and customers to accept and use the cards.

The training meeting emphasized our primary mission. The employees were coached to talk to the customers about the card in such a way that they themselves could buy into it. Having used the cards themselves helped them to explain to the customers the benefits of the cards and how to use them. We also explained the marketing activities, with emphasis placed on what the employees needed to do to be responsive to customers.

The training also involved a group brainstorming activity during which I recorded on a flipchart some conversation openers with customers. Then, the employees counted off into groups of three to practice skills in overcoming customers' objections that related to a lack of understanding about the card. In the skill-practice, one person thought of an objection, one responded, and the other observed and gave feedback. Then all three discussed the process. There was a lot of excitement and laughter during the exercise. When the group reconvened, employees shared their ideas for overcoming objections, many of which showed their depth of experience and understanding of the customers' point of view. I captured their ideas on an overhead transparency and later distributed them on paper.

The meeting concluded with two motivational activities. The OneCard committee distributed T-shirts with an embroidered OneCard emblem and Pot of Gold buttons for everyone to wear on casual Fridays. I ended the meeting by revealing a cash-filled fishbowl (the Pot of Gold) just for fun and encouraged employees to sample what it was like to draw out some cash and count it. That was truly an excitement builder as they could experience the potential of their winnings.

Additional promotional activities involved seven mystery teams and mystery goals. Team members consisted of employees in different jobs and office locations, so that employees may or may not have been on the same team with everyday co-workers. The executive secretary edited and sent a fun weekly newsletter with progress reports to all staff. For continual training and communications, the newsletter addressed questions that came up during the promotion. It also contained clues about who team members might be and who might be reaching goals, but to maintain the fun, these remained mysteries throughout the promotion. Winning customers were announced, and high-selling employees shared secrets to their success. As progress was made, we shared the additional estimated increase in annual income and related that to our annual bonus. The team urged employees on with a little friendly competition. We answered their complaints that there were no more accounts to sell to with facts such as: "We've sold cards to 42 percent of our preapproved customers; only 58 percent to go—over 2,100 accounts." The newsletter was a great source of information, fun, and motivation.

Results and Success Factors

The goal was to sell 2,000 OneCards. We came close enough to be happy with 1,931 cards sold, which was half the number of preapproved accounts. Our average OneCard sales went from 36 per week to over 200 per week. The estimated increase to annual income was $20,858. The resulting year-to-date income for the OneCard, from January through August, nearly doubled. From January through August 1997, the income was $37,184 and profits were $17,113, compared with income of $20,611 and profits of $8,837 in the preceding year. Bank management was very pleased!

Two weeks after the promotion, the bank held an evening celebration to congratulate all employees on doing a great job. At the same time, contest winners were able to grab their winnings from the Pot of Gold.

There were many elements of the program that contributed to its success. It is difficult, if not impossible, to separate what was the result of training itself or of the other pieces of the effort because they were so closely intertwined. One success factor was that very intertwining—each department was interdependent on the others for planning, implementation, and success. Frequently we couldn't do any one thing without the support of everyone. In the case of training, I needed background on how the terminals were being set up from operations and data processing, statistics from the treasurer, how-tos from bookkeeping, the intricacies of incentives and motivational factors from several sources, and so on.

A real key to my success was finding a way to build the desire to learn from the very start. The contests—first to name and design the card, then to sell—kept people asking for more information to aid them in their quest. The ongoing training and communication via several channels kept things lively and interesting.

The motivational aspect, originating with upper management, was another success factor. Everyone on the committee was expected to cheer for the program, which came very easily with our all-for-one, one-for-all attitude. The whole program was set up to be fun and exciting, with enough friendly competition for those who enjoy it but not so much as to be threatening to those who don't. The fun incentives helped; total cash awards to employees for this program amounted to approximately $2,900 with two winners of the $50 in cold hard cash contest, and 16 employees drawing around $175 cash each from the Pot of Gold. Granted, a program that offers these kind of incentives must be a top priority with management, and this was. However, the concept can be applied to many programs in proportional values.

One of the most satisfying aspects of this program was the planning and collaboration among many departments within the system, and the interconnectedness that was realized at a conscious level. Also, while maintaining high morale among the employees, we were able to positively affect the business's bottom line. It's satisfying to see such concrete results related to my work.

Lessons Learned

One thing I find most helpful in my work is the ability to see the big picture. It's essential to be able to understand the ramifications of people's actions throughout the system, particularly when employee participation and empowerment are critical. Often in training sessions, employees will have suggestions about how to improve operations or customer service. If their ideas sound reasonable, I encourage them to present their ideas to their supervisor or another appropriate person, and I share important considerations they should address so their ideas can have a higher probability of success.

If I am conducting training myself and can't bring an expert to the class, I send a trainee to an expert. For example, if in training an employee asks a technical question about the bookkeeping department, I jot the question on a flipchart so we remember it. During a break I send the employee who asked the question to a SME. Then that employee returns to tell the rest of the group what he or she learned. Often, an employee in that situation is from one of the branches, so this process gives the person an opportunity to network and learn more about the main office. Using this process, the employee learns a lot more than if I attempt to answer the question or if I seek out the answer myself.

Identifying and nurturing the relationships is critical to my job effectiveness. Making the effort to build rapport can really help. If those I rely on for information and assistance know that I respect them and their work and if I attempt to work within their frame of reference, we collaborate more. I also learn more, which is enjoyable and helpful.

One of my main challenges at first was working without a budget. In former jobs, a budget was always a big part of my planning process, and the lack of one made me uncertain. With time, I became more comfortable with the way things were done; I had to learn to work within a completely different system. The training budget is an important element of the planning process. If you don't work within your organization's budgetary process, I'd highly recommend becoming familiar with the budget and tracking your expenses regardless. Seek out your bookkeeping or finance department, and learn about the important budget line items that exist. This information will be useful whenever you need to negotiate for a budget or whenever your organization decides to assign you budgetary responsibility. By being informed, you'll have a head start.

As mentioned earlier, those I deal with have a lot of enthusiasm and energy, and we often find ourselves in the midst of many projects at once with deadlines coming up fast. An effective project planning and management process is extremely helpful as well as a means to get everyone involved to keep up good communications.

Questions for Discussion

1. With involvement in many committees and projects, time management and prioritizing are challenges, particularly when coordinating your own schedule with other people's. What steps would you take to manage your effectiveness and balance, keeping the job and time requirements of your co-workers a part of the plan?

2. If you were in a position of having no clear budget parameters, how would you establish a plan for a budget and promote it to your superiors?

3. Creating a desire to learn in your audience is not always easy and often not a conscious part of the program development process. How might you integrate motivation to learn in all your training and development programs?

4. A key success factor at Norway Savings Bank is keeping informed about and involved in the business. How did this business involvement help the success of training in the OneCard campaign? What are ways that you can be involved in your organization's business?

The Author

Barbara "Bobbi" J. Buisman is vice president for HRD at Norway Savings Bank. Former positions were with the Portland, Maine, chapter of the American Institute of Banking; cooperative extension in Colorado and Texas; community education in Kremmling, Colorado; and with the Adult Education Department at Texas A&M University as a research assistant. Her formal education includes an M.A. in adult education from Texas A&M, a bachelor's degree from the University of Southern Mississippi, and several HR courses through the University of Southern Maine. She's a very active member of the Maine chapter of the American Society for Training & Development. She can be reached at 23 Burnham Road, Gorham, ME 04038; phone: 207.839.3695.

About the Editor

Carol Prescott McCoy has more than 25 years of professional experience in education, training, and HRD management. Presently, she serves as manager for training quality assurance and as the performance consultant for customer satisfaction for UNUM Life Insurance Company of America. She has managed education and training departments ranging in size from one to five people in a variety of organizations. As a one-person HRD department for the International Consumer Banking Division at Chase, she managed training in 15 countries. Over the years, McCoy has managed the development of numerous programs in leadership, change management, customer service, communications, personal development, risk management, and many other topics. In managing small training departments, she has refined the art of the train-the-trainer process to help build the training delivery skills of both trainers and subject matter experts. Before starting her career in the financial services industry, she taught psychology at Livingston College and Rutgers University and was chairperson of a one-person social science department for a nursing school in the Bronx, New York. Currently, she teaches Managing Training and Development at the University of Southern Maine's School of Continuing Education.

McCoy received her B.A. in psychology from Connecticut College and her M.S. and Ph.D. in social psychology from Rutgers University. She is the author of *Managing a Small HRD Department: You Can Do More Than You Think* (Jossey-Bass, 1993.) As an active member of the American Society for Training & Development and a frequent conference presenter, McCoy has spoken on topics such as managing a small training department, the trainer-the-trainer process, developing leadership skills, using multirater 360 feedback, and managing resistance to change. She welcomes questions and suggestions on HRD management. She can be reached at 11 Johnson Road, Falmouth, ME 04105, or at the e-mail address Cmccoy3333@aol.com.

ical engineerin
University an

About the Series Editor

Jack J. Phillips has more than 27 years of professional experience in human resource development and management, and has served as training and development manager at two *Fortune* 500 firms, senior executive at two firms, president of a regional bank, and management professor at a major state university. In 1992, Phillips founded Performance Resources Organization (PRO), an international consulting firm specializing in human resources accountability programs. Phillips consults with clients in the United States, Canada, England, Belgium, Sweden, Italy, South Africa, Mexico, Venezuela, Malaysia, Indonesia, Australia, and Singapore. PRO provides a full range of services and publications to support assessment, measurement, and evaluation.

A frequent contributor to management literature, Phillips has authored or edited 15 books including *Return on Investment in Training and Performance Improvement Programs* (1997); *Accountability in Human Resource Management* (1996); *Handbook of Training Evaluation and Measurement Methods* (3d edition, 1997); *Measuring Return on Investment* (Vol. 1, 1994) (Vol. 2, 1997); *Conducting Needs Assessment* (1995); *The Development of a Human Resource Effectiveness Index* (1988); *Recruiting, Training and Retaining New Employees* (1987); and *Improving Supervisors' Effectiveness* (1985), which won an award from the Society for Human Resource Management. Phillips has written more than 100 articles for professional, business, and trade publications.

Phillips has earned undergraduate degrees in electrical engineering, physics, and mathematics from Southern Polytechnic State University and Oglethorpe University; a master's in decision sciences from Georgia State University; and a doctorate in human resource management from the University of Alabama. In 1987, he won the Yoder-Heneman Personnel Creative Application Award from the Society for Human Resource Management for an ROI Study of an ROI study of a gainsharing plan. He is an active member of several professional organizations.

Jack J. Phillips can be reached at the following address: Performance Resources Organization, Box 380637, Birmingham, AL 35238-0637; phone: 205.678.9700; fax: 205.678.8070.

Other Books Available in the Series

The ASTD *In Action* series examines real-life case studies that show how human resource development (HRD) professionals analyze what worked and what didn't as they crafted on-the-job solutions to address specific aspects of their work. Each book contains 15–25 case studies taken from many types of organizations, large and small, in the United States and abroad. Choose from case study collections on the following topics:

Measuring Return on Investment, Volume 1

Jack J. Phillips, *Editor*

Who's going to support a training program that can't prove itself? This volume shows you case after case of trainers proving that their programs work—in dollar-for-dollar terms. Each of the 18 case studies shows you the best (and sometimes not-so-best) practices from which every trainer can learn. Corporations demand bottom-line results from all branches of their operations, including HRD. This volume hands you the

tools—the hows, whys, and how-wells of measuring return-on-investment—to mark that bottom line.

Order Code: PHRO. Published by ASTD. 1994. 271 pages.

Measuring Return on Investment, Volume 2

Jack J. Phillips, *Editor*

This volume contains even more case studies on return-on-investment. Authors, reflecting several viewpoints from varied backgrounds, examine their diligent pursuit of accountability of training, HRD, and performance improvement programs. The 17 case studies cover a variety of programs from a diverse group of organizations, many of them global in scope. As a group, they add to the growing database of return-on-investment studies and make an important contribution to the literature.

Order Code: PHRE. Published by ASTD. 1997. 272 pages.

Conducting Needs Assessment

Jack J. Phillips and Elwood F. Holton III, *Editors*

How can you fix performance problems if you don't know what they are? This volume gives you the investigative tools to pinpoint the causes of performance problems—before investing time and money in training. Each of the 17 case studies provides real-world examples of training professionals digging deep to find the causes of performance problems and offers real-world results.

Order Code: PHNA. Published by ASTD. 1995. 312 pages.

Designing Training Programs

Donald J. Ford, *Editor*

These days, training techniques must consist of much more than setting up flipcharts, handing out manuals, or plugging in audiovisual aids. Organizations are more frequently asking instructional designers to create innovative learning systems that use a wide range of methods and media to spark participants' interest and increase retention and use on the job. This volume showcases 18 real-life examples of customized and artful programs that improve learning and staff performance. Computer-based training, distance learning, and on-the-job training are just a few of the many methods used by the organizations contributing to this book.

Order Code: PHTD. Published by ASTD. 1996. 340 pages.

Creating the Learning Organization, Volume 1

Karen E. Watkins and Victoria J. Marsick, *Editors*

It's time to take learning organizations out of the think tank and into the real world. This volume contains 22 case studies from a cross section of organizations—international and national, industry and service, government and private sector. They show you the hows and whys of creating the learning organization as HRD professionals move

beyond theory and into practice, transforming organizations into businesses that perform, think, and learn.

Order Code: PHCL. Published by ASTD. 1996. 288 pages.

Transferring Learning to the Workplace

Mary L. Broad, *Editor*

The 17 case studies in this volume cover a wide range of organizational settings. Specifically, the real-life training examples feature dramatic, large-scale knowledge and skill transfer applications that affect overall organizational performance, as well as smaller programs that affect individual employee effectiveness. As more training

and HRD professionals struggle to implement learning transfer support activities, this collection of field experiences will be an invaluable source of ideas and advice.

Order Code: PHTL. Published by ASTD. 1997. 331 pages.

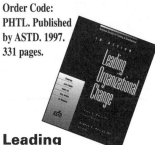

Leading Organizational Change

Elwood F. Holton III, *Editor*

HRD is concerned fundamentally with change, which is traditionally in individual knowledge, skills, and abilities. Today, however, organizations face an ever-increasing rate of change and struggle to manage change processes. HRD professionals have the opportunity and challenge to become key players in leading organizational change efforts. Covering a wide range of organizational types, change strategies, interventions, and outcomes, the 14 case studies show dramatically that HRD professionals can and should lead change.

Order Code: PHLE. Published by ASTD. 1997. 260 pages.

ASTD

1640 King Street
Box 1443
Alexandria, VA 22313-2043
PH 703.683.8100, FX 703.683.8103
www.astd.org